Writing about Literature

Writing

about

Literature

Aims and Process

JOYCE MacALLISTER
University of Richmond
Richmond, Virginia

Macmillan Publishing Company
New York

Macmillan Publishing Company
866 Third Avenue, New York, New York 10022

Collier Macmillan Canada, Inc.

Library of Congress Cataloging-in-Publication Data

MacAllister, Joyce.
  Writing about literature.

  Bibliography: p.
  Includes index.
  1. English language—Rhetoric.   2. Criticism—
Authorship.   I. Title.
PE1479.C7M33   1987   808'.0668   86–19172
ISBN   0–02–373030–7

Printing: 1 2 3 4 5 6 7   Year: 7 8 9 0 1 2 3

ACKNOWLEDGMENTS

SHERWOOD ANDERSON, "The Egg." Copyright © 1921 by B. W. Huebsch, Inc. Renewed 1948 by Eleanor C. Anderson. Reprinted by permission of Harold Ober
Associates Incorporated.

MARTIN BIDNEY, "Of the Devil's Party: Undetected Words of Milton's Satan in Arnold's 'Dover Beach'," from *Victorian Poetry* 20 (1982). Reprinted by permission
of *Victorian Poetry*.

WILLIAM FAULKNER, "A Rose for Emily," copyright © 1930 and renewed 1958 by
William Faulkner. Reprinted from *Collected Stories of William Faulkner*, by
permission of Random House, Inc.

J. F. KOBLER, "Faulkner's 'A Rose for Emily'," from *Explicator* 32 (1974). Reprinted
by permission of the author.

D. H. LAWRENCE, "The Rocking-Horse Winner," from *The Complete Short Stories
of D. H. Lawrence*, Vol. III, copyright © 1933 by The Estate of D. H. Lawrence,
© 1961 by Angelo Ravagli and C. M. Weekley, Executors of The Estate of
Frieda Lawrence Ravagli. Reprinted by permission of Viking Penguin Inc.

GIL MULLER, "Faulkner's 'A Rose for Emily'," from *Explicator* 33 (1975). Reprinted
by permission of the author.

RONALD A. SHARP, "A Note on Allusion in 'Dover Beach'," from *English Language
Notes* 21 (1983), reprinted by permission of *English Language Notes*.

ISBN 0-02-373030-7

Preface

This book is the product of my efforts to help students improve their writing, particularly their writing about literature, by offering them practical advice for studying a selection, for generating and recording ideas, and for completing and polishing a draft. And while the book does attend to concepts deemed essential to literary analysis—individual chapters are, for example, devoted to characterization, theme, point of view, and style—its primary focus is upon the process of writing itself.

Because I have spent the past several years testing its concepts in beginning composition classes as well as in courses devoted to literature, I know that *Writing About Literature* will dramatically improve the composing skills of both beginning and practiced writers. In my own classes, students have not only felt more comfortable about discussing a selection assigned but have also conquered their fears of having nothing to say or of appearing to be "unscholarly." I believe this success largely derives from the book's attention to principles from classical rhetoric and to research on the composing habits of most effective writers. Unlike many manuals that survey the subjects of literary criticism and are primarily useful as reference tools, this textbook presents each chapter as an independent unit that guides students through each stage they must complete in order to produce a polished draft about a single topic from literature.

The chapters themselves carry students through writing assignments emphasizing those aims identified by James Kinneavy in his *Theory of Discourse* as the shapers of most written and spoken communication. The sequence governing their presentation here demands a growing objectivity on the part of the writer that, in turn, leads to assignments of increasing complexity and challenge. Chapter 2, for example, analyzes the characteristics of self-expressive writing, while later chapters cover the organizations, styles, and concern for readers that we can associate with informative, persuasive, and "scientific" or researched composition.

In keeping with the textbook's process orientation, eight of its chapters include suggestions for generating and structuring material with the aid of *heuristics* or prewriting strategies and with attention to the *modes* that pattern most coherent discourse. Heuristics include simple freewriting, the journalist's questions, and the classical topics; modes studied include definition, cause-effect, classification, and comparison. Discussions of the means by which style may be polished so that it will be appropriate to its aim conclude each process sequence.

Plentiful exercises, revision checklists, and sample essays (products of work in my own classes) allow students to apply each principle to their own compositions. Specific selections upon which the sample essays are based also appear in an appendix so that those wishing to do so may study them and explore alternatives for interpreting the assignment represented. Chapter 10 concludes the book with reproductions of articles originally appearing in scholarly journals to demonstrate that the characteristics of aims studied in preceding chapters are prominent in professional as well as in student-written essays.

For students whose previous English courses have stressed process or rhetorical analysis, this book can serve as a bridge between their earlier practice and the demands of responding to literature. For those whose previous composition experience has been limited to the study of grammar or has been subordinated to the analysis of readings assigned, the book can serve as a primer for encouraging more effective practice with writing. Finally, for those whose present language courses stress reading and interpretation, this text can serve as a resource for independent composition.

ACKNOWLEDGMENTS

I want to thank a number of special people for the support they have given me over the past several years. First, I am truly grateful to James L. Kinneavy for the kindness and the help that enriched my graduate work at the University of Texas. I am also grateful to him for the theory that has given shape and meaning to my own teaching and writing; as each year passes, I am increasingly convinced that *A Theory of Discourse* is as important to the teaching of composition today as has been Aristotle's *Rhetoric* to those many generations that have had sense enough to study it. Second, I appreciate the continued encouragement I receive from Evelyn Fouraker, from Barbara Griffin, and from Janet Kotler, friends and colleagues here at the University of Richmond, whose enthusiasm for this and for all my projects adds to the pleasure I find in my work. I am similarly grateful to Wendy Thompson and to Jean Davis for their tireless efforts to keep our office running smoothly. It was Wendy, in fact, who initiated this textbook by acting on a hunch that enabled me to talk to Macmillan's English Editor in the first place. I also appreciate the help of UR's Faculty Research Committee; without its generous contribution to this project, I might still be worrying about when I could find time to get to my first draft.

I am thankful for the thoughtful supervision of my editors at Macmillan, Jennifer Crewe, Tony English, and Eben Ludlow, all of whom have been as willing to listen as to offer advice. I am thankful, too, for the skill and the imaginative vision that led my production supervisor, Pat Cabeza, and my designer, Harold Stancil, to translate my ideas into a highly appealing and exceptionally readable text. Bill Beville has also been a pleasure to work with; he encouraged this project at the outset and has continued to check in to see how the writing has progressed. The progress I have made has, moreover, been carefully guided by the following reviewers, whose invaluable comments have been both constructive and specific: Brenda H. Bell, East

Texas State University; Roger J. Bresnahan, Michigan State University; Peggy Cole, Arapahoe Community College; John W. Crawford, Henderson State University; Kenneth W. Davis, Texas Tech University; Bette Gaines, Syracuse University; Joseph Glaser, Western Kentucky University; George Gleason, Southwest Missouri State University; John K. Hanes, Duquesne University; James Kinney, Virginia Commonwealth University; John Potter, Hunter College, The City University of New York; Douglas Robillard, University of New Haven; Michael Shugrue, The College of Staten Island, The City University of New York; Lucille Johnsen Stelling, Normandale Community College; Willa F. Valencia, Valdosta State College; Lillian Wilson, The University of Charleston; and Heinz D. Woehlk, Northern Missouri State University.

My students also deserve mention for their contributions to this book; without their thoughtful responses to the ideas and the assignments that follow, I simply could not have finished the project. Neither could I have finished it without the support and the patience of my family; I offer special thanks to my dad, to my mom, and to my daughters, Elizabeth and Heather.

J. M.

Contents

I

An Introduction to Aims and Process with Literature

2

Self-Expressive Responses to Literature

3

Informative Writing about Characters in Literature 23

6

Persuasive Writing about Controlling Themes

7

Writing Persuasive Evaluations of Literature   83

8

Researched Writing: Early Stages   99

9

Researched Writing: Later Stages   III

10

The Aims in Published Writing 125

Appendix 137

Index 189

Chapter
I

An Introduction to Aims and Process with Literature

THE PURPOSE OF THIS BOOK

If you were to poll the students on almost any college campus, the chances are good that a high percentage of them would identify writing—specifically, the writing of term papers, essays, and tests—as one of the most unpleasant of their various occupations. Similarly, if you were to poll executives from almost any successful organization, the chances are also good that they, too, would reveal an aversion to writing.

In most cases, this attitude leads to habits that limit the practice of writing, and these results can be damaging; in spite of what our preferences dictate, all of us need to be continually practicing and perpetually fussing with every part of our writing. In school, those who turn in the clearest and best-defended essays will be the ones who get the highest grades and derive the greatest benefits from all of their activities in college. In many businesses and professions, those who can prepare the best reports and submit the best proposals will be the ones who enjoy the greatest rewards and find the greatest satisfaction for all of their efforts and achievements.

This book has been written to help you to relax and to improve your own writing so that you can compete favorably with those with whom you will study and work. It has also been written to help you apply strategies that promote effective expression in many different subjects to specific assignments about the nature and value of literature. Such assignments will, in turn, improve your writing in classes other than English because they will help you sharpen your responses to the compositions of others; most instructors, no matter what the course, will expect such responses to the material they assign.

Because the improvement of writing is a primary goal of this text, its assignments and discussions focus upon poems and short stories rather than upon novels and plays. And while this focus is appropriate here—based as it is upon the assumption that most short fiction is relatively easy to review for discussion and for writing—you should remember that most of the principles covered in this book are equally applicable to the other kinds of reading that may be assigned in this and in many other classes.

THIS BOOK AND THE WRITING PROCESS

Recent research indicates that many of our common beliefs about writing are truly erroneous. One popular misconception is that good writers spend little time on their writing. Another is that simply reading the "classics" will improve our composition. This last view is especially flawed inasmuch as it suggests that writing skills are, as are many diseases, the products of contagion.

Because recent studies indicate that good writers actually devote many hours to drafting and to revision, this book encourages you to extend the time you spend on all your efforts, and it describes the problems and strategies that can affect each stage throughout the writing process. The following model traces the basic steps that have been identified with the process itself:

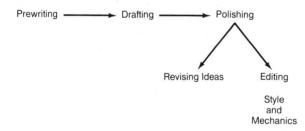

The prewriting stage involves exploring new ideas and relating them to previous experience. Prewriting occurs any time you are thinking about the writing task and about the things that could be said about the subject. Prewriting, in a sense, occurs throughout the processes of reading and reviewing a selection and of recording your earliest notes. It also occurs when you are making a conscious effort to recall experiences from the past—from conversations, from activities, and from readings—that have relevance to the subject at hand. The following chapters contain guides for improving the ways in which you can complete each of these specific activities.

This book also includes suggestions for completing the draft of a paper with greater ease and with improved results. Effective drafting demands collecting ideas and presenting them in a sequence that makes sense to those who will read or hear the composition. Most writers need to compose several drafts to meet the demands of their writing task and to satisfy the needs of their readers.

Most writers also need to spend time on polishing. Although many of us shortchange ourselves at this stage by simply looking for errors in usage, effective polishing demands a commitment to careful *revision* involving a check of ideas and a survey of form. True revision, in fact, involves a *re*-vision or a *re*-thinking of what has been said and how it has been presented, and it usually demands that we shift and rewrite paragraphs, expand or rework introductions and conclusions, and adjust the amount and kinds of details that represent our principal sources of support. Editing, on the other hand, involves attention to usage and can be improved with the aid of a handbook or the assistance of a friend.

Identifying each of these stages enables us to discuss their characteristics and to practice strategies for moving through them. Nonetheless, you should always remember that writing itself is *not* the product of a clear-cut advance from prewriting to revision; most people double back and jump forward unpredictably as they write. This unpredictability leads the experts to describe writing as a *recursive process*, with *recursive* defined as "flowing and circling back, again and again."

To provide practical help with these strategies, most chapters of this book open with a new approach to prewriting and conclude with suggestions for polishing the drafts that will result. Chapter 2 also offers a method for drafting a paper that can be applied to most of the assignments that will face you in college and beyond.

THE AIMS AND SEQUENCE

Every effective communication demands attention not only to language but also to the persons and to the sources of ideas that are essential in sharing human experience. These essential components are (1) the writer or speaker, (2) the content, and (3) the reader or hearer. This book covers ways of adapting your writing to the component you wish to stress. Identifying each of these with points on a triangle makes them easy to remember. The triangle

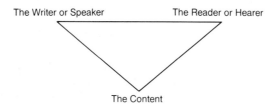

The Writer or Speaker   The Reader or Hearer

The Content

itself also stresses that all three components will be present in most written and spoken composition; as a model, it obviously reflects the belief that, if a tree falls in a forest when no one is there to hear it, there cannot be a sound.

Aside from depicting the essential ingredients of all communication, the triangle also describes the major aims that dominate all of our speech and writing. These aims are products of a heightened attention to one of the components involved. Although attention to each is always necessary, nearly every composition will be marked by a special concern for one of them, and this concern surfaces in the composition's style, organization, and adjustments to the needs of the reader. One of the following is, in fact, usually identified as a *primary aim* in materials that we read and hear. These are the self-expressive, the persuasive, the informative, and the researched aims. This triangle illustrates their relationships.

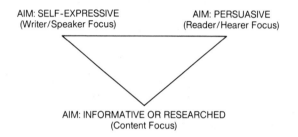

AIM: SELF-EXPRESSIVE (Writer/Speaker Focus)

AIM: PERSUASIVE (Reader/Hearer Focus)

AIM: INFORMATIVE OR RESEARCHED (Content Focus)

The triangle's left corner indicates that composition focused upon the author is *self-expression.* Self-expressive communication embodies the writer's or speaker's efforts to discover meaning or to detail personal thoughts and feelings. In fact, we usually read a self-expressive composition to learn something about its author. Examples of self-expression include diaries, biographies, editorials, and letters; Pepys' journal, Buckley's editorials, and the letters of Harry S. Truman are all dominated by this, the most personal of aims.

On the other hand, communications that are focused upon the reader or hearer in order to advance the composer's point of view are commonly known as *persuasive.* Some forms of persuasion—some political addresses, for example—simply encourage the audience to admire the personality or the qualifications of the speaker or writer. Other examples of persuasion are advertising copy, legal addresses, and sermons. Frequently, those who wish to persuade a group will actually pursue its members, a fact evidenced by the many phone calls and the armloads of mail that arrive daily from those who are seeking our votes or are trying to solicit our business.

Finally, composition that seeks to inform or to establish a point appears at the content position on the triangle. Its placement shows that conveying facts and ideas is an overriding concern of the author. Later, I will explain critical distinctions between writing to inform and writing to establish or to demonstrate a point. For now, we may simply associate informative writing with reports of data given to those for whom such material was previously unknown, and we may identify news stories, textbooks, and laboratory reports as examples of this aim in writing.

Because discovering and clarifying personal responses to experience must precede efforts with all kinds of writing, we will follow the sequence of aims described above. This book opens by describing the characteristics of effective self-expression before moving on to a study of the informative aim, which considers problems of conveying material to readers. It then discusses methods for persuading readers to accept a particular interpretation of experience, and it surveys ways to support each major assertion. These strategies will be most important to you later, when you are engaged in researched writing.

CHAPTER SUMMARY

Good writing is important to success in college as well as in many businesses and most professions. Learning to write effectively about selections in literature can help you write effectively in other subjects with many different kinds of assignments; the act of writing in response to a text involves several specific skills that are common to every discipline.

This book contains suggestions for improving your efforts at each stage in the writing process. It contains strategies for prewriting, writing, and revision as well as exercises for generating a specific paper. Chapter 2 surveys steps for beginning and completing a draft that can be used with all of your writing assignments.

This book should also help you become a better reader. Each section is devoted to explaining details that will help you evaluate examples of the self-expressive, the informative, the persuasive, and the researched aims of writing. Because exploring your own ideas is a prerequisite to all successful composition, the text opens with the self-expressive aim before moving on to each of the others.

FOR PRACTICE

1. Clip an article from your local or college paper. Underline those parts you think represent the aims that interact in most written and spoken communication. Be able, in other words, to distinguish between the characteristics of self-expressive, informative, persuasive, and researched writing.
2. List three written or spoken communications you have read or have listened to within the past week. For each, identify what seemed to have been the communicator's primary aim. Again, use the communication triangle described in this chapter as the source of your descriptions of aim. Be prepared to discuss your reasons for identifying particular aims that you can associate with each communication.

Chapter

2

Self-Expressive Responses to Literature

CHAPTER PREVIEW
Self-Expressive Writing: Its Forms and Functions

A good place to start any study of writing, including writing about literature, is with self-expressive composition. Because self-expression emphasizes the writer's personal responses to an idea or to an experience, cultivating the relaxed and personal voice and the loose, free-wheeling structure commonly associated with this aim can help eliminate many of the attitudes and habits that inhibit most writing behavior, no matter what the task. Besides, isn't it easier to communicate with others when you clearly understand your own position regarding the subject discussed?

Private and *public* are terms usually associated with self-expressive writing. Examples of private forms of self-expression include preliminary notes, first drafts of papers, and scribblings in diaries and journals. Public forms, which begin as private writing but are revised for sharing with others, include film reviews, editorials, and autobiographies.

This chapter covers ways of transforming private expression into public communication. Its opening survey of strategies for *prewriting* or recording first responses precedes suggestions for using prewriting to generate a thesis and to compose a rough first draft. Its final sections identify several characteristics of coherent style that should guide your polishing for readers. Throughout, the chapter's models are products of character analyses suggested by short stories, poems, and plays.

RECORDING INITIAL RESPONSES

Prewriting: Its Uses and Limitations

Recording notes in response to your reading is known as *prewriting;* so, too, is studying the literature you have been assigned and marking passages as you read. Both kinds of prewriting are essential to effective composition, regardless of the aim.

Prewriting helps you improve your writing in at least two ways. First, it enables you to play with ideas early in the writing process so that you know what to omit, what to include, and what to study further. Second, it encourages you to write down *something* in a hurry so that you can see that you *do* have something to say, even if you are uncomfortable with the subject.

Whereas prewriting can calm your fears and can give you some direction, one sitting rarely generates *all* the material you will need to complete an assignment. You will usually need to employ several different strategies at various stages in the writing process in order to improve your composition. You can begin building your repertoire of strategies by studying the sections that follow.

Freewriting

Freewriting is just what its name suggests—writing freely. Your primary objective with freewriting should be to let your mind and pen wander so that you can pull ideas from memory that have bearing upon the subject at hand. Learning to write quickly and to avoid rereading, judging, or editing your work will improve the chances that you can recapture a lot of the ideas you have stored. The following guidelines will help you with this process:

FREEWRITING GUIDELINES

1. First, determine the number of minutes you will write before you begin the procedure. Five- to ten-minute periods are good at project beginnings; fifteen- to twenty-minute intervals are good if you have done some research or have extensive prior knowledge about the subject.
2. Concentrate upon speed and quantity. Try to fill up one side of a page of notebook paper for every five-minute period.
3. Forget about grammar, spelling, and mechanics. Think of yourself as *talking to yourself on paper.*
4. Do *not* reread anything until the time period is over.
5. If your mind goes blank, rewrite the last word generated over and over until ideas start flowing again.

Here are some freewriting samples collected in my own classes. They were products of the freewriting activity described in the For Practice exercise below.

SAMPLE 1:

The shepherd reminds me of those silly, sugar filled novels that flood bookstores. Harlequin Romance type novels. The kind of thing women read in laundromats and watch on the television soap operas. The fantasy world that is introduced to young girls in the novels they read. In no way prepares them for the realities and truths of love. Love here is all peaches and cream but in fact love hurts and it hurts badly sometimes. This is probably why the divorce rate is so high. Too many people are living in the fantasy world of love not a true, day to day relationship that love needs to blossom and grow.

(*Christine L. Bertram*)

SAMPLE 2:

To start off this freewriting time, I am feeling nervous. I think the reason is because half the time I make it very hard for myself to understand poems. In other words I think I have a total mental block towards them. I took a poem course in high school and towards the end of the course I began to understand poems and their reasonings. I am almost forgetting what I was about to say. Back to what I was talking about. I hope this isn't going to be a hard class.

(*Jodi Murphy*)

FOR PRACTICE

Christopher Marlowe's "The Passionate Shepherd to His Love" and Sir Walter Raleigh's "The Nymph's Reply to the Shepherd" have been reproduced at the end of this chapter (p. 21). Read both carefully before spending ten minutes freewriting about them. Observe the guidelines listed above as you write. You may respond to them as a set or as single poems. Write anything you wish; the objective is to explore your thoughts and feelings as you cover your paper.

Focused Freewriting

Focused freewriting differs from general freewriting in terms of its stimulus. General freewriting begins with your subject, however broad it may be. Focused freewriting begins with a set of questions you may apply to the subject.

One set you can easily memorize and use in all your classes is called the *Five Ws Plus H*. This set is used by the journalist because its answers provide the kinds of information readers expect to find in news articles. Its questions are

1. *Who* is this material about?
2. *What* has happened?

3. *When* did it happen?
4. *Where* did it happen?
5. *Why* did it happen?
6. *How* did it happen?

Accounts, for example, of the attempt on President Reagan's life included information about the would-be assassin (the *who*), the events preceding and following the attempt (the *what*), the location (the *where*), the time and context (the *when*), the possible motive (the *why*), and the means—including the weapon (the *how*).

The guidelines recommended for basic freewriting are equally valid for freewriting that is focused with questions. Remember to determine a time limit before you begin and to concentrate upon writing quickly. Attention to spelling, grammar, and mechanics should come later.

You may answer the questions themselves in one of two ways. You can answer as many of them as possible during the time period set, or you can devote a full time period to each.

Here is a sample from one of my students. She wrote it in response to one of the For Practice exercises that follow.

> The person or the "who" that I am thinking of is the passionate shepherd who is relaying his feeling to his beloved woman. In my point of view he is acting as if everything is perfect and everything will work out. It makes life look like life will be a breeze if one is in love . . .
>
> *(Jodi Murphy)*

FOR PRACTICE

1. Try another ten-minute freewriting using the poems found at the end of this chapter. This time begin with an idea discovered in the first freewriting exercise (e.g., romantic myths, love, practicality, cynicism). Apply one or several of the journalist's questions. Include reasons for your responses.
2. This time practice a focused freewriting in response to another selection. One of the following may interest you:
   a. Paul Simon's "Fifty Ways to Leave Your Lover"
   b. William Stafford's "Now"
   c. Robert Herrick's "To the Virgins to Make Much of Time"
3. If your instructor has assigned a paper, spend ten minutes prewriting about the subject. Use the journalist's questions to help you. Save your notes; you may need to submit them with your final paper draft.

Looping: Position Statements and the Thesis

Looping refers to a second step that may follow focused as well as unfocused freewriting. The procedure involves studying a stretch of freewriting and composing a summarizing sentence that describes its main point. This sentence should include two kinds of information: (1) an identification of the passage's subject and (2) your comment about it. Because the comment makes it contestable, I call it a *position statement.* You have probably written *position papers* in school, so you can understand the appropriateness of the term. Position papers are usually subjective responses to issues of social significance.

Looping itself takes its name from the process's function. Because the position statement synthesizes most of the ideas in the freewriting passage, it closes in the gaps that separate them, thereby closing a hypothetical loop.

Here is a stretch of freewriting that is followed by a position statement. The material was written in response to the Raleigh poem mentioned earlier. Notice how the statement expresses the passage's dominant idea; it answers the question, "So what?"

> This girl may love the shepherd. We don't know. She did bother to answer him so that's something. She seems to like the idea of flowers and all but she also worries a lot about what happens when its winter and things start to die. She also must have been mixed up with some liars in the past because first thing she doubts that shepherds speak the truth very often.
>
> *Position Statement:* The shepherd's love may care for him, but she is too cautious to simply run away with him.

Writing position statements for prewriting notes helps you explore your thinking and discover ideas. Writing position statements for whole essays helps you ensure each paper's unity. A position statement that summarizes the ideas found in all of a paper's paragraphs is called a *thesis sentence.*

One way to write a thesis sentence is to complete one of the following structures. These patterns will help you remember to include the two parts that each thesis and each position statement should contain: the identification of your subject and your comment about it. Below each pattern are samples showing how each may be completed and varied.

Pattern 1: I think _____ is _____.
Pattern 2: I think _____ consists of _____, _____, and _____. (Here you may list two or more elements, problems, parts, etc.)

SAMPLES

1. I think *the boy's experience in "Araby"* is *one we all face as adolescents.* (Pattern 1)
2. We all face experiences such as that of the boy in "Araby" when we are adolescents. (Revised Pattern 1 sentence)
3. I think *the boy's awakening* consists of *his awareness of the girl's shallowness* and *his recognition of his own vulnerability.* (Pattern 2)

10

4. The boy's awareness of the girl's shallowness and his recognition of his own vulnerability are the critical components of his awakening. (Revised Pattern 2 sentence)

FOR PRACTICE

1. Try another looping practice, this time applying the strategy to a longer selection such as a short story. Begin as with an unfocused freewriting for five or ten minutes. When you have finished, write a summarizing position statement to close the loop.
2. Take the position statement you developed above and use *it* as the subject of a second freewriting and looping practice. Notice how much more limited your second position statement is.

DRAFTING AND REVISING

Writing the First Draft from a Thesis

Developing an explicit thesis is as important to the writing process as it is to the finished product. Readers need to find a thesis in order to understand your meanings; you need to produce this thesis in order to generate effective writing. What follows are suggestions for using a thesis sentence when you are ready to compose a draft.

Although everyone possesses unique composing habits, many writers may be classified into one of three groups according to the time they usually spend on drafting and revision. In her textbook entitled *Successful Writing,* Maxine Hairston has described each group's representatives and has called them *bleeders, plodders,* and *sprinters.*

Bleeders spend hours producing single sentences and paragraphs and generally find writing painful. Plodders also move slowly through first drafts, but they do not suffer as much as bleeders do because they plan to rewrite, giving themselves second and third chances to improve first efforts. Sprinters are the happiest writers of all, for they breeze quickly through first drafts and are willing to revise essays three or four times before they submit them for grades or publication.

Most of you have probably been sprinters, plodders, and bleeders at one time or another; most writers assume a variety of habits, depending upon the assignment and the situation. Many students, however, tend to avoid sprinting with school assignments because they are afraid of relaxing, even in earliest stages of formal writing. If you find yourself afraid of sprinting, you might observe the following guidelines for composing the first draft of a paper. These guidelines are the products of my reading, my own writing, and my conversations with students. They encourage an initial sprinting and, in turn, a more pleasant writing experience. Commit them to memory and return to them each time you are stumped by an assignment.

FOUR STEPS TO A FIRST DRAFT

1. First, create a comfortable environment. Assemble favorite supplies and find a favorite location.
2. Second, reserve and protect the peace and quiet you will need to complete the paper. Unplugging the phone and displaying a "Do Not Disturb" sign for two hours should help with most short essays.
3. Third, slowly reread *all* prewriting, study the thesis sentence, and carefully review any outlines made to guide the paper.
4. Fourth, set all preliminary notes aside and write the draft as quickly as possible, skipping lines on the paper and rereading nothing. The line spaces will facilitate revision. Rereading slows the drafting process; avoid it here as well as in your prewriting.

Observing these instructions will probably cramp your hand. But observing them will also give you a paper draft, and that should prove some consolation. Before proceeding to revision strategies, try the steps yourself.

FOR PRACTICE

Using any prewriting you have completed to this point, follow the four steps listed above and produce a first, rough draft for a paper for this or any other course.

Checking for Paragraph Unity and Clear Topic Sentences

Developing a clear thesis sentence and introducing it early in the paper are essential steps in readying self-expressive essays for readers. So, too, is dividing the body of the paper into unified paragraphs that open with clear topic sentences.

Most written communications, regardless of their aims, must be divided into smaller units to facilitate their reading. Such divisions help readers by indicating important shifts in ideas. Plays are spaced to show breaks within and between dialogue segments as well as between scenes and acts. Short stories, novels, and poems are broken between line and sentence groups. Just counting the stanza divisions in "The Passionate Shepherd to His Love" provides a guide to the number of reasons the young man advances to support his proposal.

The clearest paragraphs in expository composition are not only arranged to indicate shifts in thought but are also introduced with *topic sentences*. These sentences identify the subject of the unit and, because they preview *all* the ideas that follow them, are usually more general than the other sentences in the paragraph.

Even paragraphs in literature sometimes open with previewing topic sentences. Notice how the first sentence in this paragraph from "The Egg" is more general than those that follow it. It identifies that quality, the propensity for turning out badly, that is common to *all* the parents' particular endeavors.

The first venture into which the two people [i.e. the narrator's parents] went turned out badly. They rented ten acres of poor stony land on Grigg's Road, eight miles from Bidwell, and launched into chicken-raising. I grew into boyhood on the place and got my first impressions of life there. From the beginning they were impressions of disaster, and if, in my turn, I am a gloomy man inclined to see the darker side of life, I attribute it to the fact that what should have been for me the happy joyous days of childhood were spent on a chicken farm.

FOR PRACTICE

1. Skim one short story previously assigned for this course. Identify paragraphs whose first sentences preview ideas found in following sentences. These topic sentences will resemble thesis statements inasmuch as each possesses two basic components: (a) a precise identification of the subject and (2) an expression of the writer's attitude.
2. Survey one of your textbooks, identifying paragraphs with clear topic sentences as you did above.
3. Write a unified paragraph of four to six sentences about some part of a paper topic you are currently developing. Open the paragraph with a clear topic sentence.

POLISHING SELF-EXPRESSIVE STYLE FOR READERS

Just as prewriting details are initially ordered by a logic known only to the writer, so may words and sentences appear choppy and nonsensical in the earliest stages of self-expression. Choppiness and nonsense are desirable when writing is used for discovery because worry about coherence at this stage can interrupt the thinking process. But when you do wish to share ideas with others, you need to subject your draft to two tests and to rewrite it as necessary.

First, you need to check the adequacy of the support offered for the paper's important ideas. If assertions remain that may be unconvincing, you either need to drop them altogether or to add more examples to strengthen them. Revising ideas in this way should dominate most polishing efforts.

Once these changes have been made, you can proceed to the second

13

step in polishing, that of editing for style and mechanics. What follows are suggestions for editing self-expressive writing so that its style is clear and comprehensible.

Self-Expressive Language

Self-expressive style is really unlike anything taught in schools. In fact, many teachers actually discourage the use of elements commonly associated with self-expression, chiefly because self-expressive style is largely egocentric. A primary purpose of many classes is to minimize self-centered communication and to encourage dialogues between individuals and groups.

But several qualities in self-expressive language can actually improve communication, even in informative and in researched writing. The following survey of two of these qualities has been included to help you decide what to retain and what to discard.

First, use of first-person pronouns is a distinguishing characteristic of self-expression. These pronouns include *I, we, our,* and *my.* Emphasizing your own opinions about a subject naturally encourages the use of such personal words as these; attempts to avoid them often generate wordiness and confusion.

A second distinguishing feature of self-expressive style is the use of personal experience to support important generalizations. I encourage my students to incorporate examples from their own lives to support the points they make. This encouragement gives them the freedom to claim that a particular character or story incident reminds them of people and events they have known themselves. Such claims produce the specific detailing that adds interest to papers. The preceding, by the way, is an example from *my* experience.

Since self-expressive style is more relaxed than styles of other discourse aims, assessing the nature of your relationship with your readers is an important prerequisite to deciding upon the level of formality that will dominate your paper. As a rule, those readers who know little about you will expect a minimum of allusions to yourself and to your experiences. Smaller groups of readers who share problems and interests with which you can identify will be more receptive to frequent references to yourself.

Convention

No matter what the audience, readers of essays about literature will expect you to observe several conventions for discussing time and for documenting examples. The following sections summarize several principles that must be observed in all writing about literature, no matter what the aim.

Convention 1: Literary Present   Using *literary present* simply means using present-tense verbs to describe events occurring in a poem, a story, a novel, or a play. Literary present generates "Marlowe's shepherd *is* idealistic." It also produces "Joyce's character *is blinded* by his infatuation."

The rationale for present stress is that action occurring in literature will never be relegated to the past; new readers may always pick up the material to find the events occurring again and again. This conception of time is also important in writing in other disciplines. Historians use *historical present* to generate such expressions as "Lincoln is shot at the Ford Theater," and a psychologist might write that "by mid-century, schizophrenia is considered a serious disorder."

Literary present should usually dominate writing about events occurring within the storyteller's own experience. Use present-tense verbs to describe those experiences mentioned by the narrators of "The Egg" and "Araby" from the times of their earliest memories.

The only times when literary present will *not* be appropriate will be when you are hypothesizing future consequences or when you are describing events occurring *prior* to the story's opening or to the teller's participation in its action. *Perfect* verbs will be appropriate in these situations. Perfect forms include such expressions as *had done, has committed,* and *will have learned.* The following time line and descriptions should help clarify these distinctions for you.

Suppose James Joyce had given us more information about his narrator's life as he had experienced it before the opening of "Araby." Further suppose that you are imagining events which may have occurred prior to or later than those found in the story. In each case, details and speculations should be expressed with such perfect tense forms as these:

Example 1: The boy *has* probably *lost* his parents to illness.
Example 2: The boy's uncle *had* probably *supported* him in the past.

The differences between your choice of *has* and *had* may best be explained by these time spots:

——————X————————	————X————————	————X—————————	————X————
Events or conditions *completed before* present as depicted in story. Use *had* form: e.g. The uncle *had been* supportive. e.g. The boy *had* not *attended* the fair.	Events begun *before present* in story and continuing into it—use *has* form: e.g. The boy *has lost* his parents.	Present time in story— use present form: e.g. The boy *speaks* to Mangan's sister.	Time in some hypothetical future after story closes— use future, future perfect. See a handbook for these; you probably won't use them much.

A grammar handbook will provide a fuller explanation of tense alternatives. In the meantime, simply remember to use present tense unless you have a good reason for using a past form.

Conventions 2 and 3: Using Paraphrase and Direct Quotation

Concern for paraphrase and quotation is concern for support as well as for style. The following strategies for effective reference are covered here because each requires adjustments in mechanics as well as in content and language.

First, shared self-expression needs frequent and specific references to the literature itself if it is to be interesting and clear. Readers want to know what triggered the writer's response. Explaining the stimulus may require a sentence, such as this one, that has been drawn from the material: "The nymph's statement that things might be different if all shepherds told the truth suggests that she has known many who were liars." Even those who have read the poem will appreciate the reference, for it will help them to recall details they may have forgotten. It will also explain and, in turn, strengthen the writer's position. Just beware of turning your paper into a mere retelling of the story. Readers can go over it themselves if they want to, and, in self-expressive writing, they will be expecting to learn what *you* think about the material.

A second strategy for effective reference involves direct quotation from the reading itself. Although self-expression uses fewer direct quotations than do the other writing aims, incorporating a few words of dialogue or a line of poetry into the text may strengthen your assertions, particularly if the *way* in which the idea is expressed in the original source is important to your message. When you do use words exactly as they were written, you must *always* give credit to the literature's author so that the reader knows whose words they are. Failure to give credit is *plagiarism,* an extremely serious offense; using another's words without specifying the source is theft.

Essays about literature give credit in one of two ways. The first involves footnote or endnote documentation, and the second involves parenthetical notation. Most term papers assigned in high school or for other college classes have probably acquainted you with the former; you need to learn the rules that govern the second or parenthetical method because it represents the system now endorsed by the Modern Language Association and included in most handbooks describing research conventions for writing in the humanities.

The following guidelines and examples should provide sufficient information about this system to enable you to credit sources in brief essays about literature. Just remember that the advice to restrict parenthetical notations at this time to direct quotations is valid inasmuch as most assignments depicted in these chapters assume readers have copies of the selections discussed and can check on the accuracy of your paraphrases. Later, when you are writing a research paper or when you cannot assume readers have the literature before them, you *must* include parenthetical notes for paraphrases as well as for direct quotations; this issue is covered more thoroughly in Chapter 9.

The principal difference between footnote/endnote methods and the parenthetical method is that the newer system assumes that notes containing publishing information, both within the paper and in lists at the paper's end, are superfluous; parentheses listing the author's name or references to the material itself within the paper's body are considered adequate guides to the publishing data detailed in the bibliography or available to readers who have copies of the selection cited. Because of this assumption, the parenthetical approach to documentation is both simpler to learn and to complete than systems that have preceded it, and it is obviously more concise.

The method's conciseness surfaces in the content as well as in the punctuation that it includes in its notations. Instead of raised numerals directing readers to notes listed elsewhere, the new notation system uses parentheses to enclose the information the reader needs in order to find the specific reference; if the paper's subject or the surrounding sentences do not make perfectly clear the name and title of the work, the last name and an abbreviated title appear with the relevant page numbers within parentheses. These parentheses are, in turn, placed either at the sentence's end or close to the quotation itself. Commas are used to separate the author name and the abbreviated title if these are necessary; commas do *not* separate the name or title from the page number. Neither do the words *page* or *pages* or their respective abbreviations appear within the parentheses; everywhere, the emphasis is upon restricting information to just those details the reader needs in order to locate the quotation within the material or to find publishing data listed in an attached bibliography. Here are sample sentences including parenthetical notations:

FOR PAPERS DEVOTED TO ONE SELECTION (i.e., AUTHOR AND TITLE MENTIONED IN INTRODUCTORY SECTION)

Anderson's narrator opens by explaining his belief that his father was
 "intended by nature to be a cheerful, kindly man" (601).
The narrator says, "I went to work the next day, turning, so to speak,
 my back on that station" (229).

FOR PAPERS OR PAPER SECTIONS IN WHICH AUTHOR OR TITLE OR BOTH MAY NOT BE CLEAR

[All below are from D. H. Lawrence's "The Horse Dealer's Daughter."]
Mabel leaves the house when the afternoon is "grey, deadened, and
 wintry, with a slow, moist heavy coldness sinking in and deadening
 all the faculties" (Lawrence, "Daughter" 675).
Mabel leaves the house when the afternoon is "grey, deadened, and
 wintry, with a slow, moist heavy coldness sinking in and deadening
 all the faculties" (Lawrence 675).
Mabel leaves the house when the afternoon is "grey, deadened, and
 wintry, with a slow, moist heavy coldness sinking in and deadening
 all the faculties" ("Daughter" 675).

17

For Papers about a Poem

The passionate shepherd says, "come live with me and be my love"
(line 1).
[The preceding is a first reference to the poem; the word *line* establishes
lines as the bases for subsequent references. Its use in the first reference enables you to drop the word in all other notations, according
to the following model.]
The passionate shepherd says, "come live with me and by my love"
(1).

For References to Quotations from Specific Acts
and Scenes in Plays

Mary shrieks, "I will not stay. I cannot tolerate your stupidity any
longer" and leaves (2.4).

Notice that the quotation is closed *before* the parentheses in each of
these examples but that the writer's own sentence periods *follow* the parentheses. This punctuation represents another practice that should be observed in order to meet your readers' expectations.

CHAPTER SUMMARY

This chapter distinguishes between the private and public forms of self-
expressive writing by surveying the purposes and distinctive characteristics
of each. Private self-expression helps you retrieve and discover ideas at the
beginning of every writing project. It may be stimulated by prewriting strategies because such strategies encourage free and fluent writing as an antidote
to worries about grammar and mechanics that may inhibit thinking. Freewriting and responding to the journalist's questions will help you generate and
record ideas as you work to complete many different writing tasks.

Looping is an activity that may follow any of the prewriting procedures
described in this and in following chapters. Creating a *loop* or summarizing
statement helps you transform private self-expression into public or shared
writing because it suggests the content of your essay. When this statement
summarizes the main idea of the whole paper, it is called a *thesis sentence*.
Determining the thesis sentence is a prerequisite to initiating and completing
a first draft with speed and ease.

Once you have completed your draft, you need to revise its ideas, tighten
its structure, and polish its style. Here, too, the thesis will be important.
Including it in your introduction gives readers a guide for interpreting the
composition's parts.

Public self-expression also needs division into readable units and attention to conventions of style. Paragraphs or units possessing clear topic sentences are usually the easiest to read. Topic sentences, like thesis statements,

may be products of looping; each should identify the paragraph's subject as well as your comment about it. Important conventions in writing about literature include observing literary present and crediting sources of borrowed material.

To improve your own self-expressive paper, study the Revision Checklist and the student essay that follow. Use the checklist questions to evaluate the paper, identifying possible sources of change in each category, before applying the questions to your own draft. Make sure you can respond positively to each before you submit your final copy.

Revision Checklist for Self-Expressive Paper on Literature

1. *Thesis*
   Does the introduction to the paper contain a sentence that (i) identifies the subject and (ii) expresses the writer's feelings about it?
2. *Organization*
   Is the paper divided into readable units, most of which open with clear topic sentences?
3. *Style*
   a. Are personal pronouns used with a frequency appropriate to the aim and audience?
   b. Are direct quotations followed by appropriate forms for giving credit?

SAMPLE STUDENT ESSAY

"The Egg" by Sherwood Anderson is a story from which I can draw amazing parallels to my grandfather's and my father's lives. "The Egg" deals with a man who had been content with his life until he married an ambitious school teacher. Because her ambition infects him, he soon becomes a man obsessed. In an attempt to raise his social status, he sells most of his belongings and buys a chicken farm. This purchase gives him more setbacks than rewards.

My own grandfather worked on a chicken farm during the Depression, sometimes over sixty hours a week with an income barely sufficient to support his wife and son. The short-term effects of long hours and little rest that burdened him were minor troubles when compared to his lost self-esteem. Still, he refused to take charity from anyone, and that, more than anything else, was his last claim to self-respect in a time of social upheaval. He was working, at no matter how menial a job, at a time when countless other Americans were jobless and wandering the country, living off of government surpluses and unemployment benefits.

The narrator of Anderson's story bears an amazing personality resemblance to my father as well as to my grandfather. I couldn't help but feel this teller's style was impersonal. I also got the impression that his main point was to present a lesson about the effects of unrealistic expectations. This intention is obvious

19

from the first line in the story when the narrator gives us an insight into what he feels was the real personality of his father prior to his marriage. Here, he tells us that his father, he is sure, was "intended by nature to be a cheerful, kindly man" (601).

My own father lived in an environment resembling that of the narrator himself, and he, too, suffered unbearable frustration. Both men were reared in environments in which education was a luxury. Both seem to have achieved some success, at least by monetary standards. Both occasionally saw the outbursts of anger from a man frustrated by the lack of achievements in his life.

The narrator's highly objective style also reminds me of my father. He is a disciplined professional man who rarely lets his own emotions stand in the way of achieving a goal. This observation is not intended to suggest that he is cold or unfeeling; quite the opposite—his sincerity and gentleness are always present, though not always visible.

I think that the main point of this story is to expose the unnecessary pressure we sometimes put on others to meet our expectations. This is the only area in which my grandfather and the story father were different. The father in the story is driven by the ambition his wife has nurtured to a point at which he has a "half-insane light in his eyes" and he begins "to cry like a boy" (608). My grandfather, however, was driven by his own insatiable appetite to better himself as a means of bettering his son.

In retrospect, the story is about a man who thought he failed, but in reality succeeded because his son learned something important from him. This result has been the case with my grandfather as well. He speaks with such pride, it is almost as if he himself had gained the various successes my father has known. I guess he really did.

(David Coale)

SUGGESTED WRITING ASSIGNMENTS

1. Read one of the short stories listed below (or any other that your instructor may assign). Write an essay of 500 to 750 words that explains how or why you can relate to the main character's problems or aspirations. Write for a group whose members know you well and care about you. Assume this group has read the story. This means you will *not* have to spend time explaining what happens within it.

Recommended Choices:

James Joyce's "Araby"
Eudora Welty's "Why I Live at the P.O."
Ray Bradbury's "August 2002: Night Meeting"

2. Read one of the poems listed below (or any other that your instructor may assign). Write an essay of 500 to 750 words which explains what you think of the poem. Be sure to give personal reasons for thinking about it in this way. Wherever possible, add references to experiences of your own which have contributed to this opinion. Write for a group whose members know you well and care about you. Assume they have read the poem and even have a copy of it in front of them.

Recommended Choices:

John Lennon and Paul McCartney's "All You Need Is Love"
Robert Frost's "The Death of the Hired Man"
John Keats' "Ode on a Grecian Urn"

POEMS

The Passionate Shepherd to His Love

Come live with me and be my love,
And we will all the pleasures prove
That valleys, groves, hills, and fields,
Woods, or steepy mountain yields.

And we will sit upon the rocks,
Seeing the shepherds feed their flocks
By shallow rivers, to whose falls
Melodious birds sing madrigals.

And I will make thee beds of roses
And a thousand fragrant posies,
A cap of flowers and a kirtle
Embroidered all with leaves of myrtle;

A gown made of the finest wool
Which from our pretty lambs we pull;
Fair-lined slippers for the cold,
With buckles of the purest gold;

A belt of straw and ivy buds,
With coral clasps and amber studs.
And if these pleasures may thee move,
Come live with me and be my love.

The shepherd swains shall dance and sing
For thy delight each May morning.
If these delights thy mind may move,
Then live with me and be my love.

(Christopher Marlowe)

The Nymph's Reply to the Shepherd

If all the world and love were young,
And truth in every shepherd's tongue,
These pretty pleasures might me move
To live with thee and be thy love.

Time drives the flocks from field to fold,
When rivers rage and rocks grow cold,
And Philomel becometh dumb;
The rest complains of cares to come.

The flowers do fade, and wanton fields
To wayward winter reckoning yields.
A honey tongue, a heart of gall,
Is fancy's spring, but sorrow's fall.

Thy gowns, thy shoes, thy beds of roses,
Thy cap, thy kirtle, and thy posies
Soon break, soon wither, soon forgotten:
In folly ripe, in reason rotten.

Thy belt of straw and ivy buds,
Thy coral clasps and amber studs,
All these in me no means can move
To come to thee and be thy love.

But could youth last and love still breed,
Had joys no date nor age no need,
Then these delights my mind might move
To live with thee and be thy love.

(Sir Walter Raleigh)

Chapter

3

Informative Writing about Characters in Literature

CHAPTER PREVIEW
Information: What It Is and How It May Be Studied

Because the informative aim dominates most composition assigned in college and in the professions, learning to assess the informative value of your ideas and of their support can improve most of the writing with which you will ever be engaged. The following sections discuss the characteristics of material that is rich in informative value; each derives from the findings of communication specialists who note that most readers will judge a composition as *informative* when they can answer *yes* to the following questions:

1. Is it news?
2. Is it comprehensive?
3. Can its accuracy be verified?

To be informative, material must represent *news* or something previously unknown to the audience. Few readers will study yesterday's newspaper articles or reread a once-suspenseful mystery; those who do will probably have had no other exposure to current events or will have a special motive (e.g., a report or other assignment) for reviewing the now-stale thriller.

As each of these examples shows, the newsworthiness of any report must be judged with reference to a specific group of readers. One person may water ski regularly while another may just be learning; instructions for holding onto the line would obviously be wasted on the first individual. Determining the nature and the extent of information the reader or listener already possesses is a critical first step in selecting the facts and the observations that will be appropriate for any given audience.

The newsworthiness of any report also depends upon the extent of the coverage, or the *comprehensiveness,* the reader has been conditioned to expect. Some of this conditioning, as will be further detailed, is actually a product of reading the paper itself. An essay that opens with the promise to analyze point of view in "The Passionate Shepherd to His Love" but lapses into a summary of its central request will not only have failed the test of comprehensiveness but also will have damaged the credibility of its author. Such a paper, by failing to fulfill the intentions of its thesis, will leave most of its readers confused if not annoyed and disappointed as well.

Such a paraphrase will also fail if the writing misquotes the shepherd or attributes words to him that cannot be found in the poem. Readers need to be able to verify details in order to be convinced that a message is truly informative; careful quotation, paraphrase, and documentation are essential to ensuring such verification.

Because meeting these tests is critical in producing essays with informative value, this chapter emphasizes prewriting, planning, and polishing activities that will enhance the newsworthiness, the comprehensiveness, and the verifiability of the details you present in your own composition. It opens with strategies for analyzing character and for composing plot summaries of the literature you have read.

Learning to distinguish between papers that simply summarize and those that defend a thesis is important if you wish to provide your readers with information they may not have abstracted for themselves. Furthermore, the chapter's attention to sources of precision in the thesis will help ensure that your papers are comprehensive because it suggests ways to limit a paper's promises to ideas that can be reasonably and fully covered; as already noted, the thesis is an announcement of the writer's commitment. Finally, the chapter's discussion of ways to integrate and to document selected quotations is important to ensuring the verifiability of your major observations; specifying *where* material can be found in the original selection enables readers to check the accuracy of your support if they wish to do so for themselves.

PREWRITING: READING CAREFULLY AND RECORDING RESPONSES TO CHARACTERS

Reading and Responding: Thinking about Major Characters

Because most of us are drawn to the concerns of others—a phenomenon that helps to explain the popularity of soap operas—character study can be an interesting experience. Character study is also the key to an understanding of literature inasmuch as most significant themes, incidents, and symbols are the reflections of specific character behaviors.

One way to ensure that a character analysis will be highly informative is to read carefully and to take extensive notes even before starting a draft. The focused prewriting strategies covered in the last chapter will help, as will the following adaptation of questions used by journalists. Any of these methods will improve the quality of your ideas and, in turn, your writing as long as you regard them as suggestions for generating notes and *not* as sources of limitation. You should always feel free to add questions or to revise these sets in order to heed one author's advice and *write from abundance.*

These questions are best approached according to the, following two-step procedure. First, read through them slowly *before* reading the literature assigned so you know what to look for. Second, use the questions to generate prewriting notes as you did for Chapter 2. Again, aim for the speed and fluency that governed your unfocused freewriting. If several different questions elicit overlaps in ideas, don't worry. Simply move on to the next or repeat the response, modifying it as you may.

Focused Questions on Characters in Literature

(Note: Only the first set indicates plural forms; plurals may also apply in subsequent questions.)

WHO

Who is (are) the most important or interesting character(s) here?
Who may be aiding or troubling this (these) character?
Does the principal character (or set of characters) represent something
   (e.g., a class of people, a quality, a behavior, and so forth)?

WHAT

What is this character's main problem?
What does this person say about himself or herself?
What do others say about this character?
What does the behavior or appearance of this character tell us about
   him or her?

WHERE

Where does this character seem most comfortable, powerful, or exceptionally happy?
Where does this character most frequently find problems, trouble?

WHEN

When does this character's conflict begin to intensify?
When does this character or others realize the existence, nature, or
   seriousness of the problem that may trouble him or her?
When is the character's fate fixed?

WHY

Why is this character happy or unhappy, troubled, and so on?
Why does this character behave as he or she does (either habitually
   or in significant, climactic moments in the literature)?

HOW

How might this character have changed his or her circumstances?
How might antagonists have been foiled?

What follows are student notes submitted in response to this question
series. Notice the variety of responses to Matthew Arnold's "Dover Beach,"
a poem that has been reproduced at the end of this chapter on p. 41.

PREWRITING SAMPLE 1:

Dover Beach
Where: Along the sea on the French coast looking at Cliffs of Dover
Who: The narrator
What: The narrator is romantic, it seems as though trust was broken and
   he wants for them to be true to one another again. This character represents
   a mourning lover. I think the character is youthful. The conflict is that
   the two lovers have gotten into a fight and must resolve the trust.
When: Was written during the 1800s. The primary action takes place near
   the beach.
How: To resolve the conflict the two must seek another world where they
   can find dreams and escape the confusing struggles of life.

(Jennifer C. Andrus)

PREWRITING SAMPLE 2:

"Dover Beach"
most significant—narrator
primary characteristics—pessimistic, romantic, confused

represents the longing for more time: fact that life's too short
life period—middle age
social role—none in particular, could be anyone
conflict—not enough time; man vs. nature
historical period—not specified
primary action—Europe: Dover Beach

resolved—never is or will be
couldn't be otherwise settled
force—triumphs because it's nature

something beautiful bringing sadness—1st stanza
human—2nd stanza
used to have a lot of faith (sea was full)—language paints picture
now melancholy—withdrawn, retreating
wants his love to be true because the world seems like dreams
world doesn't really offer anything
doesn't want his love to disappoint the way the world did

(Karen G.)

FOR PRACTICE

1. Pick one section from the question set listed above (e.g., the "What" section) and use it to guide your reading of a narrative poem. Be prepared to discuss your responses in class when you are finished.

Recommended:

Bob Dylan's "The Lonesome Death of Hattie Carroll"
Robert Browning's "My Last Duchess"
William Carlos Williams's "Portrait of a Woman in Bed"
Theodore Roethke's "Elegy for Jane"

2. Use the question series to guide your reading of the selection you may have been assigned for your next paper.

WRITING AND REVISING: STRUCTURING INFORMATION FOR READERS

Assessing Audience Needs: Necessary Background

Public self-expression assumes its readers want to learn about the writer by studying his or her compositions. Those who write autobiographies usually expect this kind of attention. Unfortunately, few of us secure the fame or the notoriety that is necessary to drawing and holding audiences on the strength of personal attractions alone; most of us must address groups whose members do not know or care about us and are primarily interested in learning something new about another subject. In these situations, we need to anticipate the reader's knowledge about and attitudes toward the subject in order to create interest and to relate "news." What follows are suggestions for revising your own papers in order to achieve these ends yourselves.

27

The Importance of Summaries

An important first step in assessing the needs of an audience is determining *how much* most readers already know about the subject. Specialists in foreign policy will not appreciate a summary of international political conditions in an essay about the Middle East. These specialists devote most waking hours to keeping abreast of such conditions and will conclude you have not troubled to consider their status. Film critics will be similarly offended by an essay about the significance of *Citizen Kane* to a history of cinema. *Citizen Kane* is a classic, and most critics will have spent hours studying it. A class of high school students, however, may appreciate a paper discussing the film, especially if they have read nothing about it and are about to watch it for the first time.

Writing about literature is no different from writing about any other subject in terms of weighing the backgrounds of readers. Papers written in response to a literary selection are similar to the papers described above in that they, too, are most informative when built upon the reader's store of knowledge. A Chaucer scholar hardly needs a lengthy description of *The Canterbury Tales*, particularly if he or she has recently published a book or an article on the subject. A description of the *Tales* would be much more appropriate to students enrolled in a course in Middle English.

Because few of your essays will be specifically addressed to literary scholars, including a brief summary of action is justified for several reasons. First, a brief summary will help audience members recall the significant happenings in a selection. They will usually appreciate such a reminder, even if they have recently read the material; most of us process so much information each day that events and details from particular selections frequently run together in our memories and in our thinking. Second, providing a summary of events early in the paper will encourage you to dispense with the plot's details so that you can go on to discuss more meaningful observations. Too many students lapse into retelling the story when they should be developing a more informative thesis; readers can check out the book themselves if they simply want to find out what happened.

The following are suggestions for composing brief plot summaries so that readers at many different levels of expertise will be able to follow your thesis. As you will notice, effective summaries are brief and are centered upon action.

Writing Summaries

For readability and interest, summaries should be limited to one paragraph and should contain *only* the details readers need in order to understand the paper's thesis and support. Paragraphs of four to five sentences or of one- to two-hundred words usually provide adequate coverage. Placing the summary near the beginning provides a logical bridge between the introduction and the first important assertion. Limiting it to one paragraph keeps you from drifting off into a fog of detail.

Although determining what belongs in the paragraph is not easy, you can test your choices by asking if the summary accomplishes each of the following. First, does it provide a general statement about the selection's subject? If uncertain, you can begin your paragraph with "_____ is a story (or poem, play) about _____." This model will generate a sentence such as " 'Araby' is a story about a young boy's loss of innocence." Second, you should ask if the summary covers the elements and events the reader needs to know in order to follow your thesis. To test for this coverage, check to see if the paragraph provides brief responses to several of the following journalist's questions that were introduced in Chapter 2:

1. Who is the principal figure in this selection?
2. Where does most of the action take place?
3. When does it occur?
4. What are the most important events?

Here are samples of summaries written by two of my students in response to a filmed version and a printed version of two short stories. Notice that, in these samples as well as in the list above, answers to the *how* and *why* questions presented in earlier sections on prewriting are not prominent. These answers are absent because they will usually appear in the thesis sentence itself and need no mention in the summary.

SAMPLE 1:

Silent Snow, Secret Snow is a film about a boy who is trying to escape the pressures of the real world. He imagines a world surrounded by snow: a security blanket. The story flashes back and forth between the classroom and his home— the two important factors in his life. The impression is given that the boy tries to escape the real world because he finds it monotonous. In the end, he is living more in his fantasy world of snow than in the real world, for he finds comfort and adventure in his snowy wonderland.

(*Christine Adler*)

SAMPLE 2:

"Babylon Revisited" by F. Scott Fitzgerald is the story of Charlie Wales: his past life of wealth and luxury, the conflicting changes that alter this way of living for Charlie, and his determination to achieve a new and more meaningful life. With the crash of the stock market and the death of his wife, Charlie not only loses money and power, but a sense of personal identity. His daughter, Honoria, is placed under the care of Charlie's sister-in-law and her family when Charlie is placed in a sanitarium. One and a half years later, Charlie is rehabilitated, has curbed his excessive drinking and wants to live with his daughter again.

(*Sherri Baughman*)

FOR PRACTICE

1. Pick one of the stories you have read for class and write a single paragraph summary about it.
2. Write a summary of your reading for a paper for this class or another.

The Importance of the Thesis in Informative Writing

Chapter 2 identifies the thesis sentence as a source of promise to readers concerning the essay's content. As you may recall, this sentence names (1) the paper's subject and (2) the writer's attitude about it.

Although making the thesis explicit is important to public self-expression, it is even more important to informative composition because previewing content facilitates the learning process. To help you improve the previews you write yourself, the following section covers strategies for tightening the thesis sentence and for using it to draft a coherent paper.

Writing Precise Thesis Statements

Precise thesis sentences pin your promise not only to your general subject but also to the specific part of it that is covered in the paper. Making the thesis precise helps insure that the paper meets the second test of informative value, that of comprehensiveness. Readers expect comprehensive papers; they want to find that the content matches the promise. If you promise to develop the idea that "Shakespeare balances humor and pathos in his plays," but only mention *Hamlet*, the audience will feel cheated. A better course is to announce that "Shakespeare balances humor and pathos in *Hamlet*." Here are suggestions for tightening the thesis sentence by making it precise.

SUGGESTIONS FOR PRECISION IN THE THESIS

1. Wherever possible, use the specific names of objects, people or events in the thesis statement. For example:
   The *passionate shepherd* in *Marlowe's poem* is *too lovesick to plan for the future.*
   But avoid:
   The speaker in the poem isn't practical.

2. Wherever possible, insert clarifying adjectives to modify the specific nouns in the thesis. For example:
   The *reluctant* and *unfaithful young* man in *Paul Simon's* "Fifty Ways to Leave Your Lover" would like to let his *current* girlfriend assume responsibility for the *inevitable* hurt he may cause his *other, longtime* love.

But avoid:
The man in "Fifty Ways to Leave Your Lover" can't decide between two women.

The following are thesis statements that are reasonably precise. They were composed by my students in response to F. Scott Fitzgerald's "Babylon Revisited."

SAMPLE 1:

As Charlie Wales in "Babylon Revisited" establishes his new life, he encounters many conflicts, but his new source of strength and determination prevails.

(Sherri Baughman)

SAMPLE 2:

In Fitzgerald's "Babylon Revisited," Charlie has developed into a strong, determined individual who is able to overcome his complex problems because he has learned from his dismal past mistakes.

(Christine Adler)

FOR PRACTICE

1. Review the thesis you wrote for your last paper. Rewrite it, observing the suggestions given above for making it more precise.
2. Examine any prewriting you may be doing for a current assignment. Write several preliminary sentences you might use to develop compositions. Next, rewrite the sentences, making them more precise.

Using Precise Statements to Outline

In addition to providing readers with clear previews, precise thesis statements can help with planning by suggesting the sections of an outline. It is important to remember, however, that the most valuable outlines provide guidance without stifling the natural tendency to drift with new ideas during the writing process. Outlines which most encourage a creative drifting possess two characteristics. First, they include a simple list of the three to five big areas you plan to cover, and second, the list itself derives from key concepts mentioned in the thesis.

Key concepts are the clusters of ideas that emerge when you refine the thesis to make it more precise. The specific names, the modifiers, and the unusual verbs that you have added are key concepts. Below are thesis statements whose key concepts have been circled.

SAMPLE 1:

(Blindness images) in (Joyce's "Araby") give emphasis to the young (boy's early innocence.)

SAMPLE 2:

The (unhappy father) featured in Anderson's ("The Egg") suffers from (inappropriate ambitions.)

Whereas writing thesis sentences and circling clusters of ideas may help you review the parts of speech, the real value of the activity emerges when it is time to draft the paper. Identifying key concepts provides a guide to those areas that may be blocked out in the outline and developed in the paper. The first sentence above might be easily converted into the seeds of a simple outline by listing its clusters as follows:

blindness images
Joyce's "Araby"
boy's early innocence

Clusters from the second sentence could be transformed into this list:

unhappy father
"The Egg"
inappropriate ambitions

These lists or preliminary "scratch" outlines usually need to be restructured so that they are easy to follow. One common change may be to move the story title to an opening position in the outline as a reminder that the paper should usually begin with a summary of the story's action. This change appears in the following:

I. Joyce's "Araby"
II. blindness images
III. boy's early innocence

Simple outlines will not only help ensure that the paper meets the promise of its thesis but also make its writing easier by suggesting a direction for the draft. Such plans will work best if tailored to the specific needs of the assignment and the purpose. Sometimes such adjustments will involve breaking the outline into more subsections. At other times these adjustments will encourage you to expand one subsection while devoting little space to another. The variability that may characterize these expansions and contractions should not be cause for worry; few papers are readily divisible into perfectly balanced segments. The outline should work for you; you should not be working for the outline.

Here is a thesis and scratch outline developed by one of my students:

THESIS: Charlie Wales, the principal character in "Babylon Revisited," is a complex man whose emotional conflicts force him to redefine his values and goals.

(Sherri Baughman)

FOR PRACTICE

Develop a simple outline and use it to guide the draft of a paper for this or any other class. If necessary, review the suggestions for getting through a first draft presented in Chapter 2.

POLISHING INFORMATIVE STYLE

The Importance of Quotation in Informative Style

Effective informative writing demands careful reading, careful previewing, and careful planning. Informative writing also requires references to the literature that are precise and verifiable; readers want concrete evidence for assertions, and all writers need to credit those from whom they have borrowed ideas. This section covers ways of integrating quotations and of crediting their sources.

Writing Readable Direct Quotations

Chapter 2 described quoting sentence *parts* rather than full sentences as the preferable method for citing material. Borrowing parts enables you to combine your own words with those of the author so that all your sentences read smoothly. As the examples below show, combining your own words with those of an author also ensures that verb tenses, whatever their source, will be appropriately aligned. The literary present you should be using will not blend well with the past tenses often found in the sections you are quoting. Notice how much more awkward Sentence 1 is than is Sentence 2 below:

ORIGINAL (FROM CHEKOV'S "GOOSEBERRIES"):

". . . it was a still day, cool and dull."

33

SENTENCE 1 (AWKWARD VERBS):

Chekov's veterinary surgeon awakens and ". . . it was a still day, cool and dull."

SENTENCE 2 (MORE ACCEPTABLE VERB USE):

Chekov's veterinary surgeon awakens to "a still day, cool and dull."

The second good reason for favoring phrase quotation is that it lets the reader know exactly which words belong to you and which to the selection quoted. This distinction will become even more important in the chapters on persuasion and research.

For both of these reasons your writing will be most effective if you use direct quotation as it appears in the first of the following examples. Notice how the first sentence clearly distinguishes between the author of the essay and the author of the literature. Notice also the potential for confusion in the second construction. Many readers will wonder *whose* father was "intended by nature" to be kind; was it the essay writer's or Anderson's boy's?

EXAMPLES

1. Anderson's narrator tells us that he was sure his father was "intended by nature to be a cheerful, kindly man" (601). (Smooth and readable)
2. Anderson's boy's father really means no one any harm. "My father was, I am sure, intended by nature to be a cheerful, kindly man" (601). (Choppy and confusing)

For sentences as readable as the first one above, observe the following guidelines for quotation:

1. Always work quotations into your own sentences. *Never* simply include a full sentence with quotation marks around it in one of your paragraphs.
2. Lift only those words and phrases that add interest, emphasis, or support to surrounding ideas.
3. Leave out the verbs in sections you plan to quote if they are in any other than present tense. You will be using literary present yourself to complete your sentences; integrating a direct quotation with a past verb will not only sound strange but also confuse your reader.
4. Wherever possible, identify the speaker of the words you are quoting. Write such statements as *Marion says . . . , the narrator tells us . . . ,* or even an occasional *we are told that. . . .* Do *not,* however, identify the quoted words with the author of the selection. Authors usually create a different person to tell the story, so you cannot automatically assume that Fitzgerald or Anderson is actually telling us something.

FOR PRACTICE

1. Review a paper you are currently writing. Make sure all direct quotations have been trimmed so that their verbs match those in your own sentences. Also make sure *no* full-sentence direct quotations appear that are not preceded or followed by words of your own.
2. Pick a paragraph from a short story recently covered in class. Write a paragraph of your own that not only summarizes its main points but also includes word and phrase quotations.

Longer Quotations and Punctuation Guidelines

Although shorter quotations are preferable in informative and in researched writing, you may occasionally wish to reproduce several sentences or even a short paragraph. Observing the following rules for spacing and punctuation is necessary when quoting longer excerpts from a selection:

1. Direct quotations exceeding three typed lines *must* be set off from the text.
2. Set-off quotations should be indented at the left margin.
3. Set-off material should be handwritten or typed *without* quotation marks around it. The exception here, of course, occurs when you have a lengthy piece of dialogue which already contains quotation marks. In such cases, retain the double quotation marks (" ") to show who is talking.
4. Set-off quotations used to be single-spaced. Most instructors, however, prefer the new *MLA Handbook* convention that recommends double-spacing. Ask.

Even though set-off or *block* quotations give style variety, use them as infrequently as possible. Compositions filled with chunked-up indentions generally intimidate readers. You cannot afford to put readers off if your primary aim is to convey information to them.

For situations demanding quotation marks, observe the conventions described below. They will apply to the shorter quotations mentioned in the preceding section—citations most frequently requiring attention to quotation marks with medial and terminal punctuation.

Guidelines for Quotation Marks Used with Other Punctuation

1. Periods belong inside the quotation marks.
    Example: On page 25, Joyce's narrator hears the rain as "fine incessant reeds of water playing in the sodden beds."

2. Exclamation points and question marks go inside the quotation marks if they were included in the material borrowed.

   Example: Frank O'Connor's narrator, in speaking of his father's return from the war, exclaims about "the irony of it!"

3. Exclamation points and question marks go outside the quotation marks if they are yours and not your source's.

   Example: Why does Joyce's character tell us that his "eyes burned with anguish and anger"? (Here, the essay writer, not the character is asking the question.)

4. Just as in No. 3 above, place all colons and semicolons outside the quotation marks if they are yours.

   Example: The passionate shepherd promises his love to make her "beds of roses"; he also vows to make her belts of "straw and ivy buds."

5. Commas, like periods, always go *within closing* or end quotation marks; only your own commas go outside them when they precede the quoted material.

   Example: "He laughed," she said, "so I went home."

   Example: She responded, "Thank you, but I cannot go to dinner."

Do notice that these rules need modification with parenthetical credit notations. When marking borrowed material, move the end punctuation *outside* the last parenthesis, leaving the quotation marks to the left of the notation as in the following:

He says, "Her image accompanied me even in places the most hostile to romance" (p. 583).

FOR PRACTICE

Find a journal article in the library whose author is a scholar in your major or in a discipline that interests you. Read the article, noting the inclusion of block quotations and special punctuation conventions. Be prepared to discuss the value of the longer quotations you find and to identify punctuation that conforms to or violates conventions noted above.

Adding and Deleting Material

Occasionally, a direct quotation that is otherwise appropriate will contain some inessential material. You can salvage such quotations by using *ellipses*, three spaced dots that indicate where unnecessary words have been deleted. The following is a direct quotation that has been altered and properly marked with ellipses:

Anderson writes that "until he was thirty-four years old he worked . . . for a man named Thomas Butterworth."

Here is a quotation whose ending corresponds with the end of the essayist's own sentence. Correspondences of this kind require four dots: three to mark the omission and one to end the writer's sentence. Use such quotations sparingly, reserving terminal ellipses for direct quotations which, although forming complete and independent sentences within the composition, were *not* independent in the original.

ORIGINAL:

"At ten o'clock father drove home along a lonely country road, made his horse comfortable for the night, and himself went to bed, quite happy in his position in life."

ALTERATION FOR ESSAY:

The narrator notes that "at ten o'clock father drove home along a lonely country road. . . ."

Adding material may often be as necessary for clarity as is omitting extraneous ideas. Such additions are particularly important in two situations: (1) when an error belongs to the quoted author and not to you and (2) when a word demands special clarification (e.g., a noun or a pronoun).

In either case, brackets ([ ]) are appropriate signals for the addition. With embedded errors, enclose the letters *sic* within the brackets and place the set directly behind the error. This notation says, "thus I found it; the error is not mine." For example:

Mary Smith, writing in 1872, notes that "Charles Dykens [sic] found instant success with the publication of *The Pickwick Papers.*"

With additions for clarity, simply enclose your own material in the brackets and position the set as close as possible to the word to which it refers. For example:

His attitude toward the girl [Mangan's sister] was one of reverence.

FOR PRACTICE

Review the last paper you wrote that contained direct quotation. Check to see if the punctuation conforms to the rules given in preceding sections. Check also for proper placement of parenthetical and bracketed notations. Make changes as necessary to meet conventions described above.

CHAPTER SUMMARY

This chapter distinguishes between the structures, styles, and concern for audience associated with the self-expressive and the informative aims in writing. It also identifies three tests of information value and specifies ways to meet them.

To meet the first test, a composition must contain *news* or facts and ideas previously unknown to the reader. Extensive prewriting and careful analysis of the backgrounds of readers are prerequisites to determining whether or not your ideas and examples represent news. Effective writing about literature also demands a concise plot summary so that the audience has a reminder of the selection's action, even if members have already read the material. Placing the summary in the paper's introduction will also help advance its thesis because dispensing with plot details early on enables you to emphasize more meaningful observations in the space remaining.

Meeting the second test of informative value requires attention to its *comprehensiveness*. Comprehensive essays are those that meet their promises. Because the thesis sentence is a primary source of promise to readers, it needs to be sufficiently precise to describe that part of the subject the paper actually develops.

Finally, to meet the third test for value, information must be verifiable. Verifiable data may be traced to their sources by readers. To ensure verifiability in your own informative papers, observe documentation conventions that not only meet the audience's expectations but also enable its members to return to the original selection themselves.

To ensure that your own essay has informative value, review it with reference to the questions on the following checklist. Studying the student essay at the end of this chapter will also help you plan your revisions.

Revision Checklist for Informative Paper on Character in Literature

1. *Thesis*
   a. Is the thesis *precise,* i.e., does it contain specific names and sufficient adjectives?
   b. Is it stated within the paper's introduction?
2. *Organization*
   a. Does the paper include a concise summary of the literature's major events?
   b. Does the summary appear early in the paper, e.g., in the section following the thesis?
   c. Do every paragraph and every major section explicitly relate to a key concept mentioned in the thesis?
3. *Support, Style, and Mechanics*
   a. Are there sufficient and appropriate references to specific parts of the literature?

b. Do most uses of direct quotation involve words and phrases rather than full sentences?

c. Are quotations extending beyond three lines appropriately indented and spaced?

d. Does every sentence using direct quotation give credit to the author?

e. Are all quotations punctuated according to convention?

SAMPLE STUDENT ESSAY

Tennessee Williams' *The Glass Menagerie* is a play about the Wingfield family. Mr. Wingfield, who deserted the family long before the play takes place, has left his wife Amanda with many regrets about her marriage to him and about her life in general. She seems to want a second chance with her life and uses her daughter Laura's life as a way to relive the good memories of her youth and to correct her mistakes.

Throughout the play, Amanda seems obsessed with gentlemen callers. The author gives the impression that she dwells on this because her days of visits from gentlemen had given her the only truly happy memories she has. That period in her life had been carefree, and she speaks of it with joy. She loves to recount the story of how her family's slave would go to the parish house for more chairs so that all of her gentlemen callers could be seated while she entertained them with her grace, charm, and wit. Her dream is to experience vicariously that joy once more through Laura.

In the hope of finding a gentleman for Laura, Amanda asks her son Tom to invite one of his co-workers to the apartment for dinner. The gentleman turns out to be Jim O'Connor, the only boy Laura had liked in high school. Jim arouses Laura's emotions and hopes, kisses her, and then announces that he is engaged to someone else.

On the evening of the visit, Amanda's actions suggest that she not only wants to retell the story but also wants to relive this time period. For the occasion, Amanda curls her hair in girlish ringlets and dresses in the childish dress with the blue silk sash that she had worn on Sundays when she had received her own gentlemen callers.

When Tom and Jim see her, they are shocked by her aura of girlish Southern vivacity and her display of social charm. Amanda seizes the opportunity to prove her long-professed claim that she is a master of the art of conversation. She throws herself wholeheartedly into her best performance of Southern behavior as she relives her moments of glory in the spotlight. This overly enthusiastic performance embarrasses her family.

Although Amanda is a very forward and aggressive woman, she has never pursued a career. Because of this, she will always be dependent on other people. This is the reason she had pushed Laura into attending Rubicam's Business College. When she finds out that Laura had quit after the first few days, she is horrified and disappointed. She asks, "What is there left but dependency all our lives? I know so well what becomes of unmarried women who aren't prepared to occupy a position" (1.2).

Amanda speaks as though this is her own mistake. She seems to include herself in the consequences of Laura's actions. At this point she realizes the deficiency in her life caused by lack of preparation for self-sufficiency. She speaks with authority, but she refuses to admit that this gap has been the product of her own mistakes. The paradox of the situation is that she wants Laura to attend business college and to prepare herself to "occupy a position," yet she desires Laura to enter the same cycle of dependency on males that she has experienced.

Through Amanda's words and actions, we can see that she is seeking the opportunity for a second chance in life through Laura. The saddest part of the situation is that she makes the same mistakes this time. Despite her good intentions for Laura's life, her attempts backfire because she instinctively succumbs to the urge to relive the memories of her carefree youth. She arranges for Laura to have a gentleman caller, ignoring the fact that this is not in Laura's best interest and that it is the first step toward Laura's falling into the same dependency trap. Thus, in a sense, when Amanda does get the opportunity to re-experience parts of her past, she still repeats her mistakes, and Laura suffers from it.

(*Jacqueline Moenssens*)

SUGGESTED WRITING ASSIGNMENTS

1. Pick a short story containing a particularly interesting character. Using strategies covered in this chapter, develop a paper of 500 to 750 words from an informative thesis about the character you have chosen. Feel free to incorporate characteristics from the self-expressive style covered in the last chapter; these characteristics will be appropriate to the audience. Write for a group of freshman English students who have copies of your own class anthology. Assume these readers are registered in another section; this means you know few, if any, of them, personally.

Recommended:

Nathaniel Hawthorne's "Young Goodman Brown"
Bernard Malamud's "The Magic Barrel"
James Thurber's "The Catbird Seat"
Herman Melville's "Bartleby the Scrivener"

2. Follow instructions for purpose and audience in item No. 1 above but substitute a poem involving an interesting character for the short story.

Recommended:

Bob Dylan's "The Lonesome Death of Hattie Carroll"
Lennon and McCartney's "Eleanor Rigby"
Langston Hughes' "Young Gal's Blues"
Thomas Hardy's "Her Death and After"

Dover Beach

The sea is calm tonight,
The tide is full, the moon lies fair
Upon the straits;—on the French coast the light
Gleams and is gone; the cliffs of England stand,
Glimmering and vast, out in the tranquil bay.
Come to the window, sweet is the night-air!
Only, from the long line of spray
Where the sea meets the moon-blanched land,
Listen! you hear the grating roar
Of pebbles which the waves draw back, and fling,
At their return, up the high strand,
Begin, and cease, and then again begin,
With tremulous cadence slow, and bring
The eternal note of sadness in.

Sophocles long ago
Heard it on the Aegean, and it brought
Into his mind the turbid ebb and flow
Of human misery; we
Find also in the sound a thought,
Hearing it by this distant northern sea.

The Sea of Faith
Was once, too, at the full, and round earth's shore
Lay like the folds of a bright girdle furled.
But now I only hear
Its melancholy, long, withdrawing roar,
Retreating, to the breath
Of the night-wind, down the vast edges drear
And naked shingles of the world.

Ah, love, let us be true
To one another! for the world, which seems
To lie before us like a land of dreams,
So various, so beautiful, so new,
Hath really neither joy, nor love, nor light,
Nor certitude, nor peace, nor help for pain;
And we are here as on a darkling plain
Swept with confused alarms of struggle and flight,
Where ignorant armies clash by night.

(Matthew Arnold)

Chapter

4

Informative Writing about Point of View in Literature

Studying point of view is studying the story's *narrator* or teller. Often, the narrator is as compelling a character as any other. Because this individual can shape our attitudes toward the material we read, this chapter and the next are devoted to strategies for identifying and writing about narrative types and narrative influence. These chapters also include suggestions for structuring and polishing drafts about narrators so that they are coherent and are written in a vigorous, informative style.

PREWRITING: READING FOR POINT OF VIEW AND RECORDING YOUR IDEAS

Most textbooks about literary criticism give lists of common narrative types (e.g., "the objective," "the omniscient"). This chapter and the next will synthesize many of these categories by focusing upon the narrator as an individual who may or may not have been physically present during the course of the story.

Scholar Wayne Booth calls reading to discover the narrator's physical connection with the action reading to discover *narrative distance.* Determining this distance is important because it provides clues to the narrator's own interest in the material.

Two common types of narrator-action distance are the *close* and the *remote*. In the close, the narrator has been an active participant in the events described; in the remote, he or she may have been standing at some distance watching the behavior of other characters.

Close narrators usually reveal their participation with frequent references to themselves or to their interactions with other characters. They also use the personal *I* or *we*. The tellers of "Araby," "The Egg," and "A Rose for Emily" are close narrators.

Remote narrators may also adopt qualities of self-expressive style, but incidences of the first-person pronoun are usually infrequent with this speaker. Language about himself or herself has been supplanted by talk about the people and events the remote teller has observed while assuming one of two distinctive roles.

The first role is that of an all-knowing or *omniscient* presence capable of entering the minds of one, several, or all of the characters. This individual remains physically remote but is really closer than the participating narrator because of this special power and knowledge. Any time a narrator can tell more about the thoughts of a character than could be gleaned from observation or from conversation, he or she is probably physically remote but omniscient. The tellers of folk tales are usually omniscient; they can tell how frightened Red Riding Hood is and exactly what Rumpelstiltskin is thinking. "Young Goodman Brown" and "The Rocking-Horse Winner," two of the short stories that can be found in this book's appendix, are examples of tales related by remote tellers who possess omniscience.

The second position the remote narrator may assume is that of sidelines spectator. In this situation, he or she resembles a dispassionate news reporter. With this teller the self-expressive *I* and references to personal experience give way to qualities found in informative writing. These qualities include shorter sentences, simple diction, and an absence of appeals to the reader's feelings. Shirley Jackson's "The Lottery," a story many of you may have read in high school, is told by a narrator who reports events with a spectator's objectivity.

The Close Narrator: Exploring Motivation

Identifying the narrator as one whose physical distance from the tale is close or remote may in itself suggest a highly informative paper on point of view. However, papers that not only identify the narrator's distance but also explore his or her character and motivation will usually carry even more information and interest. These papers will involve close reading and well-supported arguments about ideas that may not occur to most readers during a first reading. What follows is a brief summary of common characteristics and motives that can occur with the close narrator and that can supply good centers for your writing. Much of what is explained below as a guide to reading will be further developed in the prewriting section.

The Close Narrator: Three Motives for Telling

Close narrators often have a stake in the reader's responses to a story because these narrators may have been responsible for some of its events. And although we need not assume that close narrators are always trying to justify bad behavior, investigating their motives for sharing their experiences can be interesting.

This sharing often springs from one or more of three motives. As with the aims of writing described in Chapter 1, *all* motives may be present in a narrative, but *one* will usually be primary. Primary motives will include (1) the wish to justify behavior, (2) the desire to inform or to advise, and (3) the hope that reviewing the events once more will finally reveal their significance.

The Justifier   Identifying the justifier begins with an examination of his or her environment. Because this narrator's values and behavior do not match those of others in the community, the justifier feels alienated and wishes to explain his or her side of the story. Signs of this alienation appear in the narrator's own testimony as well as in the actions and speech of other characters. Joyce Cary has created an appealing justifier in Gulley Jimson, the wayward painter who dominates *The Horse's Mouth.*

Whereas much of this novel carries Gulley's explicit justification for his *avant-garde* philosophy of art, at least half of the narrative contains implicit clues to the nature and reasons for his alienation from others. In the following passage, Gulley describes the condition of his life (as well as his studio) at his return from imprisonment for a misdemeanor. Notice how his comments reveal not only that he has suffered a loss but also that he is a sensitive and talented artist who is willing to pay a price for his unconventional behavior, even if the price saddens him at times. He notes that

When I came back, there was nothing. Wife and kids had gone back to her mama. Flat let to people who didn't even know my name. And the studio was a coal store. As for the Living God [his major project], my drawings, cartoons, ladders, they'd just melted. I hadn't expected to see the frypan and kettle again. You can't leave things like that about for a month in any friendly neighbourhood and expect to find them in the same place.

The Informer   Some close narrators want to explain their actions; a second type wants to describe them for another purpose. The informer seems to offer a tale in order to amuse or to caution against some foolish behavior. Although the nature and quality of their experiences may vary, these tellers are usually relying upon memory and describing past incidents from a changed perspective.

Narrators who share these experiences are often admirable because they have survived their early foolishness or adversity, and they have finally matured. They may have softened and may have even forgiven themselves or others for past suffering or injustice. One matured informer is Joyce's narrator in "Araby." Another is Pip in Dickens' *Great Expectations.* In both of these stories we find narrators who describe their own follies with objectivity and who draw gentle portraits of those who had shown them kindness in the past. For Joyce's narrator, this individual is his aunt, and for Pip it is his friend Joe Gargery.

The Seeker A third close narrator, the seeker, may also offer a list of woes. What distinguishes this teller from the justifier and the informer is his or her desire to detail a perplexing situation to discover its meaning. This storyteller is really still poised at the prewriting stage of thinking and writing. He or she is still seeking the thesis, although most of the facts are in. Twain's Huck Finn fits in here. His own instincts having lead him to help a slave escape his master, he feels guilty for having violated community law, which protects the master-slave tradition. Huck is still too young and inexperienced to understand that his violation of the code is a transcendant act that is more admirable than imitating the inhumanity of those around him.

FOR PRACTICE

Classify narrators from selections you have already read for this class. Mention primary sources of motivation and evidence to support your view. Also identify possible subordinate motives.

Prewriting: Particle, Field, and Wave

Particle, field, and wave is a focused prewriting strategy that involves viewing a subject from three perspectives. Each of these represents an identity most ideas, objects, events, and people may assume with reference to a particular environment.

Whenever a subject is viewed as a particle, he, she, or it is viewed as an individual with distinctive characteristics. You may be a member of the freshman class at your institution, but your own character and habits set you apart from every other freshman. Huck Finn may be broadly classed with all other protagonists in literature, but he possesses qualities that distinguish him from all the rest. These characteristics include his innocence as well as his unflagging courage. They also include his significance as a model for other protagonists in fiction.

Viewing the particle with reference to its more specific group memberships or *fields* involves identifying those qualities shared with other particles as well as those that distinguish it from them. The field perspective, if used to describe you as a member of your freshman class, would encourage thoughts concerning your resemblance to every other freshman on campus.

This thinking might, in turn, generate notes about your load of introductory courses, your concern for adjusting to serious study, and your efforts to establish a new social life. When applied to *Huckleberry Finn,* this field perspective could generate notes concerning Huck's ties to other youthful narrators and might even culminate in a comparison of his personality and values with those of Anderson's narrator in "The Egg."

Finally, the *wave* perspective leads to speculation concerning the subject's change with the passage of time or its potential for alteration in the future. Wave inquiry often leads to interesting hypotheses because many narrators are *not* true sharers and have not yet actually matured while experiencing the story's events. Wave inquiry might produce guesses concerning your success in another academic environment. Such inquiry might also generate speculation concerning the kinds of experiences Huck may face as an adult living within a community marked by ignorance and prejudice.

The particle, field, and wave strategy can be applied to any subject in any discipline to help generate material for a written assignment. Memorizing the following questions will provide a tool for analyzing people, objects, events, and ideas from these three perspectives, no matter what the subject:

1. What are the subject's unique characteristics?
2. How does it compare with other members of its class?
3. How has it changed (or can it change) with the passage of time?

These general questions can also be refined so that they are initially focused upon a particular part of a subject or a discipline. This series has been specially adapted to stimulate thinking for a point-of-view paper.

Particle	*Field*	*Wave*
What are its characteristics?	How does it compare with others like it?	How has it changed (or can it change) over time?
What personal characteristics can we identify with this narrator?	How does this individual compare with other close narrators? (e.g., is he or she a rationalizer? a matured observer? naive or troubled?)	Has the narrator changed since the beginning of the experience? If so, how?
		If the narrator has not yet changed, has he or she the potential for doing so in future?
	How does this individual's values compare with those of other members of the community (or with those of himself or herself at an earlier period)?	

Here are prewriting notes generated by the particle, field, and wave strategy. They were written in response to Matthew Arnold's "Dover Beach" reproduced at the end of Chapter 3.

Particle	Field	Wave
The narrator is melancholy; doesn't hold much hope for this sea of faith which has come to represent misery, struggle, battle. Sad.	This narrator is similar to the one of Hattie Carroll in that both are disillusioned with violence in the world. The one in Hattie Carroll is disillusioned with violence and justice and the disregard of people for others and the narrator of ''Dover Beach'' is also disillusioned with violence but also the lack of love, truth and joy in this world. Both are disillusioned and lack hope.	No feeling he'll ever lose. Is trying, though, to find hope in his love. If he doesn't become optimistic, will probably at least change into a comforted person.

(M. Hudgens)

FOR PRACTICE

1. Use the particle, field, and wave model to generate notes about the narrator for the last short story you were assigned. This may be the story you will use for your next paper.
2. Identify a topic of current media attention. Explore your own position on the topic by applying the particle, field, and wave questions.

STRUCTURING IDEAS FOR READERS

The Modes of Discourse

Most informative communications are organized according to patterns known as the *modes of discourse.* These patterns are often introduced in high school English classes with single modes dominating the structures of essays. You have used the modes yourself if you have written essays of classification, definition, or process analysis. In fact, most modes may be subsumed into four broad categories: narration, description, classification, and evaluation.

The narrative mode uses chronological order and has two common subdivisions: process and causal analysis. Description stresses the parts and qualities into which objects, people, and events can be divided. Classification and its subdivision, definition, feature the categories into which subjects may be placed. Finally, evaluation specifies the criteria against which a subject is subsequently judged.

Although each mode or subdivision may dominate a piece of writing, several or all of them usually appear within a single composition and serve to structure its parts. A history paper, governed by narration, will often include sections describing people or events as well as schemes classifying their significance. Because of these interactions, we can say that the modes behave in much the same way as do the aims of writing; in any single composition, all of the aims and modes may be present, but *one* of each may dominate.

FOR PRACTICE

1. Clip a magazine ad and underline the parts of it that are organized according to the modes described above. Be prepared to identify those you have marked as well as any prominent mode you find.
2. Follow instructions for item No. 1 above. This time, however, identify traces of the modes you can find in a recent paper written for this or for any other class.

Definition

Definition, a subdivision of classification, shapes much of our daily speech and writing. An effective expression of either side in an argument or debate usually begins with a definition of key terms; readers need to know, for example, precisely what a writer means by "negligence" and "intoxication" if these are critical terms in a defense of stricter penalties for drunken driving. Interviewers visiting campus placement offices generally expect the students with whom they speak to define their short-term and long-term career goals, particularly with reference to the profession represented, as one means of ascertaining the suitability of the applicant to the position for which they are recruiting.

In each of these situations, definition can take several forms and can sometimes even resemble description. To define an unusual object, describing it in terms of another with which it shares several common characteristics and with which readers are familiar may be the simplest solution.

A *logical* definition also uses the familiar to explain the unfamiliar, but it does so with the aid of classes or groups. It performs this function in three steps, each of which may be represented in the definition statement itself. First, it identifies the critical term and all of its relevant modifiers. Second, it identifies the term with a group of objects or events with which it may share some common quality. Third, it distinguishes the term from other members of its group by naming its distinctive features.

A review of the particle, field, and wave prewriting strategy indicates that the first step in creating a logical definition can be effected by responding to the particle question (what are its distinctive characteristics?). The second and third steps can be completed with reference to analysis of the field (how can it be compared to other members of its class?).

Most definitions can be expressed in a single sentence, although such a structure may not necessarily reflect the parts associated with the preceding logical definition. Most of these sentences can, however, be rephrased so that they conform to the logical definition pattern; such conversions may be useful in suggesting the broad outline of an essay, even if their structures do not actually appear in the paper's final draft. Such conversions, furthermore, are possible with most of the thesis sentences derived from using the particle, field, and wave strategy as a source of prewriting.

Here are two sentences—products of prewriting using the particle, field, and wave strategy—that have been converted from the writer's earliest expression of opinion into structures conforming to the logical definition pattern. The purpose of these conversions is more fully covered in the next section, which details a method for creating a simple outline from a sentence of logical definition.

> *Original, Sentence 1:* The matured narrator of "The Egg" warns us
> against obsession.
> *Original, Sentence 2:* The troubled narrator of "A Rose for Emily" is
> still upset by the horrors he has experienced.

Term	Class	Distinctive Features
The narrator of "The Egg"	is a close narrator	who has matured and is warning us against obsession.
The narrator of "A Rose for Emily"	is a close, seeking narrator	who is still troubled by the horrors he has seen.

Notice that groups identified in the second column can vary in size. Certainly the group entitled "close narrators" will be larger and will denote many more individuals than will the group of those who are not only close but also seeking answers to troubling questions. More limited groups will usually generate more precise thesis sentences for you.

FOR PRACTICE

1. Write a sentence of logical definition for each of the characters about whom you have written for this class. You need not restrict yourself to story narrators here.
2. Study recent prewriting notes you have developed for this or for any other class. Use them to suggest a logical definition thesis you could use for an upcoming paper. Write the sentence. Then check it for precision and circle its key concepts.

Transforming the Definition into a Simple Outline

No matter what the term, the group, or the distinctive features, a definition thesis will help organize a paper by suggesting the divisions of a simple outline. The definition thesis is, therefore, comparable to the precise thesis sentence covered in the last chapter. The primary difference between the two is that a precise thesis derived from other means suggests outline sections with its modifiers and special verbs; the thesis of definition suggests sections that follow the definition pattern itself. A logical definition produces a plan that introduces the term, devotes a section to its similarities to other group members, and concludes with an explanation of its distinctive characteristics.

Those definition examples focused upon the narrator and surveyed above could be transformed into the outlines that follow:

A. Thesis: The narrator of "The Egg" is a close narrator who has matured and is warning us against obsession.
   I. Narrator (what he's like, and so on)
   II. Close and Matured
      A. Evidence of closeness ("I, references to self," and so on)
      B. Evidence from text of maturity
   III. Warning
      A. Obsession—in his family
      B. Obsession—its consequences

B. Thesis: The narrator of "A Rose for Emily" is a close, seeking narrator who is still troubled by the horrors he has seen.
   I. Narrator—summary, and so on
   II. Close and seeking
      A. Traces of closeness, participation
      B. Traces of search
   III. Still troubled
      A. Horrors
      B. Possible questions about horrors

Obviously, these models are more detailed than the outlines surveyed in the last chapter. The second, capital letter levels have been added to suggest content; you may or may not choose to add this much detailing to your own plans.

FOR PRACTICE

Write a logical definition and a simple outline that you could use for a paper in this or in any other course.

POLISHING INFORMATIVE STYLE
FOR READERS: ADDING VIGOR

For centuries, variety and vigor have been recognized as sources of interest and as important components of the informative style. Clearly, interest is important in discourse designed to inform; without interest, a composition cannot retain and inform a reader. This chapter section surveys strategies for maintaining interest by adding strength to language. The next chapter will survey ways of varying sentence style.

One way to create vigor is to use the *active* rather than the *passive* voice. Sentences using active voice put the *performer* of an action in the *subject* position; sentences using passive voice fill the subject slot with the action's recipient. In passive sentences, the actor is either not named or is named following the word *by* and appears in a non-subject position. The first sentence below uses active voice, and the second uses passive. In both, subjects and verbs are italicized.

> *Active: Emily refuses* to accept a changed society.
> *Passive:* A changed *society is refused* (by Emily).

Eliminating the passive voice altogether is neither necessary nor desirable, but most writers would improve their styles by reducing its incidence. Because using passive voice usually increases wordiness, you should limit its use to sentences in which identifying the actor with the subject would be either impossible or unnecessary. The passives below represent instances in which active voice would actually divert attention away from the writer's true concern.

1. The *townspeople* were swept with horror by Emily's secret.
2. The *law* was broken continually by those who did not respect it.
3. The Court's *decision* was not contested.

FOR PRACTICE

Write five sentences that you could use to support the thesis of a paper you are writing. Next, rewrite them, converting them into "passive" voice. Be prepared to discuss differences in emphasis and sentence length you find as you study your pairs.

CHAPTER SUMMARY

This chapter covers ways of reading to identify the personal characteristics of narrators found in literature. Because identifying the narrator's motives can generate highly informative papers, the chapter's sections survey three narrators who have participated in a story's action: the justifier, the informer, and the seeker. These categories reflect the teller's primary motive in offering the tale. The justifier wishes to explain behavior, the informer wishes to share experience, and the seeker wishes to review events in the hope of understanding their significance.

Particle, field, and wave analysis can provide a good beginning for papers describing these motives. This analysis represents a prewriting strategy that seeks answers to three questions: (1) What are the subject's unique characteristics? (2) How does it compare with other members of its class? and (3) How has it changed (or can it change) with the passage of time?

The *modes* of informative writing can provide the structure for a draft built upon notes generated by this prewriting. These modes represent patterns by which information is usually structured. Definition is one pattern that can provide a clear conception of your subject; a logical definition identifies the subject with a class of similar objects, events, or people. It then differentiates it from other members of its class. An example of a thesis on point of view that has been shaped by logical definition is "The speaker in 'Dover Beach' is a participating narrator who is seeking hope in an otherwise dreary world."

The chapter closes with a review of active vs. passive constructions and with the recommendation that most sentences be written in active voice. Active sentences generally add strength to informative style by keeping sentence length to a minimum and by making the performer of an action the subject of the sentence.

The following checklist for revising your point-of-view paper incorporates principles covered above. Here, as in other chapters, the list should help you locate areas in your own or in others' papers that may need further rewriting.

Revision Checklist for Informative Paper on a Close Narrator in Literature

1. *Thesis*
   a. Does the thesis reflect the precision of a logical definition?
   b. Does it link the close narrator to a class based upon motivation (e.g., the justifier, the informer, the seeker)?
2. *Organization*
   a. Does the paper include a brief summary to inform those who have not read the material or to prompt the memories of those who have?
   b. Does the structure follow the thesis and reflect an effort to put the narrator into a class and to distinguish him or her from its other members?
   c. Does the paper observe principles of paragraph unity and coherence?

3. *Support, Style, Correctness, and Mechanics*
   a. Does the paper conform to conventional rules of support, grammar, and punctuation?
   b. Are most sentences written in *active* voice?

SAMPLE STUDENT ESSAY

The speaker in Matthew Arnold's "Dover Beach" is a seeker. He appears to be trying to make sense out of his life and out of the problems which plague him. At times, he even seems to be a matured informer, owing to his attempts to give advice in the last stanza. There, however, he seems so desperate that we cannot fully believe in his conviction.

Early in the poem, the narrator laments his loss of faith and happiness. He uses the sea as a symbol of his present status in his personal life, as well as a symbol of what his life used to be and should be. He also tells us that we should be true to one another and do our best to show love because the world is such an unloving place.

The poem does open with a positive note. The narrator paints a peaceful picture of the sea; it soothes and calms, and the waves roll in and up upon "the moon blanched land" (line 8). I think that this calm portrait of the sea represents the happiness that the narrator used to feel. But the tranquil tone changes abruptly when he uses the word "grating" (9) to describe the "roar of pebbles which the waves draw back, and fling . . . up the high strand" (10–11). This change provides the first clue that the narrator has a problem which he is trying to deal with. This early contrast sets the tone for the entire poem.

The poem's disturbing tone continues with the narrator's reference to "the eternal note of sadness" (14) which he uses to describe the sound of the waves hitting the shore. He tells us that Sophocles heard the same sound, and it made him think about "human misery" (18). The narrator is as disturbed by this sound as Sophocles was, and he searches for a reason. At this point, he is clearly a naive seeker of truth; he seems to be searching for some sort of answer for this sad note.

The narrator then tells us that the "Sea of Faith" (21) was once a full body but has become desolate and empty. Indeed, he hears a "melancholy, long withdrawn roar" (25) which comes from the sea and haunts him. This is the most disturbing part of the poem. I think that when a person's faith becomes gray, he loses a great part of his identity and purpose. Again, the narrator becomes a naive, participating narrator who is trying to make some sense of his messy life.

In the last stanza, however, he assumes the role of the matured informer; he gives readers a piece of advice. He says, "Let us be true to one another" (29–30). He explains that we must try to love one another because the world is deceptive. It appears to be full of love and hope but is really a terrible place which "hath really neither joy, nor love, nor light" (33). He identifies love as man's only source of salvation.

This troubles me because I think much of his unhappiness stems from previous experience. The entire poem suggests that both his faith and his trust in others are gone. Why, then, does he insist upon looking outside himself again for hope?

By taking a naive participating stance in most of the poem, the narrator forces the reader to analyze his problems and questions about the loss of faith and love. But in the last stanza, by becoming the matured observer, he tries to demonstrate his maturity in giving advice. In my opinion, Arnold's narrator believes he has questioned and answered his own problems. Unfortunately, he has not fully considered the implications of his past experience and has foolishly leaped to the conclusion that he has profited from his past. I think he remains in the dark.

(*J. Christopher Gibson*)

SUGGESTED WRITING ASSIGNMENTS

Write an informative essay of 500 to 750 words about a close narrator. Begin with a definition thesis that places your narrator in a general class and distinguishes him or her from other members of the class. Write for an audience of interested college students who have *not* read the literary selection. This means that you will have to provide a summary.

Recommended:

William Faulkner's "A Rose for Emily"
Herman Melville's "Bartleby the Scrivener"
Henry James' "The Turn of the Screw"
Robert Browning's "My Last Duchess"
Richard Eberhart's "The Groundhog"

Chapter
5

Informative Writing about More Distant Points of View

CHAPTER PREVIEW
Those Who Shape Our Perceptions of Stories

Whereas Chapter 3 investigated the motives of tellers who have participated in their stories' events, this chapter explores the influence of narrators who have *not* been involved in the action they describe. Because all tellers, no matter how distant, can be powerful forces in shaping the reader's responses to literature, learning to identify their sources of influence not only leads to a clearer understanding of the stories, poems, and novels that we read but also suggests significant and interesting topics to focus the essays that can be written about them. Learning to identify ways an author may use a teller to influence the feelings of readers also illuminates the control that distinguishes excellence from mediocrity in literature.

One way to understand the significance of narrative control is to think of all those who create or participate in a selection as observers who transfer information to readers. The varying distances from a selection's action and the ways each observer influences the audience's vision can be illustrated with a diagram resembling a framed picture:

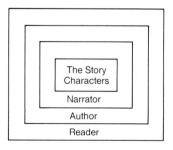

At the center are the characters and the action described in the story itself. Readers never get this close to the action; they receive information that has been filtered through the perceptions of both the narrator and the creating author. Only the author knows what really might have happened. Readers can only investigate the character of the narrator to determine the extent to which the author has enabled this individual to alter the imagined story.

Although no one can ever provide an irrefutable argument concerning what really might have happened in a literary selection, you can at least avoid some common pitfalls in building a reasonable case for your own conclusions. A frequent slip occurs when writers ignore the narrator altogether and preface comments with "The author says. . . ." Such statements are risky insofar as they involve assumptions that further reading and study may prove invalid; an author may well have created a storyteller whose character and philosophy bear no resemblance to his or her own beliefs. Only literary scholars possess the credentials that enable them to assume the writer is speaking to the reader, and even they are generally cautious about such generalizations.

Remaining aware of your position as a reader-critic is also important insofar as it helps you clarify your own identity with your style. The link between style and identity will be fully addressed in Chapter 7. In the meantime, this chapter will prepare you to clarify the varying roles of writers and characters by surveying the powers distant narrators may wield, by introducing a prewriting strategy for recording notes on narrative function, and by describing organizational patterns generated by causal analysis.

PREWRITING

Reading: Identifying Strategies of Narrators

Authors give distant or non-participating narrators one or more of three resources for influencing the responses of readers. The first is *omniscience*, the second is *tone*, and the third is *focus*. Identifying these resources when reading is in itself a form of prewriting that is as helpful to generating ideas as is any other prewriting strategy that can be used.

Omniscience *Omniscience* denotes a capacity for entering the minds of one or more characters to reveal what they are thinking and feeling. Omniscience is an important source of influence because readers generally notice and sympathize with individuals whose thoughts they understand.

Omniscience is sometimes difficult to identify because its occurrence may be subtly drawn. Compare the kinds and amounts of knowledge revealed in the following passages:

His first feeling was one of awe that he had actually, in his mature years, stolen a tricycle and pedalled Lorraine all over the Etiole, between the small hours and dawn. In retrospect it was a nightmare. Locking out Helen didn't fit in with any other act of his life, but the tricycle incident did—it was one of many. How many weeks or months of dissipation to arrive at that condition of utter irresponsibility?

(*F. Scott Fitzgerald, "Babylon Revisited"*)

He had cast up his eyes in astonishment, and, looking down again, beheld neither Goody Cloyse nor the serpentine staff, but his fellow-traveller alone, who waited for him as calmly as if nothing had happened.

(*Nathaniel Hawthorne, "Young Goodman Brown"*)

In the Fitzgerald selection, the narrator obviously possesses omniscience; the first clue surfaces with "His first feeling. . . ." Unless a character describes his or her feelings, no one else can discover them without entering the individual's mind. Nowhere in this passage are the quotation marks that would suggest that the individual who is remembering his past has actually voiced his feelings.

Omniscience in the Hawthorne passage is not as readily apparent because the distinctions between thoughts and simple description are not as clear. The narrator first tells the reader that the character, Goodman Brown, has looked up to the sky and then back down to the ground again. The speaker then explains that Brown can no longer see the staff and the old woman who had formerly caught his attention; now he is left with only his walking companion.

Here, the word "beheld" can be deceiving, for it describes what Brown *saw,* not what he *looked at.* Any observer could identify what the character looked at, but only an omniscient viewer could enter his mind to describe exactly what he saw. After all, Brown could have looked at the area and, owing to a bit of dust in his eyes, failed *to see* the traveller before him.

Because good arguments *for* as well as *against* omniscience arise in many selections, you need a guide for describing the narrator's power. The simplest and most widely accepted is that which evaluates the narrator's knowledge in terms of information commonly derived from observation and dialogue. This principle argues that if you find the narrator telling *more* about a character's thoughts than could have been grasped from watching or talking to that character, the narrator is probably omniscient.

Tone *Tone* is the second power a narrator may use to influence the reader's responses to literature. Tone denotes the attitude revealed by the speaker's choices of language. This attitude appears most clearly in words used to describe a character and those objects identified with him or with her. Most readers warm to those who are described with positive tones; narrators are expressing such tones whenever they seem to be admiring, sympathetic, or amused.

Any time the influence of word choice in a passage seems doubtful, substitute more objective terms for its nouns, verbs, and modifiers and notice how the attitude shifts. Consider Pip's description of the aged and eccentric Miss Havisham in Dickens' *Great Expectations:*

We had stopped near the centre of the long table, and Miss Havisham with her withered arms stretched out of the chair, rested that clenched hand upon the yellow cloth. As Estella looked back over her shoulder before going out of the door, Miss Havisham kissed that hand to her with a ravenous intensity that was of its kind quite dreadful.

Few readers can find Miss Havisham appealing, and few find her obsessive concern for Estella, her young charge, particularly healthy. To better understand the sources of these responses to her, we can underline key words in Pip's description and substitute terms that are more neutral or positive. Here are two sample revisions that demonstrate the power of the narrator's tone. The first substitutes neutral terms, and the second uses positive ones for those that draw negative responses in the original.

REVISION 1:

We had stopped near the centre of the long table, and Miss Havisham, with one of her *slender* arms *extending from* the chair, rested a *small* hand upon the *pale* cloth. As Estella looked back over her shoulder before going out at the door, Miss Havisham kissed that hand to her, with a *motion* that was of its kind quite *restrained.*

REVISION 2:

We had stopped near the centre of the long table, and Miss Havisham, with one of her *graceful* arms *adorning* the chair, rested a *delicate* hand upon the *ivory* cloth. As Estella looked back over her shoulder before going out at the door, Miss Havisham kissed that hand to her with a *warmth* that was of its kind quite *endearing.*

Focus *Focus* is the third major source of narrative power. Focus refers to the amount of space and attention devoted to some component of a story. Identifying the objects of a narrator's focus should include attention to those elements that have been ignored; that which goes unmentioned may have earned its neglect for an important reason, possibly to conceal a characteristic that the narrator wants to suppress for fear of discrediting the portrait he or she has drawn.

Usually, distinguishing between components that command attention and components that do not will help illuminate areas of significance in literature. Readers generally understand those characters and happenings best which dominate the selection's pages. Browning mentions at least four characters in his poem, "My Last Duchess," but the reader's attention is focused upon only two, the duke and his deceased wife. In spite of the dialogue and the descriptions of his art collection, most of us immediately guess that it is the duke's relationship with his duchess that merits our full attention.

FOR PRACTICE

1. Review "The Passionate Shepherd to His Love" and "The Nymph's Reply to the Shepherd" found at the end of Chapter 2. Mark words, lines, or stanzas to show how the tones of each narrator influence the reader's responses to the shepherd's proposal.
2. Rewrite an episode from a popular folk tale, this time using a narrator who admires the villain. Give this narrator an omniscience that excuses a character's bad behavior. Be careful to choose words and details that contribute to a favorable tone. Your point-of-view selection could include that of the wolf in "Red Riding Hood," the cruel stepmother in "Cinderella," or the evil puppeteers in "Pinocchio."
3. Try to recall the last television newscast or documentary that you watched. Explain how the narrator's tone and focus upon particular objects or events influenced your response to its content.

Using Cause and Effect to Explore and to Record Notes

The modes of discourse identified in Chapter 4 can be used not only to organize informative writing but also to guide the prewriting that provides its content. The cause-and-effect mode, a subdivision of narration, is especially helpful for generating ideas about the influence that distant narrators can wield.

An important principle to remember about causal analysis is that causes and effects often occur in chains. One cause may produce an effect which, in turn, becomes the cause of another effect. Thorough analyses will, therefore, involve responses to the following questions:

1. What is the significant event?
2. What are its causes?
3. What are its consequences?

Applying causal analysis to the Three Mile Island nuclear incident suggests that the potential melt-down was the significant event. This application further suggests that causes of this near-disaster included the facility's poor design and the inadequacy of its staff's training. Finally, the conclusion of such an analysis might stress that consequences of this scare have included efforts to strengthen federal control of nuclear facilities and more vigorous protests against the use of nuclear energy by the public.

Special prewriting questions can help us identify the important causal chains that reflect a distant narrator's influence. The following questions are adaptations of those listed above and are particularly helpful for papers on distant points of view.

1. What is the significant character or action?
2. In what ways has the narrator influenced my particular response to this character's behavior or to this action, i.e., how has the narrator used omniscience, tone, or focus?
3. What are the effects of the behavior or the action?

Here are notes generated by periods of freewriting and of reviewing the material read. They were written in response to D. H. Lawrence's "The Rocking-Horse Winner" found in the appendix at the end of this book.

WHAT

I feel sorry for Paul. He is crazy to get his mother's attention, to make her happy. Like most children, he feels too responsible for her, feels her happiness or unhappiness depends upon him. This feeling's not appropriate. I also feel sorry for his mother. She spends too much money but this is probably not her fault. We learn that her family had money, so she's probably just trying to live the way she once did. In fact, she almost seems to feel guilty for her bad luck.

WHY

I feel sorry for Paul mostly because of the narrator's tone. As the story goes on, the narrator uses words like "frail" to describe him. In other spots he's "feverish" and "strange" (652). By the end of the story, when he's dying, his eyes are wild and like "blue stones" (653). We can see him going completely crazy as time passes. The mother, though, gets my sympathy mostly because of the teller's omniscience. While I learn at the story's beginning that she couldn't love her children, by its end I also know she feels worried and anxious about Paul. We are told she rushes to him when he collapses with all her motherly feelings covering her. Even though she never seems to change drastically, we know she is a better mother by the story's end. This is because of the omniscience.

HOW

My feelings for Paul and his mother make me pay special attention to her brother, Oscar Cresswell. She does tell Paul that gambling caused a lot of trouble in her family and I think this shows up in Uncle Oscar. He learns to use the boy and doesn't even seem too disturbed at the end when his nephew dies. All he seems to care about is Malibar's winnings. My sympathy for Paul and his mother also makes me notice how absent and weak his father is. We don't learn much about him—just that he goes to work and isn't very successful. Still, he seems happy to live way beyond their means, too, and doesn't do much to help his wife.

FOR PRACTICE

1. Briefly review one of the literary selections covered in an earlier chapter. Identify your general response to one of its characters or events and then list all the causes and all the effects you can associate with this response. Feel free to identify causes other than those surveyed in this chapter. When you have finished, return to the selection itself to find specific parts that may be quoted or paraphrased to support your answers.
2. Clip a newspaper article of interest to you. Map out the event, its causes, and its effects. Fill in any other critical causes and effects that seem to be missing from the article itself.

WRITING AND REVISING: USING CAUSE AND EFFECT TO STRUCTURE INFORMATION

Prewriting generated by the cause-effect questions can lead to a thesis identifying the narrator's capacity for shaping responses to literature. Here is a sample thesis written by a student who had studied the Lawrence story:

> In "The Rocking-Horse Winner," the narrator's omniscience causes us to sympathize with the mother.
>
> *(Margaret Hudgens)*

This thesis suggests at least three options for organizing a cause-and-effect paper; each may be developed with any subject that interests you. These options include developing papers that stress causes, that emphasize effects, or that balance attention to both.

A cause stress could generate an outline that details the omniscience concept identified in the thesis. Attention to the effect, that of evoking sympathy, would be limited, and the following pattern would guide the draft:

I. Omniscience
   A. With mother—limitless (cause 1)
      1. Example 1 from story
      2. Example 2
      3. Example 3 and so on
   B. With son—limited (cause 2)
      1. Example 1
      2. Example 2
II. Sympathy—general impression (effect).
   Summary of impression

The thesis might also be developed into a plan that stresses the sympathy evoked by the narrator's omniscience. This effect-centered outline could include the following divisions:

I. General response—sympathy
(*Effect* of narrator's style but *cause* of following reader responses)
II. Response 1—we can understand her preoccupation with money (Effect 1)
  A. Example 1—obsession with luck
  B. Example 2—spending anonymous gift
III. Response 2—we can understand her sense of failure (Effect 2)
  A. Example 1
  B. Example 2 and so on

Finally, a balanced outline would devote equal space to both the causes and the effects of the narrator's control. Most balanced analyses of literature, however, are best reserved for such longer papers as those that incorporate the findings of extensive research. Papers within the 500- to 750-word range are better developed according to such plans as those already described, principally because their limited scopes promote the careful detailing that marks effective composition.

FOR PRACTICE

1. Identify a cause-and-effect essay you have recently written for another course. Diagram the pattern that has given this paper its form.
2. Study the editorial page of your local paper and clip an essay that uses causal analysis. Diagram its pattern and evaluate the nature of its assumptions about the causes and the effects that it details.

POLISHING STYLE FOR READERS

Readers of informative writing expect not only a logical organization but also a clear and interesting style. One way to achieve clarity is to eliminate words that add nothing to the meaning of sentences. One way to secure interest is to vary the placement of modifiers. What follows are suggestions for evaluating the levels of clarity and interest in your style at the polishing stage in writing.

Eliminating Wordiness

Wordiness promotes confusion and boredom in popular as well as in scholarly writing. Fortunately, wordiness is currently under attack by prominent writers and critics, many of whom identify the following as common sources of cloudiness and inflation in style: (1) superfluous relatives and prepositions, (2) "it is" and "there is (are)" openers, and (3) frequent nominalization.

Common relatives (or relative pronouns) are *who, which,* and *that.* Commonly used prepositions include *of, for, to, at, by, as, in,* and *with.* These combine with nouns to form *prepositional phrases.*

Both relatives and prepositions are frequently overused, particularly by those who are trying to appear scholarly. Notice the differences in clarity in the sentence pairs below. In each example, the extra relatives and prepositional phrases clouding the first sentences have been deleted or replaced by single words in the second constructions.

1.a. Charlie Wales goes *to the bar that* he had frequented *in the past.*
1.b. Charlie Wales goes to the bar he once frequented.
2.a. The narrator claims *that* he became gloomy because *of the years that* he had spent *on the chicken farm.*
2.b. The narrator claims his gloominess came from long years spent on the chicken farm.
3.a. The long, gray hair *on the pillow in the room which* contained the body *of Homer Barron* gave *to the townspeople* a sense *of shock.*
3.b. The long, gray hair found on the pillow in the room containing Homer Barron's body shocked the townspeople.

Although eliminating *all* relative clauses and *all* prepositional phrases is neither necessary nor desirable, most of us write sentences that need trimming, and these structures should usually be among the first to go. These exercises provide practice in eliminating them.

FOR PRACTICE

1. Rewrite each of the following, deleting as many unnecessary relatives and prepositions as you can.
   a. The narrator of "Dover Beach" seems to regret that he has lost the faith of an earlier period in his life.
   b. Bartleby is the kind of person who never looks toward a goal or into the future of his career.
   c. Marion Peters has only the worst of opinions for her sister's husband, partly because of her memories of the money that he had squandered.
2. Write five sentences about some part of a current writing project. Use as many relatives and prepositions as you can. When you have finished, rewrite these sentences, trimming away the excesses.

Using many "there is (are)" and "it is" sentence openers as well as nominalizing are two further contributors to wordiness in style. One habit suggests the writer's fear of informality, and the other indicates his or her desire to impress the reader.

Some writers seem to use "there is (are)" and "it is" openers because they are afraid of choosing personal pronouns. Notice how much clearer the first sentences are in the pairs below when they are compared to the second ones; the first use a more natural and personal voice while the second structures open with superfluous padding.

EXAMPLES:

1.a. We cannot decide whether or not the boy actually hears the names of racehorses in "The Rocking-Horse Winner."

1.b. It is difficult to decide whether or not the boy actually hears the names of racehorses in "The Rocking-Horse Winner."

2.a. We have reason to believe the matchmaker set up the meeting between the rabbi and his wayward daughter in "The Magic Barrel."

2.b. There are reasons for believing the matchmaker set up the meeting between the rabbi and his wayward daughter in "The Magic Barrel."

Although each of these sentences could be recast many ways, making *we* the subject is an effective option for several reasons. First, because it frequently appears in scholarly writing, more readers will find *we* free of the stigma usually associated (however unfairly) with the singular *I*. *We*, therefore, lends a naturalness that is rarely objectionable. Second, *we* suggests an identification with readers that most of them find appealing. As long as you really can identify with an audience's thoughts, feelings, or status, you might as well express the connection with your style.

Causes also stand better chances of attracting readers when arguments for them are expressed with a minimum of nominalizing. *Nominalization* is the process of transforming verbs or action words into nouns or words that name. Frequent occurrences of words ending with *-ness, -ment, -tion, -ance,* or *-ence* signal nominalization. In addition to plumping up sentences with empty verbage, nominalizing usually annoys readers because it indicates a misguided conception of scholarly style. Even scholars are learning to avoid the distracting language that pervades the first sentences in the pairs below and to use the active verbs that dominate the second structures.

1.a. The shepherdess *betrays a hesitation* when she considers the shepherd's proposal.

1.b. The shepherdess *hesitates* when she considers the shepherd's proposal.

2.a. The boy's father never *secures an improvement* in their lives on the chicken farm.

2.b. The boy's father never *improves* their lives on the chicken farm.

3.a. The narrator *reflects a condition* of disappointment in "Araby."
3.b. The narrator *reflects* disappointment in "Araby."

FOR PRACTICE

Rewrite each of the following to eliminate unnecessary words:

1. There is a feeling that the supernatural is in operation in this house.
2. A hope for a better life is a part of the boy's thinking.
3. Charlie will not join the celebration of his old friends because he has a hesitation about getting mixed up with them again.
4. It is clear that Marion will not develop a forgiveness for Charlie which is what he needs.
5. Bartleby does not exactly achieve an advancement in the company, but he does win the attention of his employer.

Varying Sentence Structures

In addition to expecting sentences that are free of empty phrases, readers of informative writing also appreciate structures that have been varied as a safeguard against monotony. For centuries, most writers and scholars have, in fact, identified sentence variety as a prerequisite to effective informative style.

One way to vary sentences is to alternate the positions of modifiers. Fortunately, most modifying phrases and clauses in English can be freely shoved from sentence openings to sentence middles to sentence ends, depending upon the words they modify and upon the writer's emphasis. Good candidates for such shifts are participial phrases.

Participles are verbs that are serving to modify nouns in a particular sentence. In each of the following, the italicized words function as *verbs* because they express action or existence; the boxed words, on the other hand, function as modifiers rather than as verbs because they are describing and *not* denoting action. We need to forget for the moment that these boxed words usually serve as verbs because in these specific sentences they are performing quite different functions.

1. The child, | hoping | for a cookie, *smiled* and *cleaned up* the toys.
2. The mother, | tired | and | saddened |, *comforted* her discouraged husband.

In the first sentence, *hoping* is describing the child's condition while *smiled* and *cleaned up* explain what he is actually doing. Similarly, in the second sentence, the mother's action involves *comforting* her husband while *tired* and *saddened* are describing her appearance.

Participles can be recognized not only for their functions but also for

65

their *-ing* or their past verb form endings (e.g., tired, grown, gone). They also join other words in adding details to the words they describe; when they do so, the whole group is called a *participial phrase.*

Participial phrases are among the most flexible structures in English, appearing as they do at the beginnings, middles, and ends of sentences. The range of their mobility is checked only by the rules that require them to (1) appear close to the words they modify and (2) be marked by commas when they open or interrupt a sentence.

Here are further examples of ways participial phrases can serve to vary style. Notice the slight shifts in emphasis between the *a* and the *b* sentences as well as the confusion generated by the placements in those that are marked with a *c*. In the *c* sentences, the rule concerning placement has been violated, and the reader cannot easily link the modifying phrase with the noun to which it should be adding meaning.

1.a. *Depressed by his view of the world,* the narrator exclaims, "Ah love, let us be true to one another."

1.b. The narrator, *depressed by his view of the world,* exclaims, "Ah love let us be true to one another."

1.c. (AVOID) The narrator exclaims, "Ah love, let us be true to one another," *depressed by his view of the world.*

2.a. *Realizing the rabbi is smitten with his wayward daughter,* the matchmaker mutters "prayers for the dead."

2.b. The matchmaker, *realizing the rabbi is smitten with his wayward daughter,* mutters "prayers for the dead."

2.c. (AVOID) The matchmaker mutters "prayers for the dead," *realizing the rabbi is smitten with his wayward daughter.*

FOR PRACTICE

Copy the following sentences, adding participial phrases to modify the nouns that are italicized. Then rewrite the sentences, moving the participial phrases to other positions.

1. The passionate *shepherd* begs his love to come and live with him.
2. *Miss Emily Grierson* apparently murdered Homer Barron.
3. The *duke* has hung a painting of his last duchess on the wall.
4. *The mother* decides they need to leave the chicken farm.
5. The *boy* rides his horse and shrieks, "It's Malibar."

CHAPTER SUMMARY

This chapter examines three sources of power authors give their distant narrators to influence the responses of readers. The first is *omniscience,* the ability to explain the thoughts and feelings of characters; the second is *tone,* the ability to describe characters and events with language that both reflects and evokes specific emotions; and the third is *focus,* the ability to indicate significance by committing varying degrees of attention to particular characters, events, or issues.

One way to develop and organize material about the narrator's influence is to engage in causal analysis. Three questions common to most cause-and-effect studies are: (1) what is the significant character or event? (2) what are its causes? and (3) what are its consequences? Notes generated by these questions can be organized later according to one of three common cause-and-effect patterns: (1) the cause focused, (2) the effect focused, and (3) the balanced.

Informative writing about the distant narrator ultimately needs polishing so that its style is clear as well as interesting. Clarity is generally improved by trimming sentences of three common sources of wordiness. These sources include unnecessary relatives, superfluous prepositions, "it is" and "there is (are)" sentence openers, and bulky nominals. Varying its sentence modifiers is, furthermore, one way of enhancing style's level of interest; participial words and phrases are particularly good candidates for variation.

To improve your own paper on narrative function, study the checklist below as you consider your revisions. Then study the sample essay that follows, noting areas that could be improved with attention to principles found in this chapter.

Revision Checklist for Informative Paper on the Influence of Distant Narrators

1. *Thesis and Support*
   a. Does the paper open with a sentence that identifies (a) a reader response and (b) sources of influence the narrator uses to cause this response? (Common sources are omniscience, tone, and focus.)
   b. Does support include specific examples (e.g., words, phrases) of the influence identified in the thesis?
2. *Organization*
   a. Does the paper develop an idea promised in the thesis sentence?
   b. Has the paper an organization reflecting one of the basic cause-and-effect patterns?
3. *Style*
   a. Have sentences been trimmed of unnecessary relative clauses, prepositional phrases, nominals?
   b. Are "there is (are)" and "it is" openers kept to a minimum?
   c. Are sentence modifiers (especially participial phrases) positioned to create sentence variety?

SAMPLE STUDENT ESSAY

In Lawrence's "The Rocking-Horse Winner," the narrator's omniscience in describing the mother makes us understand her anxieties and conflicts. The mother wants to love her children but cannot.

The story-teller's omniscience helps us understand the mother's desire to love her children even though she is incapable of such love. Without this omniscience we would believe that she is a good, loving mother for, according to the narrator, "Everybody else said of her: 'She is such a good mother. She adores her children.' " He also tells us, however, that "Only she herself, and her children themselves, knew it was not so." Whenever she is with her children, she always feels "the centre of her heart go hard" (646).

Nonetheless, this mother does want to love them. The narrator's omniscience alerts us to the mother's anxiety, particularly that which she feels each time she thinks about Paul. Late in the story, she notices the pressure her son is under, and with a "heart curiously heavy because of him," she encourages him to go to the seaside (652).

Still later, this anxiety drives her to call the nursery governess to check on the children. Judging from the governess's surprise, this act is inconsistent with the mother's normal behavior. Also, when Paul takes his final rocking-horse ride, he collapses, and his mother, with "all her tormented motherhood flooding upon her" rushes to him (653).

Without this narrator's omniscience, we would see Paul's mother as an adoring parent who showered her children with gifts but who was somewhat careless of keeping track of her family. The omniscience helps us realize the depth of the mother's conflict with her emotions.

(Margaret Hudgens)

SUGGESTED WRITING ASSIGNMENTS

Read one of the selections listed below and write an informative essay about the influence of its narrator. Stress *causes* of a particular response, extended *effects* of it, or both. Write for classmates who have studied narrative influence but who have *not* read your specific selection.

Recommended Selections:

Shirley Jackson's "The Lottery"
Bernard Malamud's "The Magic Barrel"
D. H. Lawrence's "The Horse Dealer's Daughter"
Richard Wright's "The Man Who Was Almost a Man"
Robert Browning's "My Last Duchess"
John Keats' "The Eve of St. Agnes"

Chapter
6

Persuasive Writing about Controlling Themes

CHAPTER PREVIEW
The Significance of Persuasion and Theme

Daily, those who want us to do or to believe something fill our lives with their written and spoken communications. Advertisers highlight the benefits of using their products, friends embellish the miseries that they share, and employers push us into working longer hours. Because their bids pervade so many of our waking moments, a study of persuasion's strategies is essential to generating and to interpreting effective composition.

So, too, is a study of theme in literature. The ability to identify literary themes not only helps us understand the significance of a selection but also enables us to discover its relevance to daily experience. To help you improve your skills in studying and writing about material that you read, this chapter explains ways of analyzing themes in literature and identifying and polishing appeals in persuasion. It opens with a guide to determining theme and then goes on to survey methods for recording notes, for organizing material, and for revising and editing style.

PREWRITING ABOUT CONTROLLING THEME

Reading to Discover Theme

A *theme* in music is a melody that is repeated throughout the composition; in informative writing, the theme is the thesis that pulls ideas together.

In literature, theme is the central idea about the human condition that is supported by characterization, by images, and by symbols.

Characterization is the act of creating character. Authors develop characters with dialogue, action, descriptions of physical appearance, and the responses of those around them. Careful attention to these resources helps reveal patterns of characterization that are significant insofar as they point to and support a theme. Here is a statement about a characterization pattern in "The Rocking-Horse Winner":

> Paul's characterization stresses his vulnerability: he is slight of build, unhealthy, and his speech reflects his passive nature.

Images are descriptions that appeal to the senses; they help us to see, hear, feel, smell, or taste that which is being depicted. Images are products of concrete diction and figurative language. *Metaphor* and *simile*, the figures of comparison, are found in many images.

Although imagery is most prominent in poetry, important image patterns often surface in short stories, novels, and plays. In "The Bride Comes to Yellow Sky," Stephen Crane describes a railroad car with words and figures that remind most readers of caskets used for burial. These funeral images, coupled with the story's other symbols of death, suggest and support Crane's theme that the primitive West is fading and is being replaced by an advancing Eastern culture.

Symbols function as do images and methods of characterization because they, too, create patterns that provide support for themes. Symbols are objects, beings, qualities, and behaviors that have meaning beyond themselves.

Whereas some symbols have limited, subjective value, many others elicit predictable responses in readers owing to their prominence in the culture. The American flag evokes thoughts of patriotic duty for most of us in the United States while a smile evokes feelings of warmth and friendship for people in most parts of the world.

Recording: Writing a Tentative Theme Statement

Theme statements can be expressed in a variety of ways, even with reference to a single selection. This variety is the product of the different emphases readers detect and is *not* a sign that literary pieces possess limitless numbers of central ideas. Nonetheless, several varied statements about a selection may be compatible even though they reflect different concerns.

Theme statements will also vary because of the differing generalization levels with which they can be expressed. Such statements fall into at least one of three categories. These can be (1) a general, unqualified comment about humanity; (2) a particularized comment about a specific life situation; and (3) a qualified statement that adds meaning to either a general or a particularized observation.

General theme statements can complete this pattern:

A theme of _____ is that _____ is (are)
_____.

Here are examples of general theme statements:

1. A theme of *"A Rose for Emily"* is that *social change is inevitable.*
2. A theme of *"The Egg"* is that *the American dream of success is not within the reach of everyone.*
3. A theme of *"The Rocking-Horse Winner"* is that *greed is a primary source of cruelty in people.*

These general statements say something about life as nearly everyone experiences it, and they provide good beginnings for lengthy papers, especially those that are products of research. For short essays, particular or conditional statements provide more effective beginnings because they demand an appropriately limited focus.

Particular theme statements describe a specific quality or condition that can be identified with types or groups of people or with particular stages in life. They also describe the consequences of possessing this quality or condition. Particular statements can fill this sentence pattern:

A theme in _____ is that _____ who
_____ can or may _____.

Here are examples of particular theme statements:

1. A theme in *"A Rose for Emily"* is that *people* who *cannot accept change* may *become desperate and dangerous.*
2. A theme in *"Araby"* is that *young people* who *become obsessed with romantic fantasies* may *suffer humiliation and disappointment.*
3. A theme in *"The Rocking-Horse Winner"* is that *greedy people* who *live beyond their means* can *provoke tragedy.*

Although general and particular themes both demand some degree of precision, both can be further refined with statements of *conditions.* Such statements usually involve the addition of clauses preceded by *when.* The following are conditional theme statements derived from general as well as from particular statements:

GENERAL, CONDITIONAL STATEMENTS

1. A theme in *"A Rose for Emily"* is that *change is inevitable* when *the middle and lower classes increase in number and win economic advantages.*
2. A theme in *"The Egg"* is that *economic success is uncertain* when *an individual lacks training and talent.*

71

PARTICULAR, CONDITIONAL STATEMENTS

1. A theme in *"A Rose for Emily"* is that people who *refuse to accept change* can become *dangerous* when *they fear loss.*
2. A theme in *"The Egg"* is that people who *adopt another's ambitions can never be happy* when *they haven't the capacity to pursue the other's ideals.*

FOR PRACTICE

1. Write a general theme statement for a selection you have recently read for this class. When you have finished, write particular and conditional statements for the same selection.
2. Write general, particular, and controlling theme statements for selections assigned in previous chapters. These include:

    "Dover Beach"
    "My Last Duchess"
    "Bartleby the Scrivener"
    "A Rose for Emily"

Recording Responses: Prewriting for Discovery and Support

Once a tentative theme statement has evolved from a careful study of the literature, you need to review the material itself in order to provide specific examples for the paper's most important observations. Supporting details are especially important to persuasion because of its concern with encouraging readers to adopt a particular view of the subject. Effective persuasive writing contains appeals to the audience's reason as well as to its feelings, and both forms of appeal demand plentiful and appropriate facts and examples.

Once again, the journalist's questions can offer help at this particular stage in your writing. If a tentative theme statement does not emerge with a first reading of the literature, these questions can guide successive reviews. If a tentative theme has surfaced, the questions can help you to record notes from memory or to select specific references to the text. Regardless of the recording method chosen, trying to respond to as many questions as possible and writing answers as quickly as you can will heighten the effectiveness of this procedure.

Here is an adaptation of the journalist's questions that should help generate ideas and support for an analysis of theme. Feel free to add to the set and to further subdivide questions as may seem necessary; the collection is a tool and not a source of limitation.

FOR SUPPORT FROM CHARACTERIZATION:

1. *Who* supports my theme statement?
2. *What* does he or she do to support it?
3. *What* in his or her speech, action, or appearance supports it?
4. *What* in other characters' responses to this character supports it?

FOR SUPPORT FROM IMAGERY AND SYMBOL:

1. *What* comparisons, symbols, or terms appear in descriptions of major characters or incidents?
2. *How* do they contribute to my theme statement?

Here are sample notes written in response to Nathaniel Hawthorne's "Young Goodman Brown," a short story reproduced at the end of this book. Each set of notes was the product of a five-minute stretch of freewriting.

CONTROLLING THEME STATEMENT

People who see evil in others cannot live happy lives when they cannot be forgiving.

CHARACTER SUPPORT

Mostly Brown supports the idea that some people never recover when they find out that others are bad. He goes home and looks sadly at Faith, spends his whole life afraid his church will fall down, and is buried with a sad tombstone message. He starts out really worshiping the people he thinks are good, even suggests the traveller's been wrong when he says his relatives had beaten Quakers and burned Indian villages. Spends his early life feeling sure his family and neighbors were too good to be evil. Later doesn't ever smile again, gets epitaph showing his disillusion was so strong that those who lived around him and carved his tombstone knew about it.

Of course everything Brown does adds to the idea that we can get too bitter. Guess the unhappy part of the theme goes well with all the other unhappy things that go on in the story. There are lots of ugly actions on the part of nature that he notices—in the woods the wind howls, trees creak. I also noticed the parts where the blue sky keeps getting covered up by the ugly dark cloud. All these dark things seem to prepare us for the dark part of the theme— Brown's unhappy end.

IMAGE AND SYMBOL QUESTIONS

Symbols—words pointing to things not explicitly mentioned. Let's see—Faith's name and her pink ribbons. She's obviously a symbol of his faith—she adopts evil ways, though, and he loses his faith. Name's really important. Makes us think about what happens to him *after* the forest. Also devil's stick—everything about the traveller reminds us of snakes, things we think about when we think about the devil. I guess the snake in the Garden of Eden. Also, many times the people at the meeting in the woods are described as "grave." Grave and death. Brown's happiness and trust die.

FOR PRACTICE

1. Carefully reread a literary selection you might use for a paper on theme. Then write out prewriting notes in response to the questions above. Spend about five minutes freewriting on each section.
2. If you are not yet working on a paper about theme, apply the preceding instructions to the selection that centered your last paper.

Determining How Much Support Is Enough

Although no fool-proof formula for guaranteeing persuasion exists, effective writers at least try to anticipate the needs of the readers they address. If readers have already studied the selection upon which the paper is based, you can provide a short summary that is limited to brief descriptions of major characters and events. If your readers are skeptics, or have not studied the material, you can provide more examples and facts to fortify the main points of the argument.

As long as the reader has been identified, the following questions will suggest the notes you can use in completing an *audience sketch* to further guide the paper's planning and revisions. These questions generate ideas about those factors that specialists in analyzing audiences (e.g., advertisers, politicians) identify as significant influences upon the responses of readers and hearers.

The most useful audience sketches are collections of freely written notes that can be used for later reference. My own students submit these notes with their final paper drafts so that I can understand their choices of support, of structure, and of style.

QUESTIONS FOR AUDIENCE SKETCH

1. What is the age of most of my readers?
2. What is the sex of most of my readers?
3. What is the educational background of most of them?
4. What is the occupation of most?
5. What are their personal goals?
6. What knowledge of and attitudes toward the subject do most already possess?

Here are notes written in response to these questions.

AUDIENCE SKETCH
(Assigned group—college-educated adults)

All are in their 20s and 30s
All live in a small town
Of the middle to upper-middle class
Have graduated from state schools

Have at least heard about many classics and short stories
Value family, job success, home, religion, social acceptance, money

Have read this story in college or in high school but may not remember much about it. Maybe they remember that at its end the villagers stone one of their members. Probably most just remember they were upset, though, when they read it but cannot remember exactly why. Because they are themselves from small towns, I can't be too hard on these kinds of people—ought to stress more that this group has been victimized by the ones who came before and who forced them to accept tradition. Maybe I'll just leave out the parts that stress the small town business—maybe I can just work on the point, which is true, that they all know each other well. This could happen in any kind of town. They will need a quick summary, especially one that explains the roles the main characters play among themselves.

I don't want to turn them off so words and style should be simple—like choices I'd make in a letter to someone I know.

FOR PRACTICE

1. Write an audience sketch for a group you must address with a paper-in-progress (assigned for this or for any other class). Your audience may be your professor; if so, be careful to put down details you've learned over the course of the semester (i.e., don't stereotype him or her).
2. Go to the library and pick up a popular magazine. Survey its feature articles; skim the styles and ads you find. Write an audience sketch for those you identify as the magazine's target readers.

WRITING AND REVISING: STRUCTURING PERSUASION FOR READERS

Using Classification to Strengthen Support and Structure

Classification is the process of grouping experiences according to their common characteristics. An integral part of most complex thinking, classification helps us sort information and blend it with ideas we have already stored in our memories. Without this process, children would not learn to protect themselves by distinguishing between acts that bring pleasure and acts that are followed by pain; most two-year-olds need touch a hot stove only once before classing the experience with falling off tricycles and scraping their knees as "things that usually feel awful."

Because classification is so important to thinking and learning, sharpening skills in grouping ideas is essential to improving your writing and speech. By clarifying the relationships between experiences, classification can strengthen support as well as guide the structure of papers. Developing a *classification tree* from prewriting notes is one way of beginning this process.

A classification tree is a diagram whose branches show how the specific products of an experience are related to each other. The top of each tree represents a group of ideas, objects, events, or people that share a common characteristic. In a study of literature, the class *characterization* would include those strategies authors use to develop the people they depict: dialogue, physical appearance, actions, thoughts, and the responses of others. The class *setting* would include those details writers use to create a distinctive environment: time of day, date, furnishings, dress, and weather.

The individual branches of classification trees indicate the individual members of the class. These projections derive from responses to the question, "What kinds of _____ are there?" Each branch or kind can, in turn, become the name of a new class from which new sets of branches will project. Here is an extended version of the characterization tree described above:

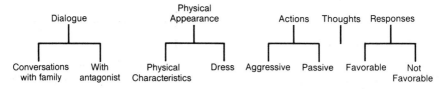

Notice that branches near the bottoms of trees name classes whose memberships are more limited than are those named near their tops. This movement from larger to smaller class sizes is worth noting insofar as it is common to all extended classifications. Observing this movement in your own tree structures will help you to evaluate your support and to supplement it as necessary so that its persuasive potential is strong.

Tree structures representing responses to reading will often begin with classes denoting the selection's general characteristics. Subsequent divisions into *kinds* or class members will gradually assume levels of increasing specificity until no further divisions are possible. Those levels from which no further divisions or branches can project will usually list words and phrases referring to particular examples from the literary selection itself.

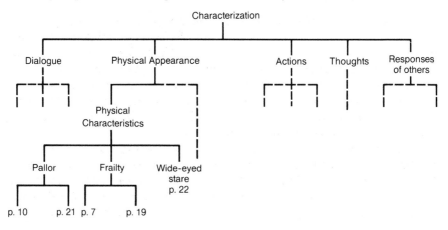

Notice how this fragment of the tree described above has been extended to its limits. Notice the page numbers on the bottom branches; these can be added when you return to the text for additional support or later before you begin the first draft.

FOR PRACTICE

Create a tree structure for the paper assigned in this class or for one you are writing for another. The structure may describe ideas that will govern the whole paper or simply one of its sections.

Classification trees can suggest patterns for organization as well as areas needing additional references to the selection. Once you have diagrammed your ideas, you can develop a logical plan by studying the tree and by transforming words and phrases from its branches into a simple outline.

The characterization tree described above could be transformed into the following outline. This transformation reflects a left-to-right consideration of the tree's classes. Although the left-to-right movement usually generates a logical plan, you may re-order your class sequence in your outlines; keeping class subdivisions together is important for clarity, but maintaining the original sequence of classes in your paper's organization is sometimes unnecessary.

CHARACTERIZATION

    I. Dialogue (as source of theme support)—Conversations with family
       A. Supportive
          1. p. 22 Molly
          2. p. 21 Charles
       B. Antagonistic—p. 20 aunt
    II. Physical Appearance
       A. Physical characteristics
          1. Pallor
             a. p. 10 standing before mirror
             b. p. 21 at reception
          2. Frailty
       B. And so forth

FOR PRACTICE

Convert a tree structure of your own into a simple outline. Be sure that the extent of your outline detailing matches the number of levels marked by different branches on your classification tree.

Clarifying the Paper's Organization

Because of their complexity, papers on responses to literature that classify evidence need to specify the kinds of evidence used early in the essay. Readers need this kind of preview to help them follow your arguments, particularly in compositions devoted to theme.

Here are sample paragraphs written by my students. Used to introduce their papers, each provides a guide for readers by specifically stating the kinds of evidence used to support the theme identified as well as the theme itself.

SAMPLE 1

"A Worn Path" by Eudora Welty is an appealing story because it details the strength and perseverance of an old woman who cares for a grandson who is chronically ill and in pain. Its theme is that love can motivate people to care for others who are in need, even when those who help are suffering the physical and psychological disorders of old age. Welty develops this idea throughout with careful characterization.

(Andrew Payne)

SAMPLE 2

"The Lottery" is a haunting story with a surprise ending. Part of our discomfort comes from its theme about tradition. Its main idea is that people who become obsessed by tradition sometimes forget to question their beliefs and become monsters. Shirley Jackson's characterization, imagery, and action emphasize this point throughout.

(Cesar Madarang)

FOR PRACTICE

Write an introductory paragraph that specifies evidence for a paper on the theme of a literary selection. This selection may be one you are currently writing about or one you studied for another paper.

POLISHING STYLE FOR READERS

Modifying structures known as *appositives* can add interest and clarity to persuasive style. These qualities are as important to persuasion as they are to informative communication; with either aim, readers must remain interested in the paper and be able to follow its assertions so that they do not give up and stop reading altogether.

Using appositives to clarify style is also important to persuasion because it can enhance the writer's *character appeal,* that image projected to attract and hold the audience. Because appositives explain important words and phrases, they help readers to understand the message and, in turn, to appreciate the writer's concern for their comprehension.

Appositives resemble the participial phrases described in Chapter 5 insofar as both can be used to vary sentence structures. Both can be placed in the beginnings, the middles, and the ends of sentences as long as they are close to the words they modify.

In spite of their common flexibility in placement, appositives are unlike participials in terms of their composition. While participials open with verb forms, appositives usually consist of nouns and noun phrases that *rename* the words they describe. The appositives are italicized in the following examples; the words they modify are circled.

1. (Emily Grierson,) *a last symbol of the older Southern tradition,* locks herself away from the younger generation.
2. *The product of his journey into the forest,* (Young Goodman Brown's cynicism) haunts him until his death.
3. The family's greed destroys (Paul,) *the young man.*

FOR PRACTICE

Rewrite the following units, converting the second and third sentences into appositives as best you can. When you are finished, underline all appositives and circle the nouns they modify as has been done in the preceding examples. Watch your punctuation.

1. The townspeople learned to leave Emily alone.
2. The townspeople were a group without tradition.
3. Miss Emily was a woman who was aloof and stubborn.

1. The man is looking out over the white cliffs.
2. The cliffs stand silent and are wave-swept and cold.
3. The man is a sorrowful and disillusioned person.

1. Bartleby perishes in the Tombs.
2. Bartleby is a man without friends, ambition, and comfort.
3. The Tombs is a debtor's prison.

CHAPTER SUMMARY

The purpose of this chapter is to survey strategies for discovering and for supporting theme statements about selections from literature. The chapter also describes ways to write essays about these discoveries so that readers will be persuaded to accept a specific interpretation of the material.

Identifying a selection's theme is important in understanding the literature read and in grasping its relevance to our daily experience. The products of careful attention to characterization and to the use of images and symbols, theme statements can be expressed in at least three ways: with sentences that are general, are particular, or are qualified with limiting clauses.

Persuasive papers on theme demand special attention to support because readers usually agree with an interpretation if its assertions are carefully defended. Rereading the material itself will help strengthen support because it will suggest specific examples to cite. Questions on characterization, image, and symbol provide effective guides to rereading and to recording your references.

To double-check the strength of evidence and to organize a draft, you can use the classification mode to organize and describe this evidence. Classification trees, diagrams depicting the kinds and nature of available support, can help the writer evaluate the adequacy of notes and plan an outline. Studying the trees can also suggest a logical presentation.

Explaining or defining unusual or significant terms in a draft can further strengthen an analysis of theme. Appositives, words and phrases that rename nouns, are useful for adding necessary definitions and varied structures to persuasive style. Efforts to explain and describe will contribute to a positive character appeal because readers appreciate efforts to help them understand a communication.

To improve your own essay on theme, use this checklist to guide your revisions and study the sample essay that follows it.

Revision Checklist for Persuasive Paper on Theme in Literature

1. Thesis, Content, and Support
   a. Does the introduction contain both a theme statement and an identification of the *kinds* of support that will follow?
   b. Are the amounts and kinds of support appropriate to the audience addressed?

SUGGESTED WRITING ASSIGNMENTS

1. Write a paper of approximately 750 words. Try to persuade your audience that your conception of a literary selection's theme is sound. Include in your introduction not only the theme statement but also the *kinds* of evidence you plan to use for support (i.e., characterization, action, imagery). Use classification as the primary mode of organization for the whole paper or for one or more of its sections. Write for a group of readers who understand what a controlling theme is but who have *not* read your selection. Develop an audience sketch for assessing the needs of this group.
2. Follow the instructions in item 1 above but substitute a recent film for your selection from literature.

---

2. Organization
    a. Does the presentation reflect a careful analysis of the subject and of the support used to defend the thesis?
    b. Is the sequence of observations and support both clear and logical?
3. Style
    a. Have appositives or other modifying structures been used to add variety to sentences?
    b. Have these structures been positioned close to the words modified and have they been punctuated correctly?

SAMPLE STUDENT ESSAY

When we witness evil in others, we often find it hard to continue to live with them. Knowledge that evil does exist sometimes leads to disillusionment. Hawthorne develops this theme with images and symbols in his short story "Young Goodman Brown."

In this tale, the main character does witness evil in several people. The naive Brown, feeling mildly guilty as he leaves his young wife alone for the night, sets out on a strange journey. Walking through the "deep dusk" of the forest, Brown meets the devil (478) who leads him to a gathering of sinners who have already been baptised into an evil society. As they walk toward their destination, the old man "of the serpent" reveals familiar people with whom Brown has been acquainted (479). All of these people, whom Brown had once considered devout, are at the devil's gathering in the "haunted forest" (482). Even Faith, his wife, is there. Brown eventually resists the power of evil, but the knowledge he gains of the sins of these pious people greatly disillusions him.

This disenchantment with trusted people is supported by several important symbols. Faith's pink ribbons, symbols of her child-like goodness and beauty, float away, and she becomes a "pale wife" (484). Brown learns that his grandfather, a constable, had lashed a Quaker woman in Salem's streets and that his father had burned an Indian village. Brown also notices that his traveling companion, the devil in disguise, always carries a walking stick that resembles a great black snake. This stick is an appropriate symbol of its bearer's evil.

Hawthorne also uses images in describing the forest path which add to this sense of newly discovered evil. Many of these words refer to unpleasant, negative things. Everywhere he looks, Brown sees "uncertain light" (479), a "twisted staff" (479), "withered" branches (480), and "uncertain sorrow" (481). The trees creak, the wind laughs loudly, and the brotherhood is "loathful" (483). Wickedness is everywhere.

Wickedness is likewise depicted in the dreadful setting of the sinners' "communion" (483). This hell is "hemmed in by the dark wall of the forest" (482). An altar of rock is "surrounded by four blazing pines" (482), and it is set in front of a demonic "congregation" (483). Blood is used "to lay the mark of baptism upon their foreheads" (484), and familiar faces are "wretched" (483).

When Goodman Brown leaves home, Faith hopes that he will find all is well when he comes back. Unfortunately, when the young man does return,

81

he is no longer able to believe naively that those he had considered holy are even moderately pious. No longer can Brown believe their lives are "of righteousness and prayerful aspirations heavenward" (483).

His new knowledge of their evil causes him to avoid friendship ever after and to live the rest of his life alone with his gloom. This is a fitting conclusion to a story that shows us how devastating evil can actually be.

(Jean Hawxhurst)

Chapter

7

Writing Persuasive Evaluations of Literature

CHAPTER PREVIEW
Evaluation as a Tool in Learning

Evaluation, the process of judging and assigning value, governs most of our learning and our communication. Every day we evaluate experiences and use the resulting judgments to decide which experiences we will repeat and which we will try to avoid. If a department store clerk is rude, the chances are good that we will take our business elsewhere. Similarly, if a newly opened restaurant offers good service and excellent food, we will probably recommend it to others and will return to it frequently ourselves.

Although evaluation is an important guide to choices of friendships, recreation, employment, and shopping, it is also an important tool for learning in college. Evaluating literary and nonliterary texts with care helps us distinguish between writing with limited and ephemeral value and writing that is destined to endure.

To help you improve your own skills in evaluating the materials that you read, this chapter opens with a guide for describing the value to be found in many different kinds of literature. It also offers an adaptation of the particle, field, and wave prewriting strategy, and it surveys the structures and styles found in essays about literature that are particularly appropriate to analyses of value.

PREWRITING

Reading for Ideas

Scholars advance many different criteria for determining the quality of literature; a large proportion of them will however, identify *unity*, the skillful integration of parts, as a characteristic, that marks selections of enduring value and separates them from material that is mediocre. The careful integration of parts leaves readers feeling that every detail contributes in some way to the theme and that nothing is without purpose. When you have finished reading a fully integrated selection, you can look back and understand how most descriptions, dialogues, and incidents add something to its lingering, dominant impression.

Although studies of theme and studies of unity share a common concern for purpose, papers on unity usually survey a broader range of literary devices than do papers on theme. Literature is often unified by plot, setting, and point of view as well as by the characterization, imagery, and symbolism that interest the writer who analyzes theme.

Reading for Ideas: Looking for Unity

Analyses of unity in literature often include thesis statements of two kinds: those that identify the degree to which the selection reflects an integration of parts and those that identify the relative prominence of those elements that pull the selection together. ''_____'s unity is flawed by inconsistency'' is an example of the first type of thesis, and ''Hawthorne's '_____' is unified by its setting'' is an example of the second type.

As a rule, thesis statements identifying prominent sources of unity are more precise and thus more desirable for short essays about literature than are statements that focus upon degree. Statements of degree are best reserved for lengthy studies involving extensive research. A first step in developing either thesis, however, is to determine and study the selection's controlling design; a second step is to survey the elements that support it.

Controlling Design Determining controlling design involves identifying a theme and studying its key concepts, steps surveyed in the last chapter. The following sections review these processes and survey the ways literary elements can support key concepts.

Key Concepts and Controlling Theme Theme statements include not only the subject of the theme and the comment the selection makes about it but also those modifying words and clauses that limit the statement to particular persons or conditions. In the sentence, ''Hawthorne's theme is that those who are obsessed by evil find misery,'' the theme of obsession is limited to those who see evil. In the sentence, ''Melville's theme is that Christian charity is not always rewarded," the writer limits the concept of charity to that concept dictated by the religious ideal.

These limitations are products of the theme's *key concepts*. In Chapter 6, key concepts were identified as (1) modifying words and phrases attached to important nouns and (2) verbs used in an unusual or controversial way. Distinguishing key concepts from other parts of the theme statement is important because literary elements may stress the concepts themselves as they contribute to the unity of the whole selection.

If you were to develop the first of the preceding theme statements, you could circle key concepts and then search for support for each. This search would lead you to evidence supporting the senses of *evil, obsession,* and *misery* you identified as pervasive within the selection. If you were to develop the second theme, you would look for traces of *Christian theology, charitable behavior,* and *the lack of reward* that comprise the key concepts of the full theme statement.

FOR PRACTICE

Write out a theme statement for a selection you have read recently. Circle its key concepts and then underline those key concepts for which you can provide the strongest support. List the sources of support that you can remember.

Sources of Support   In addition to studying characterization, imagery, and symbol—the sources of support for themes surveyed in the last chapter—analyses of unity invite attention to two other elements that bind a selection and its theme's key concepts together. These are plot and setting.

The *plot* is the pattern of incidents found in a selection. These incidents are usually linked to each other by cause-effect relationships, and they frequently involve a conflict and resolution. The plot of "Bartleby the Scrivener" follows its narrator's experiences with the puzzling clerk; it begins with their first meeting and ends with the news that arrives following Bartleby's death of his link to the Dead Letter Office.

An analysis of plot contributions will answer one or both of the following questions. The first is, "What does the *sequence* add to theme or to its key concepts?" The second is, "What does each *event* contribute?"

Questions of sequence generate speculation concerning the changes in theme or dominant impression that would have occurred if incidents involving major characters had followed a different pattern. You might ask if Emily Grierson's fate would have been different had Homer Barron arrived in town *before* her father died. You might also ask if the sense of decay would have been as pervasive had the townspeople visited Emily earlier in her life to ask that she pay her taxes. As it is, they find a puffy-faced old woman in a musty and sunless parlor.

Questions of *incident contributions* generate ideas concerning the significance of seemingly inconsequential events. Speculations of incident, like speculations of sequence, are most productive when they begin with major events and major characters. Every major happening and every action of a character consists of smaller events that of themselves may go unnoticed. Careful attention to these constituents usually generates ideas about their larger contributions.

An analysis of incident for "A Rose for Emily" might prompt a consideration of how Emily's clipped conversation with the druggist adds to the impression that she is trapped without connections to the changing world around her. Such an analysis might also ask why Faulkner had Emily purchase the initialed vanity set shortly before Homer's disappearance. What does this purchase add to the theme or to its associated ideas?

FOR PRACTICE

1. List five to ten incidents involving the major character of a short story, play, novel, or poem with which you are familiar. List them first in the order that actually governs the selection. Then transpose several of them and spend five to ten minutes freewriting about how these changes would affect the selection's outcome and its theme. Share your conclusions with the class.
2. Spend five to ten minutes freewriting about what each incident listed in item 1 contributes to some part of the theme.

Setting, like plot, also deserves attention in evaluations of unity. Next time you watch a film, pay particular attention to the locations and to the weather conditions dominating its important scenes. You will probably find that these have been chosen to match the feelings or the actions depicted. Depressed characters often appear in empty streets with cloudy skies or rain. Families often reunite in sunny rooms or gardens in springtime.

Attention to setting should begin with an identification of the geographical location. You need to identify the political territory—country, state, town—at the outset. Then you can concern yourself with the immediate space—the building, the room, the chair.

When the immediate space is important, setting becomes more than location; it includes the details of dress, decorative furnishings, and even the climate and season. Setting thus becomes a *stage* upon which actions unfold.

Occasionally, however, setting details will be so nonspecific that you cannot guess when and where the action occurs. This in itself may be significant. The author may be suggesting that the theme message is applicable to anyone, regardless of time and place.

A close look at setting reveals meaning that might otherwise be lost to casual reading. Attention to setting shows how appropriate the chicken farm with its sickly stock is to Anderson's story about a man's painful struggle for success. Attention to setting indicates the significance of the law office's partitions in Melville's story of the antisocial scrivener.

FOR PRACTICE

Identify a theme statement for each of the selections below. Circle key concepts. Be prepared to discuss how each of the settings or setting details listed contributes to a key concept in the theme statement.
   a. The white cliffs in "Dover Beach."
   b. The rocking horse in "The Rocking-Horse Winner."
   c. The interior of Emily's parlor in "A Rose for Emily."

Prewriting: Recording Notes

Identifying those elements that contribute to the unity or dominant impression of a selection needs to be followed by a careful reading of the material. Reading and rereading the literary selection are important steps in analyzing its content and in recording your ideas. If you find yourself returning to the text again and again during the prewriting stage, you are probably completing this stage as most effective writers do; studies of unity demand an especially close reading and review.

No matter what the method of reviewing and recording used, the wave, particle, and field strategy described in Chapter 4 can guide your studies and your prewriting about unity in literature. The following adaptation can be especially helpful. The column listings provide a left-to-right progression from responses that are very specific to those that are more speculative. Notice that the questions assume a controlling theme has already been identified.

Some responses to these questions may involve listing words and phrases; others may involve generating longer stretches of connected freewriting. The plot and style questions most particularly demand lists of major events and elements of style from significant passages, particularly with the particle or "What is it?" questions. Either recording mode is acceptable as long as it works for you.

Basic Questions

Particle	Field	Wave
What is it?	How is it like or unlike others of its kind?	How might it be changing?
		What is its potential for change?

Adaptation for Analyzing Support

Particle	Field	Wave
Plot—What is it, i.e., what are the major events in sequence?	To what key theme concepts does the plot relate?	How might the plot have been different?
	Is its contribution relatively major or minor?	How would the difference have affected the theme?
Plot Incident—What is it?	To what key theme concept does the incident relate?	How might the theme have been different with its absence?
Character—Which one?	To which key concept does this character's presence relate?	What would be lost in his or her absence?
Style—Which passage is relevant e.g., which description of major or minor character or event?	To which key concepts does this word or comparison relate?	What other language choices might have been made?
	What is the strength of the contribution?	What influence would these choices have had upon the theme?
Which words?		

Here are sample prewriting notes written in response to "My Last Duchess" by Robert Browning. A copy of the poem appears on page 97.

CONTROLLING THEME—People who are arrogant and egotistical are capable of murder when they feel threatened.

PLOT—WHAT IS IT?

Actually 2 stories in one. The Duke is involved in one story—his negotiations for his next marriage. The other plot is the one he tells the representative about his last wife. Both are important. Story he tells helps us know his present one.
Present plot:
Event 1—Duke pulls back curtain to show portrait of wife.
Event 2—tells story (2nd plot). Wife liked everyone. Smiled and blushed for every gift. Duke had her killed.
Event 3—Duke says he expects bride's father will be generous but notes he's mostly interested in the bride herself.
Event 4—Begins to lead visitor downstairs.
Event 5—Points out a statue.

PLOT—HOW IT COMPARES TO OTHER SUPPORT

Plot mostly supports key concept about Duke's arrogance. Tells of how he's willing to kill. Tells about the silly things that drive him to kill his wife. They are all insignificant—only important to him.

Plot—How Things Would Change

If Duke had begun by talking about new marriage plans before going through story of last duchess, the representative of his new bride might have seen the story as a threat. So would we. As is, the sequence causes us to be pulled in before we realize what a horrible person he really is. By saving his confession of having given commands and his comments about the forthcoming marriage until the end, we don't just chalk him off as a devil at first. Instead, we pay attention and then feel how evil he is at once.

Plot Incidents—What They Add

Duke's pointing out Neptune statue at end adds to idea of his arrogance and egotism. He's just been talking about his beautiful dead wife yet slips easily into showing off again. Also—fact that he opens up curtain to show off portrait of wife is interesting. Sounds like he keeps the painting covered except when he wants to show her off. Apparently he hates her so much still he can't stand looking at her at other times.

Character—Duke

Not much to add. He's so completely bad, controlling theme has no room for any sympathy. Not like a lot of more modern literature that has some characters that are both good and bad.

Character—Duchess

Although info comes just through his eyes, she seems innocent, child-like. Makes us really hate him—she's so defenseless. All the things she does to annoy him are positive—thanking someone who picks her some cherries or smiles at her. No hint at all that she's capable of deliberately doing something to make him unhappy. Her greatest sin is in just being herself. Without these details, we might actually think he's had a bad wife.

Style

Monologue, so not a lot of description. Still, some comparisons. Word "read" in line 6. Says some people read the passion in her face. Interesting—shows Duke's arrogance causes him to think people read a lot into every little thing in his life. Later refuses to "stoop." Stoop is ugly word for bowing, bending. Duke won't bend, won't even talk and give her a fighting chance. No wonder he's gone through so many wives.

FOR PRACTICE

Use the particle, wave, and field questions to generate notes concerning unity in a selection you have read recently. Don't forget to write a theme statement; you need one to focus the questions. Spend five to ten minutes on each support element (plot, characterization, and so on).

WRITING AND REVISING: STRUCTURING AN EVALUATION

Using Evaluation to Write a Thesis

Evaluation is a mode of organization that is usually neglected in composition studies. This neglect probably comes from the common misconception that objectivity precludes evaluation. Such a conception of objectivity is unwarranted inasmuch as strong evaluative presentations can reflect careful reasoning as well as a desire to be persuasive.

Distinctions between persuasive and ineffective evaluations do, in fact, depend upon the use of evidence and reason. Weak evaluative assertions are usually little more than expressions of personal feeling. Such unqualified statements of preference as "I like Fitzgerald" or "Hemingway is terrible" are weak and subjective evaluations.

A strong statement, on the other hand, includes not only an expression of preference but also an explanation of the criteria against which the subject has been judged. The fullest explanations include a list of qualities that could be associated with an idealized or "perfect" example of the subject, if such an example could ever exist. These full explanations also include a point-by-point description of how the subject in question actually measures up to the components on the list of ideal qualities.

The sample thesis statements presented earlier in this chapter represent effective beginnings for strong evaluative presentations about unity. Any time you can specify the components supporting a dominant impression, you are listing those areas in which the selection approaches a hypothetical ideal.

Here are several more thesis sentences that promise to explain the bases of their evaluations:

1. Hawthorne's "Young Goodman Brown" has unity by virtue of its plot, characterization, and style.
2. Malamud's "The Magic Barrel" is unified primarily by its point of view.
3. Setting strengthens the unity in "A Rose for Emily."

Writing a thesis that describes the sources of unity not only prepares readers for an analysis but also suggests a plan for the paper's final draft. A good place to begin this plan is with the introduction the thesis suggests.

Using Evaluation to Write an Introduction

Any introduction to an extended evaluation should begin with the writer's conception of some hypothetical ideal and should list those characteristics the paper's subject actually shares with this imagined model. Accepting the belief that unity leads to value in literature usually leads to an imagined model selection that is bound by some clearly dominant center. An obvious center in most is a theme with its associated concepts.

Here are introductory paragraphs developed from the thesis statements presented above. Notice how each names the theme, its key concepts, and its support.

EXAMPLE 1:

Hawthorne's "Young Goodman Brown" has unity by virtue of its plot, its characterization, and its style. Hawthorne uses these to develop the controlling theme that some people never recover from the experience of finding evil in others. All three elements support the idea that evil is everywhere; plot incidents support the idea that some cannot recover.

EXAMPLE 2:

Malamud's "The Magic Barrel" is unified primarily by its point of view. The narrator's omniscience supports the idea that one of its main characters, a rabbi, is experiencing conflict. This, in turn, supports the controlling theme that some people experience serious conflict when they learn the truth about themselves.

EXAMPLE 3:

A controlling theme in "A Rose for Emily" is that some people are driven to desperation when they see their cherished reputations deteriorate. Setting, particularly the Grierson house, unifies the story by stressing the idea of deterioration.

FOR PRACTICE

Review any prewriting notes you have generated concerning a selection's unity. Then use them to develop a thesis paragraph you could use to introduce your evaluation. Remember to include the following: (1) your thesis sentence, (2) the selection's controlling theme, (3) references to significant key concepts, and (4) a statement linking specific support elements to specific key concepts. Study the preceding models for extra help.

Using Evaluation to Plan a Draft

An extended evaluation indicates two patterns for developing the draft of a literary evaluation. The theme's key concepts provide the pattern for one, and the unifying elements themselves provide the plan for the other.

Here is a tentative outline for a paper on "Young Goodman Brown" that features the theme's key concepts:

THEME STATEMENT: Some people never recover from the knowledge that evil exists in others.

- I. Plot Incidents—no recovery
  - A. Brown's behavior at return from forest
  - B. Details of his later life
- II. Evil Everywhere
  - A. Plot
    - 1. Journey
    - 2. Events in woods
  - B. Characterization
    - 1. The mysterious traveler
    - 2. Goody Cloyse
    - 3. Faith
  - C. Style
    - 1. Words
      - a. Those that describe setting
      - b. Those that describe actions in the woods
    - 2. Figures
      - a. Comparisons to snakes
      - b. Comparisons to devil
      - c. Comparisons to savage animals

Here is an outline for the same subject that features the sources of unity:

THEME STATEMENT: Some people never recover from the knowledge that evil exists in others.

- I. Plot Support
  - A. No recovery
  - B. Evil is everywhere
- II. Characterization Support
  - A. No recovery
  - B. Evil is everywhere
- III. Style Support
  - A. No recovery
  - B. Evil is everywhere

FOR PRACTICE

Study a thesis paragraph composed for the preceding exercise. Use it to write a simple outline covering its major ideas. Use either a *key concept* or a *support source* development. Return to your textbook or to your prewriting as necessary for listing all relevant details.

POLISHING STYLE FOR READERS: VARYING REFERENCES TO ACTION

Past chapters have surveyed ways of varying modifiers for the sake of maintaining interest in informative and persuasive writing. Readers most appreciate writing that presents messages in language that is neither confusing nor boring.

This section covers ways of securing interest by varying the references used to describe the actions involved in essays about most printed texts. It includes a survey of the kinds of references that can be used as well as a guide for using these references so that they are appropriate to the audience and the purpose of the writing.

To begin, most literary and expository writing involves *action* of some kind; authors *write* about human experience, the characters they depict *suffer* conflicts, and readers *study* and *respond.* The following diagram covers these kinds of action and the types of reports that usually describe them:

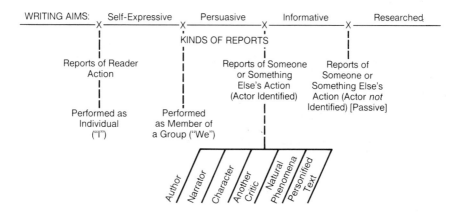

Each major category denotes a type of report that can be used in essays about literature, about history, and about many other areas of human and cultural experience. Each takes its name from the *actor* whose behavior is reported; compositions about literature describe the thoughts, the actions, and the visions of any or all of those listed here.

The report of reader action depicts the thoughts the essay writer experienced when reading the selection. These depictions identify this person in one of two ways: (1) as an individual or (2) as a member of a group that includes *us* as readers. Reader action reports include such phrases and sentences as the following:

1. *I see* the character wallowing in his grief. (As individual)
2. *We share* the narrator's surprise. (As group member; we, the readers, are also members of this group)

Reports of text action and reports of someone or something else's action dominate informative and persuasive writing. Reports of text action personify the material; the language suggests that the literary selection is alive and is doing something by itself. The following are examples of textual personification:

1. The *story opens* . . .
2. The *climax comes* as a shock.
3. The *conclusion devastates* us with its abruptness.

Reports of someone or something else's action resemble text reports insofar as they name the performers of the action. These reports produce such expressions as

1. *Faulkner writes* of Yoknapatawpha County.
2. The passionate *shepherd has* no practical sense.
3. The *vase tumbled* to the floor.
4. *John Doe has examined* this idea in his critical biography.
5. *The hurricane caught* the villagers by surprise.

Action reports that fail to identify the actors often dominate *researched* writing. These reports usually include passive voice constructions that add unnecessary words. To avoid wordiness, you should keep these forms of report to a minimum using them only when nothing else conveys the emphasis you intend. Here are sample reports by unidentified sources:

1. The shepherd's request *is followed by* a refusal.
2. The iron-grey hair *is found* on the pillow.
3. Arnold *has been studied* for decades.

To ensure that your own reports of action are both interesting and effective, be sure that they are appropriate to the essay's or the passage's specific purpose. The horizontal line drawn above the diagram of reports provides a guide to the kinds of reports most frequently found in published models of writing. Each *X* indicates the writing aim for which a particular reference is most appropriate. While *all* types of reports will appear in most compositions, the type appropriate to a specific aim should be the one that dominates the paper.

CHAPTER SUMMARY

This chapter describes the nature and the sources of unity in literature. Although opinion of literary value remains divided, many scholars consider unity the characteristic that distinguishes good literature from efforts that are mediocre. A selection possesses unity if every part contributes to a single theme or impression. Characterization, image, symbol, point of view, plot, and setting are all sources of unity.

This chapter also describes the evaluative mode as a source of organization for informative and for persuasive writing. Strong evaluations explain the criteria by which the subject is being judged, and these evaluations suggest ways in which the subject measures up to a hypothetical ideal. Many strong evaluative thesis sentences about literature assume that a unified paper represents an ideal model, and they specify those literary elements that contribute to the selection's dominant impression.

The evaluative thesis can be expanded into an introductory paragraph that not only prepares readers for the paper's major assertions but also suggests a logical outline for the draft itself. Evaluative drafts may be organized according to key theme concepts or according to prominent sources of unity.

The chapter closes with a survey of the kinds of reports of action that can be used in informative and in persuasive writing. These include reports of reader behavior, reports of other actors or objects, and reports of unidentified sources. Because reports of action by unidentified sources usually involve passive-voice constructions, these should appear infrequently in most of your compositions.

Use the following checklist to proofread your own evaluative essay and then mark strengths and weaknesses in the student essay that follows.

FOR PRACTICE

1. Clip a movie or book review from your local or college paper. Mark the kinds of reports it contains as follows: (a) *underline* words, phrases, and sentences that are reports of reader action; (b) *double underline* reports of the actions of others when the other *is* identified; and (c) *circle* reports of action whose actors remain unidentified. After determining the author's primary aim, be prepared to discuss how well he or she has observed the principle of appropriate dominance.

2. Follow the instructions in item 1, using a paper of your own. You may have written this paper for this or for any other class. Be prepared to discuss the appropriateness of your references to the writing aims that dominated the composition.

Revision Checklist for Persuasive Paper on Evaluation

1. *Thesis, Content, and Support*
   a. Does the paper open with a thesis and an introductory paragraph that identify the unifying elements found in the selection?

b. Does the introductory paragraph identify a theme for the selection and link specific literary elements to its key concepts?
2. *Organization*
Is the paper clearly organized according to key theme concepts or to unifying elements themselves?
3. *Style*
Can you mark types of action reports you have used and find that those which dominate are appropriate to your writing aim?

SAMPLE STUDENT ESSAY

A theme in "Bartleby the Scrivener" is that a person can lose his desire to live when he becomes isolated from society. Herman Melville's short story has unity, for its setting, characterization, and distinctive style contribute to its theme.

This story is about a man named Bartleby, who slowly loses his desire to live. His job as a scrivener is to copy documents for the narrator. He is isolated in a small corner of the narrator's office where he works, eats, and lives. One day for no reason, Bartleby stops working. After refusing to leave the office after many requests, he ends up living in the Tombs, a debtor's prison, where he eventually stops eating and dies. The narrator then discovers that Bartleby had once worked in the Dead Letter Office in Washington.

Melville constantly shows how Bartleby is an outsider who gradually loses his will to live, and he stresses Bartleby's isolation with the setting. Bartleby works in a small corner in the office where he is separated from the narrator and the rest of his co-workers by a high screen that hides him. Later, he even decides to live in this tiny space, far away from relatives and friends.

Bartleby's characterization also emphasizes his separateness. When he first comes to work, he works hard all the time. He is never willing, however, to give advice or to share his opinion. He always refuses to work with the rest of the people in the office. When asked to complete any task, he always says, "I would prefer not to" (753). This reply reflects not only his isolation but also his apathy.

Melville's distinctive style also helps focus Bartleby's growing separation from humanity. Melville's word choices consistently portray him as an isolated and dull human being with nowhere to go; he is always "pallidly neat, pitiably respectable, incurably forlorn" (751).

Even word choices used to describe Bartleby's work space convey a sense of isolation and emptiness. The description of the "pale window behind the screen, upon the dead brick wall" heightens this empty feeling (757). It reminds us of Bartleby's emptiness as well.

Because of this story's setting, characterization, and style, we see that when a person becomes isolated from society, he may lose his desire to live. Melville explains this message by using Bartleby as an example.

(*Cesar Madarang*)

SUGGESTED WRITING ASSIGNMENTS

1. Study one of the following selections and write a persuasive paper that evaluates its unity. Write for a group whose members value unity but have not studied the selection about which you are writing.

Recommended:

John Cheever's "The Country Husband"
Shirley Jackson's "The Lottery"
Franz Kafka's "A Hunger Artist"
William Wordsworth's "Ode: Intimations of Immortality from Recollections of Early Childhood"
A. E. Houseman's "To an Athlete Dying Young"
Amy Lowell's "Patterns"

2. Read a short story from a popular magazine. Write a persuasive paper that evaluates the story in terms of the presence or absence of unity. Write for a group whose members subscribe to the magazine and like to read it.

My Last Duchess

Ferrara

That's my last Duchess painted on the wall,
Looking as if she were alive. I call
That piece a wonder, now: Fra Pandolf's hands
Worked busily a day, and there she stands.
Will't please you sit and look at her? I said
"Fra Pandolf" by design, for never read
Strangers like you that pictured countenance,
The depth and passion of its earnest glance,
But to myself they turned (since none puts by
The curtain I have drawn for you, but I)
And seemed as they would ask me, if they durst,
How such a glance came there; so, not the first
Are you to turn and ask thus. Sir, 'twas not
Her husband's presence only, called that spot
Of joy into the Duchess' cheek: perhaps
Fra Pandolf chanced to say, "Her mantle laps
Over my lady's wrist too much," or "Paint
Must never hope to reproduce the faint
Half-flush that dies along her throat:" such stuff
Was courtesy, she thought, and cause enough
For calling up that spot of joy. She had
A heart—how shall I say?—too soon made glad,
Too easily impressed; she liked whate'er
She looked on, and her looks went everywhere.

Sir, 'twas all one! My favor at her breast,
The dropping of the daylight in the West,
The bough of cherries some officious fool
Broke in the orchard for her, the white mule
She rode with round the terrace—all and each
Would draw from her alike the approving speech,
Or blush, at least. She thanked men—good! but thanked
Somehow—I know not how—as if she ranked
My gift of a nine-hundred-years-old name
With anybody's gift. Who'd stoop to blame
This sort of trifling? Even had you skill
In speech—(which I have not)—to make your will
Quite clear to such an one, and say, "Just this
Or that in you disgusts me; here you miss,
Or there exceed the mark"—and if she let
Herself be lessoned so, nor plainly set
Her wits to yours, forsooth, and made excuse,
—E'en then would be some stooping; and I choose
Never to stoop. Oh, sir, she smiled, no doubt,
Whene'er I passed her; but who passed without
Much the same smile? This grew; I gave commands;
Then all smiles stopped together. There she stands
As if alive. Will't please you rise? We'll meet
The company below, then. I repeat,
The Count your master's known munificence
Is ample warrant that no just pretence
Of mine for dowry will be disallowed;
Though his fair daughter's self, as I avowed
At starting, is my object. Nay, we'll go
Together down, sir. Notice Neptune, though,
Taming a sea-horse, thought a rarity,
Which Claus of Innsbruck cast in bronze for me!

(*Robert Browning*)

Chapter
8
Researched Writing: Early Stages

CHAPTER PREVIEW
The Characteristics of Researched Writing

Researched writing differs from other kinds of writing in at least four ways. First, it uses resources outside the literature itself to strengthen its major points. Second, it integrates a greater number of documentation conventions than do other kinds of writing. Third, it assumes an audience of demanding and knowledgeable readers, and fourth, because of its many references to different resources, it produces essays that are longer than those of most other assignments given in college and in many professions.

Because the research process demands attention to many details, two chapters of this book are devoted to its stages and conventions. This chapter covers preliminary inquiry and planning; the next traces the later stages of revising an outline, writing early drafts, and polishing style for readers.

This chapter opens with a preview of paper topics appropriate to writing about literature and then offers prewriting strategies for limiting these topics and for planning careful reading. It finally examines ways of surveying materials and of taking notes that will reduce the number of false starts that can inhibit your writing progress.

PREWRITING

Options for Research in Literature

The comparison mode dominates many published papers about literature; the process of reading and comparing several different selections by a single author produces interesting and significant writing. Here are several research assignments from my own classes; they invite comparisons and have generated successful student papers. While they are *not* offered as an exhaustive list of all the possibilities open to you, these assignments may provide you with some direction at this early stage in your exploration. Surveying them will also help you understand the prewriting, structuring, and polishing examples included in this chapter and the next.

Suggested Researched Writing Assignments

1. General Specifications
   a. *Audience.* Students in this class. Remember that they have been studying literature all semester and will have even completed Chapter 9 on documentation conventions before you have finished your own project. This background indicates that they will expect heavy support and careful attention to form. They may *not*, however, have read the literature you cite, and they certainly have not studied the outside resources you will use.
   b. *Length, Form, and Bibliography.* Lengths will vary according to the subject, but most college research papers cover eight to twelve typed, double-spaced pages.
   c. Documentation should conform to guidelines specified in the *Modern Language Association Handbook* (the *MLA*). MLA form is acceptable in researched writing in the humanities and is that form specified in most of your composition and grammar textbooks.
2. Recommended Thesis Choices
   a. *Paper 1 Choice.* Thesis identifies a subject or idea that recurs in the controlling themes of several of an author's selections.
      Example: D. H. Lawrence develops themes about the consequences of irresponsibility in three of his short stories.
   b. *Paper 2 Choice.* Thesis compares the kinds, motives, or effects of narrators that are used by an author in several different selections.
      Example: James Joyce uses a close narrator who shares his foolishness with us in three of his short stories.
      Example: The narrator's tone and omniscience cause us to respond both positively and negatively to major characters in two Fitzgerald novels.
   c. *Paper 3 Choice.* Thesis either evaluates the unity or the relative strengths of the sources of support in one or more literary selections.
      Example: Melville's characterization does not consistently support his themes in two of his short stories.
      Example: Setting and style are important sources of unity in "A Rose for Emily" and "Delta Autumn."

FOR PRACTICE

If your instructor has assigned a research paper that requires you to select the author or thesis yourself, list three writers who interest you. Listing three provides some leeway should you later reject selections by your first or second choices. Once you have made your list, start reading the literature you might use for the paper itself.

Prewriting for a Tentative Reading Outline

Once you have an author, a tentative thesis, and a body of literature in mind, you need a tentative outline to focus the research so that you won't be sidetracked by interesting but irrelevant material. The most effective reading outlines devote space to primary as well as to secondary materials.

Primary resources, as you may recall, are those that can be studied and analyzed without reference to anyone else's opinions. A taped interview, bearing your subject's own words, is a primary resource. In your writing for this class, your primary sources have been the literary selections themselves.

Secondary resources, unlike primary resources, include the perspectives of at least two people: (1) the subject involved and (2) the individual who has interpreted the subject's words or actions. If a journalist from *Newsweek* had secured a taped interview with Barbara Walters and had used it to write an article about her, the article would be a secondary source, the offering of an intermediary—in this case, the journalist—whose own background and biases may have influenced the representation of what Ms. Walters had said. An accurate evaluation of this particular representation would demand some information about the journalist and about his or her biases. The writer may well have ignored statements Ms. Walters had made that would have detracted from the positive or negative image he or she was trying to create.

Many different secondary sources can derive from the same primary materials. In writing about literature, for example, two different scholars may produce two different studies of theme in response to "The Rocking-Horse Winner." Because of their subjectivity, the critical compositions would be labelled *secondary* sources while "The Rocking-Horse Winner" would be considered the *primary* material.

An important point to remember here is that the strongest researched papers about literature are those that stress the literature itself and use secondary material for backup. If you will learn to read carefully, to trust your own observations, and to fortify them with specific references to the selections, you will create papers that are both readable and interesting. If, on the other hand, you have somehow assumed that researched writing involves assembling bunches of secondary source quotations, you will end

101

up with something resembling a patchwork quilt. It might contain interesting bits of information, but it will be sadly lacking in focus.

First Notes: General   After reading the primary sources that will dominate the paper, you need to explore the ideas that have been generated by the material as well as by the assignment itself. One place to start is with prewriting notes developed in response to the classical topics.

The *classical topics* are questions we have inherited from antiquity. Throughout the classical period, most citizens needed skill in political and forensic address so that they could protect their property and secure employment within the community. Most believed an important component of this skill was the ability to speak freely and fluently on almost any subject introduced in a public forum. For this reason, distinguished speakers and teachers developed lists of questions that could be memorized, applied to any subject, and, therefore, used as insurance against "blanking out" or being left with nothing to say. The word *topics*, incidentally, referred to *places* for finding ideas and not to the subjects of the compositions themselves.

While these lists were first devised for speakers, they are equally helpful to writers. Here, for example, is an adaptation of topic questions described by Aristotle that will generate first notes about most research assignments. As with all prewriting questions, you can freely respond with lists or with notes. The objective at this stage is to find out what you already know. You might be surprised by what you find.

One particularly helpful way to work with them is to follow this two-step procedure. First, respond to the questions with reference to each of your literary selections; run through them as many times as necessary, using each single selection as your subject. Then, answer with reference to some part of the thesis you are developing. If your assignment choices resemble those listed at the beginning of this chapter, you might address the questions to "the subject of the controlling theme" or "the narrator in '_____.'"

TOPICS FROM ARISTOTLE

DEFINITION
1. How do most people define the subject?
2. How do I define it?

COMPARISON
1. To what other subjects of the same class may my subject be compared?
2. How is it similar to or different from these subjects?

RELATIONSHIP
1. What causes my subject to occur as it does?
2. What are the effects of its nature?
3. What, if any, contradictions appear in relation to my subject?

CIRCUMSTANCE

1. Would it be possible for my subject to occur in a different form or to be transformed?
2. What, if any, precedents would support these changes?
3. What would be the result of these changes?

TESTIMONY

1. Which, if any, authorities support my attitude (or any part of it) toward my subject?
2. Which do not?
3. What statistics can I identify for its support?
4. Which maxims or ideas in popular culture support my perspective?

Here are sample notes written in response to D. H. Lawrence's "Odor of Chrysanthemums." The *subject* to which questions are addressed is characterization, i.e., that of Elizabeth Bates, the young widow. Notice that some of the topic questions are not as applicable to the subject as are others. Don't let these trouble you; simply answer what you can and move on.

DEFINITION

Elizabeth Bates is the wife who is widowed and left even poorer, in worse shape than she was before. Most people would see her as a pitiful creature. But because her husband's death makes her aware of how little she knew of him and of how miserable marriage can sometimes be, I'd define her as a person who has just awakened, not as somebody who is miserable.

COMPARISON

Elizabeth reminds me of other wives who find out that they hadn't really known their husbands at all. This happens sometimes with absence, other times with death. I remember an old movie that was just on TV again—*Midnight Lace*. I think this woman gets all these murder threats but finds out in the end that they had been coming from her husband. Wasn't that what that old Grace Kelly movie, *Dial M for Murder* was all about, too?

Elizabeth is different from a lot of other wives, though. I remember reading about Tess in *Tess of the D'Urbervilles*. Her husband, Angel, wins her over but if you ask me he was so rigid and so harsh in judging her, he had the wrong name altogether. I think Tess and Elizabeth Bates are different because Tess never seems to see her husband's weaknesses while Elizabeth finally does.

RELATIONSHIP

Elizabeth seems to have stayed a suffering wife because of the period and the social conditions she was living in. Today she might have become a runaway wife. The period keeps her unhappy and long-suffering. Still, there's some contradiction. She really is strong after all. Strong enough to protect her children. Stronger than her mother-in-law whose grief just knocks her out.

CIRCUMSTANCE

As I said above—if Elizabeth were living in the 1970s and 1980s she'd probably not be stuck. She'd probably have custody of the kids, have them in day-care centers, and be back in school herself working on a degree so she could get them out of the rut.

TESTIMONY
I don't know yet which authorities or critics support my ideas. Guess that's what the library research is going to be all about. Same with statistics. Maxims. I wonder if this counts—the one that says the evil we do lives after us. Shakespeare. Probably Elizabeth will remember this. Still—she's kind enough to hold onto what memories of the good she can find for him. Other maxims? Maybe those about how we really never know people even when we think we do. Guess I'm going to have to think about more maxims.

FOR PRACTICE

Use the classical topic questions to secure a set of preliminary notes for a research paper of your own. Remember that you may best respond to the sequence several times by changing the *subject* to which each question refers. Subjects will include ideas from individual reading selections as well as from your choice of the paper's thesis.

Second Notes: Specific to Thesis If you have used the classical topics to produce several sets of notes and are still without a tentative thesis, you might try the following questions to narrow your subject further. These questions should look familiar inasmuch as they were suggested by the assignments described above and because they ask questions covered in preceding chapters.

PREWRITING QUESTIONS FOR SPECIFIC THESIS CHOICES

FOR THESIS COMPARING CONTROLLING THEMES
For each selection, what is a controlling theme?
For each, what are key concepts? (Circle them.)
What similarities or differences appear in reference to the group of controlling themes?
What are major forms of support for each theme? (e.g., characterization, plot, plot incident, setting, style—especially images, symbols, figures)
What, if any, similarities exist among controlling themes in terms of their respective support?

FOR THESIS ON NARRATOR TYPES
(Respond to each item for each selection you are using.)
Is the narrator close or distant?
If close, what might be his or her reason for telling the story, e.g., to rationalize, to share, to seek or explore?
If distant, how do this narrator's characteristics and powers affect us as readers, i.e., his or her omniscience; tone; degree of attention to particular characters, objects, or events?

What, if any, purposes do the specific choices of narrator for each selection serve?

FOR THESIS ON UNITY AND SUPPORT

What controlling theme dominates each selection?

Does each possess unity, i.e., do most elements of plot, character, setting, style contribute *something* to a dominant impression or theme?

What, if any, inessentials appear in any or all selections?

For each, what are the conspicuous sources of support for unity?

What, if any, changes would you recommend for any selection whose potential for unity seems flawed?

FOR PRACTICE

Respond to the thesis-specific prewriting questions for a paper you may be writing about literature. To broaden your options, work through all three sets.

Developing and Using the Tentative Reading Outline

Writing a tentative thesis is especially important in researched writing because the thesis itself will suggest your reading outline. This outline, if roughed out early in the project, provides help in two ways. First, it indicates areas that demand further research; sometimes knowing what you do *not* know about the subject is more important than knowing what you do. Second, the reading outline provides limits that will enable you to cover the subject well while meeting the paper's deadline. In its absence, you might waste precious time reading about inessentials simply because they are interesting or because materials about them are easy to obtain.

Here is a tentative thesis and reading outline to guide early research for a paper on theme in D. H. Lawrence. You may wish to compare it with the final outline submitted with the student paper reproduced in Chapter 9. Clearly, the tentative reading outline is intended as a *guide* and, as such, is subject to change.

TENTATIVE THESIS: D. H. Lawrence writes short stories with themes about unhappy or greedy people.

I. Summaries
   A. "Horse Dealer's Daughter"
   B. "Rocking-Horse Winner"
   C. "Odor of Chrysanthemums"
II. Unhappy people
   A. "Horse Dealer's"
   B. "Rocking-Horse"
   C. "Chrysanthemums"

III. Greedy people
    A. "Horse Dealer's"
    B. "Rocking-Horse"
    C. "Chrysanthemums"
IV. What critics say about themes, unhappiness, greed in Lawrence

---

FOR PRACTICE

Use your prewriting to identify a tentative thesis and tentative reading outline to help you with a research assignment for this or for any other class. Feel free to break your outline into more subheadings than those detailed in the preceding section. Most reading outlines for research should, however, extend at least to the capital letter level.

The Reading Outline as a Guide to Notes

Because the reading outline limits the materials you will study, it provides an index to the numbers and kinds of notes that you need to take. What follows is a survey of ways to improve note-taking and of standard resources that you should consult once you have limited the territory.

Assembling a Tentative Bibliography Whatever the subject, first trips to the library should be devoted to assembling the *tentative bibliography,* a list of the most promising resources for the project. For best results, you should compile this list as soon as the assignment has been made, and you should record the items on three-by-five cards, each of which contains a single resource. Card references should include the data that belongs in the bibliography; taking a handbook to the library to make sure that the documentation is correct is a good idea. Careful recording of data at this stage will enable you to simply alphabetize the cards later and to type their notes in order.

Here is a sample bibliography card. Notice its form and call number; including the call number helps should you need to make later trips to the library to check the resource again.

```
PR
6023
A93      Delavenay, Emile.
Z62355   D. H. Lawrence: The Man
         and His Work.
         Carbondale, Ill.: Southern
         Illinois UP, 1972.
```

Resources for the Literary Bibliography   Important stops for beginning a bibliography in literature include the encyclopedia shelves, the public or card catalog (if your library uses one), and the indexes to periodicals. Consulting each of these is also essential for research in other subjects as well.

Encyclopedias are helpful because they not only present brief overviews of most subjects but also provide lists of relevant publications. Encyclopedias also suggest other possible entries for the tentative bibliography. You may well begin with encyclopedia articles written *about* your chosen author before looking for articles on subjects that dominate his or her writing. D. H. Lawrence sets many of his stories and novels in villages where coal mining is the principal occupation; turning to "coal mining" may supply some valuable background.

Checking the author's name in the card catalog is another essential step. The cards succeeding the name refer to books written *by* as well as *about* a writer. Plan to spend some time with the catalog and be choosy. Note and check out those secondary sources that have been most recently published. These will often include summaries of earlier scholarship that will save you the time you might otherwise spend looking through dated criticism. As a rule, recent books will also discuss materials by or about an author that had not been available to early critics.

Indexes to periodicals will also provide references to the most recent scholarship about your subject. Again, begin with the most recently published indexes and then work back through time.

Good subject headings to consult in indexes include the author's name as well as the title of specific selections that he or she has written. Articles dedicated to literature you are not using may also be helpful if article titles include references to ideas listed in your own tentative thesis. Discovering what one critic says about greed in Lawrence's *The Rainbow* may prove valuable to your study of short stories if you can draw parallels between the critic's view and those you have drawn on your own.

Recording Notes: Card Size and Function   Most of you have, doubtless, experimented with a variety of ways for recording notes on cards. The specifications and card types that follow have proved helpful to me and to my students for most of our research assignments.

To begin, recording notes on four-by-six cards is usually the most effective system for at least two reasons. First, because their size so readily distinguishes them from the bibliography cards described above, the chances of misplacing or confusing notes are limited. Second, four-by-six cards are sufficiently large that you can record most notes on their faces without having to clutter their backs. Keeping notes posted on one side only is also helpful later because it simplifies the process of revising the tentative outline.

The most effective notes, then, are those recorded on cards that can be read faceup and can be shuffled and rearranged later as you begin to structure ideas for readers. Effective notes are also those that reflect your own careful thinking and *not* your fears of running out of things to say. One way to collect effective notes is to devote most cards to summary and paraphrase and to limit those that bear lengthy quotations.

Recording Notes: Effective Content Summary and paraphrase notes are similar insofar as both reflect the writer's attempt to express another's ideas in his or in her own words. They are different inasmuch as summaries usually cover lengthier stretches of material than do paraphrases. Notice in the following card samples how the summary card provides an overview of the original passage while the paraphrase centers upon one of its areas.

ORIGINAL:

In an analysis of the evolution of the themes of Lawrence's short stories of this 1912–13 period, undertaken quite independently of the present study and indeed before this was conceived, we have shown, in the final pages of *Sons and Lovers* and the stories of the same period, the sudden appearance in Lawrence's mind of certain themes on consciousness, love, death and the self which are highly relevant to the present discussion. These can be briefly summarized here.

> Delavenay claims his analysis of *Sons and Lovers*, especially of themes in its final pages, is "highly relevant" to his current study.
> Delavenay, p. 112

> Delavenay argues that the sudden appearance of "themes on consciousness, love, death and the self" on the last pages of *Sons and Lovers* is significant.
> Delavenay, p. 112

Notice also that both notecards contain direct quotations. Integrating direct quotations into summary and paraphrase cards is fine as long as it's important to reproduce the exact words of the author.

FOR PRACTICE

If presently involved in a research assignment, try taking notes on four-by-six cards according to the principles and specifications described above. Aim for a dominance of summary and paraphrase card types.

Recording Notes from the Literature

Effective research papers incorporate references to both primary and secondary resources. This principle holds true in research about literature as well as in research about any other subject. If you fail to summarize, to paraphrase, or to quote from the primary, literary selections, the final paper will neither reflect your own thoughts and feelings nor provide an adequate number of references to the literature to convince readers that its important assertions are true. Secondary materials should always represent backup for ideas you have generated and have organized yourself. This has been the case with preceding essays; no reason exists for shifting the perspective now.

Primary Sources: Guidelines for Notes and Page Numbers Previous assignments in this textbook have assumed that readers have had access to the anthology and to the specific selections upon which the writing was based. This assumption has legitimized the practice of limiting page number references for primary sources to paper sections containing direct quotations. When you are writing longer research papers, however, and are using a wider range of materials, the assumption that readers can check on references themselves will rarely remain valid. When readers cannot check examples by surveying their own materials, you need to include page numbers for other details from the literature. What follows are some guidelines for limiting cards and references to those which are essential.

First, because most papers will include summaries of the selections read, you may omit page number citations in later references to this material. The summary itself credits these details and events to the author, and most general readers could verify their appearance. In a paper about "A Rose for Emily," you could probably omit documentation with references to Emily's seclusion or to the fate of Homer Barron. Page number citations would be better applied to references to Tobe's disappearance or to Emily's lessons in china painting.

Second, because most readers who are familiar with a selection would probably remember its significant repetitions, you may omit notecards and page numbers for details and events that are repeated throughout the material. In a paper about "The Rocking-Horse Winner," you could omit page references to the house's cries for money or to Paul's continued rides upon the horse.

FOR PRACTICE

If you are writing a paper according to this chapter's specifications, review your reading outline and the notecards you have completed to this point. Make sure that at least half of these cards contain references to your primary sources. When in doubt as to whether or not a card and a page-number citation will be necessary, err on the side of caution; you can always jot a question mark at the top of a card and reconsider it later.

CHAPTER SUMMARY

This chapter surveys the early stages of researched writing. It opens with a description of researched writing as composition that uses secondary as well as primary resources to establish the high probability that its arguments are significant and valid.

Because effective research needs focus, an early section in this chapter offers the classical topics and a set of thesis-specific questions for generating prewriting and, eventually, a tentative thesis. This thesis is especially important because it can suggest a reading outline or tentative plan for limiting materials and for exploring relevant parts of the subject.

The chapter closes with a discussion of ways to write effective notecards. It emphasizes that cards that are dominated by summaries and paraphrase will generally lead to the most readable of papers. So, too, will notes that balance primary and secondary sources; balanced notes encourage researched writing that reflects the writer's own well-defended thinking. Ways to best express this defense appear in Chapter 9.

Chapter

9

Researched Writing:
Later Stages

CHAPTER PREVIEW
Planning for Yourself and Your Reader

Once the reading and note-taking stages are over, it's time to structure, to draft, and to polish ideas so that they make sense and are interesting to readers. This chapter offers several strategies for completing these stages as painlessly and as effectively as possible. It opens with a plan for writing and revising a draft, and it concludes with suggestions for reporting and for crediting resources.

WRITING AND REVISING: STRUCTURING RESEARCHED WRITING

The first step in drafting a researched paper is to study your notecards so that you can pull all of their ideas together. Because the weight, the bulk, and the content of the cards may make this review a formidable task, the following sections detail ways to ensure that you, not the cards, remain in control of this important stage in your writing.

Outlining with Notecards

Pulling ideas on the cards together requires that you put them into a logical order, a procedure that should be relatively easy if you have used a reading outline to guide your note-taking process. Writing *slugs* or descriptive words and phrases across the tops of cards can further simplify the process; labelling cards in this way makes it easy to identify their content and to link them to the outline-in-progress.

The process of assigning slugs works best when it is broken into two steps. The first step involves reading through the cards and adjusting the reading outline so that it accurately reflects the kinds of information and the structure that you now want to dominate the paper. Words and phrases on this outline provide the content for the slugs you write on the cards. The second step involves reading the notecards again, dividing them into piles of related ideas, and writing the appropriate slug at the top of each card. Paper clips or rubber bands might help you keep each pile together at this point.

Do feel free to eliminate cards to which slugs cannot easily be assigned. These cards can be collected into a separate pile for later retrieval if necessary; the objective now is to clear away deadwood and to focus upon those notes that now fit into the overall plan.

FOR PRACTICE

If you are currently writing a paper, follow the steps listed above to organize its notes. Keep revising your reading outline until it reflects the points you really wish to make in your paper.

Writing from a Card Outline

When all the notecards have been labelled and grouped, they need to be arranged into the sequence suggested by your outline. The uppermost pile of related cards should correspond to the *I* on the outline, and it should be followed by cards representing the outline's subsequent divisions. Arranging notecards in this start-to-finish order makes it easy to review them once again before beginning the first draft of your paper.

While you may be tired of the cards at this point, slowly reviewing them and setting them aside makes completing the draft easier because the content of the cards will be fresh in your mind. Reviewing and setting cards aside also provides insurance against the common habit of arbitrarily stringing card ideas together in the hope of filling up space and meeting paper deadlines. The process will be more pleasant and will generate a better draft if you really know your subject well before you sit down to write.

This reviewing process has been incorporated into the following guidelines for writing a researched draft. While some of the procedures may seem time-consuming or awkward when first you practice them, observing them will soon become habit to you, and they will truly improve your writing.

1. Find a block of two to three hours of quiet time. Take the phone off the hook if necessary and put a sign of caution on the door.
2. Have all writing materials assembled before you begin.
3. Start the draft with a fifteen- to twenty-minute final review of the notecards. Read them slowly, following their outline sequence.
4. When you are finished reading the cards, set them aside and try to avoid rereading them unless it is absolutely essential to do so.
5. Write a first draft as quickly as possible, skipping lines and writing on one side only of the paper.
6. As with freewriting, try not to stop or to reread and avoid worrying about grammar and mechanics until later. At this stage, it's important to get a lot down as quickly as possible.
7. When finished, reread each draft section to identify spots that need parenthetical notes. Pull the appropriate cards to mark the names of authors, titles, and page numbers in the spaces above your written lines. Mark an *X* in spots that might need revision or additional support.
8. Now set the draft aside for several hours. A full day is even better. Time away from the writing is important because it enables you to approach it with a fresh perspective for revision.

FOR PRACTICE

Use the guidelines above to write the first draft of a paper you are now preparing for this or for any other class. Don't worry if it is messy at this stage; the objective is to have something down to revise when you come back to it later.

Revising the Draft

Revision is best done after a break; you need time away from the paper in order to return to it with greater objectivity. One of the best ways of determining what, if any, changes will be necessary is to compose a postdraft outline.

Some students consider drafting an outline *after* the paper has been written a useless waste of time. This attitude needs modifying because a postdraft outline can serve as a good check on how well the paper hangs together. The need for such checks of coherence is especially great with researched writing because of the added complexity that comes with its added length.

You can compose a postdraft outline fairly quickly with attention to each of the steps below. Using pens or pencils with colors that are different from those used in the first draft of the paper will enhance the readability of the outline as well as the revisions.

REVISING WITH A POSTDRAFT OUTLINE

1. Read each paragraph very slowly and write a word or phrase in the paper's margin that describes the main idea of the unit.
   Example: Setting shows family is poor
2. Read through each marginal description and identify the key concept from the thesis to which the paragraph relates. Circle it.
   Example: Setting shows family poor (Economic problems)
3. Reread all paragraph descriptions and key concepts. Adjust or delete any paragraphs which do not obviously contribute to a key concept. Rearrange any paragraphs that need to be grouped with other common key concepts.

FOR PRACTICE

Follow the steps described above to outline and to revise a paper of your own.

POLISHING STYLE FOR READERS

Although researched style is partly dominated by rules for citing resources that no writer can ignore, the character we project in the text itself need not be stiff and rigid. Remembering that the paper is really a long essay reflecting our own considered opinions can help offset the tendency to assume the distant voice that audiences soon find boring. Attention to the suggestions which follow for reporting action and for crediting others will also help you hold your readers.

Reports of Action in Research

As you probably remember, Chapter 7 discussed the various kinds of action reports found in all of the aims of writing. These included reports of writer behavior (those using *I* and *we*), reports of the text as actor (those using expressions such as "this chapter opens"), reports of identified others (those reflecting the views of author, narrator, or characters), and reports of others who remain unnamed (those employing such passives as "it was decided").

Although reports of action by those unnamed often dominate the style of researched writing, a trend toward greater personalization is growing in many different disciplines. Increasingly, many accomplished writers are adopting reports with writer, text, and identified-other orientations. Here are suggestions for using these reports in the papers you write.

114

Reports of Others: Authors and Critics Many preceding sentences feature reports of the behavior of characters and narrators. Two "others" that are prominent in effective researched style are the critic and the author. Reports of critics are important to this aim of writing because they contribute a positive character appeal by indicating the breadth of your reading. Most readers respond to the ideas of writers who have done their homework. Identifying critics is also important because it highlights your support; naming the critic the first time his or her material appears helps readers determine *where* the borrowed material begins. Failure to name the authors of resources blurs the distinctions between your ideas and those of others you have read.

Here are some examples from student papers that suggest options for incorporating reports of the actions of critics. Notice how opening the borrowed material with the critic's name and closing it with a parenthetical citation distinguishes it as a borrowed unit. Notice also how first and last names are both mentioned; identifying both is usually appropriate to first references to an individual. Later references can use last names only for convenience (e.g., Taylor says . . . , Brown writes that . . .).

EXAMPLES:

Emile Delavenay verifies this by noting that Paul "is trapped in a web of mystified greed that she [Hester] has woven" (423).

(Michael Barrs)

According to one critic, May Brown, the attitudes of the Compsons emphasize the "dehumanization of Nancy by the whites."

(Cesar Madarang)

Dr. Welford Taylor of the University of Richmond feels that because no names are ever given to the three characters in "The Egg," we can assume the "universality of their plight."

(Sandra Hulbert)

As Michael West notes, the father "becomes a grotesque dancing with rage like Elmer Cowley."

(Gregory J. Silvi)

FOR PRACTICE

Review a research paper of your own that was written for this or for any other class. Circle the names of authors you have included to indicate the sources of borrowed ideas. Rewrite as necessary to name authors wherever possible.

Earlier assignments have recommended identifying the *narrator* rather than the author as the individual who is telling the story or describing the scene. Identifying the narrator is the wisest course when you have studied only one or several selections by a particular writer. In these situations, your limited experience has not provided the amount and the kinds of knowledge that lead to valid statements about an author's habits.

The extensive reading, however, that accompanies researched writing will usually provide the background that permits some cautious yet meaningful generalizations about a specific writer. No one can determine how many primary and secondary sources you must actually read in order to become an expert; however, most researched assignments incorporating the amount of material that is recommended here should provide the experiences you need in order to enjoy some degree of authority.

Most statements you make about your author—otherwise known as reports of author action—will appear in the thesis paragraph. They appear in this position because many assignments in literary research relate to the author's technique or philosophy. Further references to the author in the body of the paper help readers remember the thesis or major assertions that preceded them. Here is a thesis paragraph from a student's paper that uses these reminders well. Following it are several sentences from the body of the paper that help readers remember that the paper's subject is Edith Wharton's sources of control over her material.

EXAMPLE

Edith Wharton uses a close narrator in "The Looking Glass," "Charm Incorporated," and "Roman Fever." In each case, the narrator's character has been shaped by a rigid society with rigid demands. Although each narrator first seems to be manipulative, he or she is, in fact, the real victim of manipulation. We can say, therefore, that Wharton is really using the narrator to fool her audience.

. . .

However, Wharton leaves the reader with a sense of despair.

. . .

Wharton uses Attlee as a tool to manipulate her audience.

. . .

Wharton is showing characteristics which do not fit the previous portrait.
(*Nancy B. Errichetti*)

FOR PRACTICE

Review a research draft of your own for reports of author action. Add any that may be necessary to highlight a passage's connection to your thesis.

116

Crediting Sources

Readers of researched writing are usually so well educated that they expect scrupulous attention to data on resources. Such data is what documentation is all about: crediting those who have contributed ideas and providing directions for finding the resources themselves. Failure to give full and proper credit damages your character appeal because it leaves you looking irresponsible and guilty of *plagiarism.* Plagiarism is such a serious offense that it is usually punished by expulsion from school and even by litigation. Plagiarism is the theft of someone else's ideas.

What follows are brief descriptions and models of common noting and bibliographic forms; studying these models and using them to indicate the material you have borrowed will protect you against inadvertently plagiarizing the ideas of another. For most extensive coverage of appropriate forms of documentation, consult the *MLA Handbook* or your grammar textbook.

Notes   As Chapter 2 explains, the latest Modern Language Association guidelines substitute parenthetical notes for the endnotes and footnotes that once dominated research in the humanities. Because the assignments and the models in this book have recommended and have used this system throughout, you should already understand the rules for marking citations within the body of a paper; if you wish to review these rules, you need only reread the sections on polishing style that are found in Chapters 2 and 8. The following summary of the situations that may demand an *information note* is designed to supplement your knowledge of citations.

Information notes provide an opportunity to give readers supplemental information, which, if included in the paper, would represent a confusing or time-consuming digression. Although the numbers of notes used should usually be limited, you may use this form if the supplement is sufficiently interesting or important to merit the reader's time or additional research.

Information notes are signalled by elevated numerals appearing in the body of the paper and are usually placed at the end of the sentence for which the note has relevance. If your paper contains more than one information note, number the notes consecutively throughout the text and list each note with its accompanying details on a sheet entitled NOTES. This sheet will eventually precede the bibliography when the manuscript pages are bound together. Here are sample information notes representing the kinds that bear inclusion:

[1]Fitzgerald also writes about this subject in "Winter Dreams."
[This note refers the reader to the Bibliography within which this entry is listed.]
[2]I use this term to denote action as well as objects that suggest ideas beyond themselves; Smith provides a different definition, however.
[This note also sends the reader to the Bibliography—this time to look up Smith's work. It also makes perfectly clear the meaning the writer is attaching to a specific term.]

FOR PRACTICE

If you are completing a research paper of your own, check its body for unusual terms or for associated material that should be cited in an information note. Write out any notes that are relevant on a separate sheet entitled NOTES. Then add numerals in appropriate spots in the text and number the notes consecutively throughout the paper as well as on the sheet upon which they are listed.

Bibliography   The bibliography is a separate page listing resources in alphabetical order. While some bibliographies list *all* materials studied, even if some are not mentioned in the paper, most bibliographies assigned in college list *only* those that are actually cited. The following forms and guidelines will be appropriate in either case:

1. The bibliography is organized alphabetically by the name of the author or by the title. Titles are presented in alphabetical order when no author is identified or when several selections by the same author appear.
2. Each unit of bibliographic information is separated by periods, parentheses, or by the colon.
3. First lines of bibliographies are flush with the left margin; subsequent lines are indented.
4. Bibliographic entries for articles from periodicals and for chapters or stories from books carry *inclusive* page numbers. Inclusive page numbers specify the first and last page numbers of the article, thereby telling readers how long it is.

SAMPLE BIBLIOGRAPHY ENTRIES

FOR A BOOK:
Delavenay, Emile. *D. H. Lawrence: The Man and His Work.* Carbondale, Ill.: Southern Illinois UP, 1972.
[Note: "UP" refers to University Press.]

FOR A STORY IN COLLECTION WITH AN EDITOR:
Faulkner, William. "Delta Autumn." *Modern Short Stories: The Uses of Imagination.* Ed. Arthur Mizener. 4th ed. New York: Norton, 1979. 714–35.
―――――――――. "Dry September." *Fiction 100: An Anthology of Short Stories.* Ed. James H. Pickering. 3rd ed. New York: Macmillan, 1982. 334–40.
[Note: the dash shows that this author is the one named above, i.e., Faulkner.]

FOR A PERIODICAL WITH VOLUME OR ISSUE NUMBER:

Bride, Sister Mary. "Faulkner's 'A Rose for Emily.' " *Explicator* 20 (1962): 26–7.

[Note: when you have *both* volume and issue numbers, separate them with a period, e.g., 20.3]

FOR AN ARTICLE IN A WEEKLY MAGAZINE:

Updike, John. "Reflections: Kafka's Short Stories." *New York* 9 May 1983: 121–26.

[Note: with a monthly magazine, simply leave off the day's date, e.g., leave off the *9* in the entry above.]

FOR A PERSONAL INTERVIEW:

Taylor, W. D. Personal interview. 14 Feb. 1984.

FOR AN INTRODUCTION, PREFACE, EDITORIAL COMMENTS:

Hoggart, Richard. Introduction. *Lady Chatterley's Lover.* 2nd ed. London: Penguin Books, 1969.

FOR PRACTICE

Alphabetize those bibliography cards that represent the materials you have cited in a researched paper of your own. Type your bibliography sheet with the aid of preceding examples. Title the sheet BIBLIOGRAPHY unless your instructor has specified something else.

CHAPTER SUMMARY

This chapter offers strategies for easing the processes of structuring and polishing the notes collected in research. Because writing a researched paper is a difficult and time-consuming experience, learning strategies for facilitating the process is important. The structuring section of this chapter surveys one way of classifying and ordering notecards so that they may serve as keys to producing a paper; it also lists eight steps for completing and revising a draft. Sorting the cards into piles of related ideas and assigning them *slugs* that correspond to the revised reading outline will help you get ready to write. Reviewing the cards and setting them aside will help you finish the process.

Setting the draft aside is important because it provides the break you should take before attempting revisions; a break helps you approach this task with a heightened sense of purpose and a better eye for identifying areas needing changes.

The revision strategy featured here involves creating a *postdraft outline.* This outline, a product of writing brief paragraph descriptions in the paper's margins, provides a final check on each section's contributions in developing the research thesis.

The chapter's section on polishing is devoted to suggestions for creating an appealing voice while observing the conventional rules of documentation. It includes a survey of options for using the "we" form for reports of writer actions and the author-and-critic emphasis in reports of identified others. The "we" report is cited as an effective alternative to those reports of unidentified actors that too often pervade the researched aim in writing. The author-and-critic reports are identified as effective strategies for distinguishing between your own ideas and those of other writers. Varying all three types of reports within a paper will help generate a positive character appeal, one source of attraction for your readers.

The following checklist will help you evaluate your own appeals as well as the other details that are important to researched writing. Review it as you revise your paper, and use it to evaluate the student essay that follows.

Revision Checklist for Researched Writing

1. *Thesis, Content, and Support*
    a. Does the thesis conform to assignment specifications?
    b. Is it clearly expressed in a single sentence or in a thesis paragraph?
    c. Could most of the content be described as a reflection of the writer's own thinking, i.e., is support from reading used primarily as backup?
2. *Organization*
    a. Does every paragraph and every section clearly relate to the thesis?
    b. Are paragraph and section sequences logical in terms of the thesis?
3. *Style and Mechanics*
    a. Are borrowed ideas clearly marked throughout the body of the paper?
    b. Is the bibliographical documentation correct?
    c. Is the style natural and relatively free of passive structures?
    d. Are reports of action predominately author- and critic-centered?

CENTRAL THEME IN THREE WORKS BY D. H. LAWRENCE

Michael Barrs
English 102
May, 1983

OUTLINE

THESIS: Three short stories by D. H. Lawrence, "Odor of Chrysanthemums," "The Horse Dealer's Daughter," and "The Rocking-Horse Winner," possess the same central theme that relationships deteriorate when economic problems obsess the people involved.

CENTRAL THEME IN THREE WORKS BY D. H. LAWRENCE

Three of D. H. Lawrence's short stories, "Odor of Chrysanthemums," "The Horse Dealer's Daughter," and "The Rocking-Horse Winner," all share the same central theme. This theme is that relationships will deteriorate when economic problems dominate a household. In "Odor of Chrysanthemums," the relationship between a husband and wife has deteriorated because of the poverty that has driven him to escape home whenever he can. In "The Horse Dealer's Daughter," the relationship between three brothers and their sister deteriorates when they have to find new lives at the collapse of their fortunes. In "The Rocking-Horse Winner," the relationship between a mother and her son deteriorates because of her desires to live beyond the family's means.

"Odor of Chrysanthemums" is the sad story of Elizabeth Bates and of her unhappy marriage. She has an uncommunicative husband who spends the family's money at the local tavern after his day in the coal mines. When he is killed in a mining accident, Elizabeth is forced to admit that her marriage has been empty and that she must make a life for herself.

Setting as well as characterization indicate the family's poverty. The Bates cottage is located "three steps down from the cinder track" where "a large bony vine" clutches "at the house as if to claw down the tiled roof" (531). This sense of empty dreariness is further sustained by the grim adjectives that describe its exterior. It looks "wintry," "ragged," "dishevelled," and "foul" (531). Immediately, we visualize a house and a family that are impoverished in many ways.

In spite of the family's needs, the father habitually goes straight from his work to his drinking. We learn that "he isolates himself from his family, and his wife responds with bitterness and resentment" (Draper 131). We see this resentment when Elizabeth says, "It is a scandalous thing as a man can't even come home . . . past his very own door he goes to get to a public house" (535). Her father agrees with her and claims it is a pity "when a man can do nothing but make a beast of himself" (535).

It is only after she learns of his death that Elizabeth realizes the truth of their marriage. We gather this from a monologue in which she admits, "I have been fighting a husband that did not exist. He existed all the time" (548). According to Tony Slade, it takes death for Elizabeth to finally become "aware of the transitoriness of life and her own past error in allowing the ordinariness and mundaneness of her lot to stifle her feelings and demean her character" (99).

"The Horse Dealer's Daughter" resembles "Odor of Chrysanthemums" in that it, too, features the deterioration of a relationship in the presence of economic setbacks. It centers primarily upon a young woman named Mabel who becomes involved in a struggle with her brothers after their father's death. Because the father has left the family in debt, they are forced to sell their farm. The brothers, feeling confident about their own futures, immediately begin to badger Mabel about her own. Their meddling, however, only forces her to isolate herself until she can no longer cope with the pressure and attempts suicide. Fortunately, she is saved by the village doctor, Jack Ferguson. At the story's end, the pair have fallen in love and are attempting to establish their relationship.

The characterization in this story repeatedly stresses that money and power exert significant influences upon relationships. Although Mabel is twenty-seven years old, her brothers still dominate her life because she has no income of her own. In fact, at the story's opening, the brothers are discussing where she should go since everyone else is going in his own direction. We learn that Mabel is so numb with powerlessness that this discussion does not even seem to distress her. We learn that her brothers have "talked at her and around her for so many years, that she hardly hears them at all" (637).

This powerlessness and its consequence, paralysis, are so destructive that they even form a chain. Mabel's failure to respond to her brothers causes one of them to mutter that she is "the sulkiest bitch that ever trod" (638). Another notes that "You could bray her into bits, and that's all you'd get out of her" (638).

Mabel, however, has finally started to look into herself and believes that she "holds the keys of her own situation" (639). In order to escape it, she attempts suicide and is lucky enough to meet Ferguson as a result. It is in her relationship with Ferguson that Lawrence suggests the solution to the dilemma she has suffered: only warm, human relationships may provide us with salvation.

"The Rocking-Horse Winner" also carries this vision inasmuch as it is filled with episodes showing that money is not the answer to happiness. It centers upon a woman who is greedy and who cannot love her children. It is this lack of love that encourages her son, Paul, to bet on the horses. In an effort to please her, he somehow learns to determine the winners by riding his rocking horse. In this way, he amasses a small fortune which he hopes will satisfy his mother's greed and leave her time to love her children. Unfortunately, no amount of money satisfies her, so Paul's obsession increases. In the end, he becomes ill, falls off his horse, and dies.

From the story's beginning we know that greed has replaced love in Paul's mother's heart. The narrator tells us that she always feels "the center of her heart go hard" whenever her children are present (646). She seems to resent them because they are the products of her marriage to a man who has little money and no promising future.

From the story's beginning we also know how difficult life is for the children. They sense their mother's hostility. Lawrence indicates this with his references to their house. He tells us that it is haunted by the repeated phrase, "There must be more money! There must be more money!"

The fact that only the children can hear this is significant. It shows how damaging a person's greed can be for those who are close to it. Charles Koban argues that these voices begin for the children because the mother "makes them insecure and self-conscious" (393).

Lawrence further suggests that, once greed takes over, nothing can stop it. Emile Delavenay verifies this view by noting that Paul "is trapped in a web of mystified greed that she [Hester] has woven" (221). This shows up clearly in the scenes following Paul's anonymous gift to her. Even though he has given her a substantial amount of money, she still wants more. This gives him an even greater determination to make her happy, and this has tragic consequences. As he puts more effort into his concern, the voices in the house become more intense. Lawrence uses them to show us how insistent is their pressure. They scream for more money—"Oh, now, now-w! More than ever" (652).

Lawrence underscores the evils of this pressure at the story's climax. This is where we are told that "the little boy . . . rides himself to death on his rocking horse" (Hobsbaum 120). Hobsbaum's reference to Paul as "the little boy" emphasizes the vulnerability we find in this child. He is shown as not only young and subject to the whims of adults but also at the threshold of insanity.

Beyond this point, Paul can never expect any more control, so he simply dies. We see him "madly surging on the rocking horse." When his mother questions what he is doing, he screams in a strange and powerful voice, " 'It's Malabar!' " He then falls "with a crash to the ground" where he is knocked unconscious (653). He remains this way, and in several days, he dies.

Concern for money and for comfortable living is prominent in D. H. Lawrence's writings. In three of his short stories we find this concern can serve as a deteriorating force. In "Odor of Chrysanthemums" worries of making ends meet and the escape habits of a young husband have torn apart a marriage. Here, the leading character finds being alone is better than trying to be happy with another person. In "The Horse Dealer's Daughter" money tears up a family of brothers and a sister. Money means power, and those who have it meddle in the concerns of the one who does not. Fortunately, Mabel, the leading character, finds a love that is free of concern for material power. This gives her a reason for wanting to live. Paul, the leading figure in "The Rocking-Horse Winner" is not so lucky. He loves a mother who cannot return his feeling because she is so consumed by greed. His story carries Lawrence's message to its worst conclusion by showing that greed can sometimes pull people so far apart that they can lose all hope for salvation in the future. This is what happens to Paul's mother when she loses her son to death.

BIBLIOGRAPHY

Delavenay, Emile. *D. H. Lawrence: The Man and His Work.* Carbondale, Ill.: Southern Illinois UP, 1972.

Draper, R. P. *D. H. Lawrence.* New York: Twayne, 1964.

Hobsbaum, Philip. *A Reader's Guide to D. H. Lawrence.* New York: Thames and Hudson, 1981.

Koban, Charles. "Allegory and the Death of the Heart in 'The Rocking Horse Winner.' " *Studies in Short Fiction.* Columbia, S.C.: R. L. Bryan, 1978. 391–98.

Lawrence, D. H. "The Horse Dealer's Daughter." *Fiction 100: An Anthology of Short Stories.* Ed. James H. Pickering. 3rd ed. New York: Macmillan, 1982. 636–45.

———. "Odor of Chrysanthemums." *Modern Short Stories: The Uses of Imagination.* Ed. Arthur Mizener. 4th ed. New York: Norton, 1979. 714–35.

———. "The Rocking-Horse Winner." Pickering. Macmillan, 1982. 646–54.

Slade, Tony. *D. H. Lawrence.* New York: Arco, 1970.

Chapter
10
The Aims in Published Writing

Unlike preceding chapters that have described the processes by which the aims of writing evolve, this chapter contains examples of the products themselves. It has been included to show that the principles of style and structure that are associated with the self-expressive, the informative, the persuasive, and the researched aims can, indeed, be found in the published works of scholars.

These essays have also been reproduced to demonstrate how several of the aims will compete for dominance within a single essay. Although assignments in preceding chapters have encouraged composition that is clearly governed by *one* of the discursive aims, the chances are as good as not that most of the writing assigned in other courses will be characterized by combinations of content, style, and organization suggesting that at least two of the aims are controlling the writer's presentation. These combinations are certainly represented in the following models.

In fact, only one aim seems to be weakly represented in these essays, and that is self-expression. Two reasons can account for its apparent absence. First, until recently, self-expression has been discouraged in academic writing by editors and specialists in many fields. Second, in most published writing, self-expression probably initiated the project in the prewriting stage but was later polished to conform to the standards of a primary aim that is less subjective. Just remember as you read that even though an occasional ''I'' and ''we'' appear to be the only traces of self-expression in an essay, every other part of its thought and wording are probably the descendants of the aim; self-expression is always present, no matter how formal the writing or how limited the traces.

The following selections represent honest and effective attempts to inform and to demonstrate (i.e., nearly prove) assertions for the scholarly audiences they address. Each composition is accompanied by a brief discussion that explains why a particular aim could be identified as dominant. As you read each selection, be sure to underline additional sentences and passages not mentioned in the commentary that reflect the influence of other, nondominant aims. If you can identify these influences and can explain what they contribute to the author's primary aim, you are well on your way to becoming a skilled evaluator of your own writing as well as the writing of others.

MODEL 1: INFORMATIVE AIM— "FAULKNER'S 'A ROSE FOR EMILY' " BY GIL MULLER

All five sections of William Faulkner's "A Rose for Emily" contain imagery drawn from art, and Miss Emily reveals herself as an expert in the aesthetics of the grotesque. Statuary, architecture, calligraphy, water coloring: these are some of the art forms mentioned in the first section alone. Throughout this story, Faulkner investigates with consummate skill an artistic realm which is rose-colored and immortal and a woman who literally attempts to fuse the worlds of art and existence.

In her very being, Miss Emily aspires to the permanency of art. She variously resembles monuments, idols, and "angels in church windows—sort of tragic and serene." And the townspeople remember Emily and her dead father in artistic terms: "We had long thought of them as a tableau." For a while, Emily gives art lessons to children, but then turns inward to erect her masterpiece.

The last section presents the culmination of Emily's artistry in that locked room which is at once a manifestation of grotesque art and a revelation of the interior life of the artist. When the townspeople break into this hidden tomb of artistic treasures, they encounter carefully arranged artifacts constructed on a superhuman and almost supernatural scale. Here is a three-dimensional tableau that is at once bridal and funereal, a tribute to Miss Emily as supreme artist and penultimate cosmetician.

Emily preserves love by removing it from life. She savors her lover as he petrifies and gradually becomes an art object. And her art is revealing, because the emotions of a lifetime are seen in her handiwork. She is the artistic rebel who pursues the absolute with an intensity that is sublime and perverse. Flouting social conventions and defying mortality itself, she is the artist as outsider and as visionary. From the world of the living, she retains only her black servant, secure in the knowledge that after her own death he will open her macabre museum to the visiting public, and that her masterpiece will finally be discovered. The artistic network which Faulkner has so carefully created in "A Rose for Emily" achieves an unnerving effect as the townspeople and the reader (wanderers at a strange exhibition) observe a perfect replica of grotesque art.

This essay reflects principles presented in Chapter 7. Muller's thesis is that Faulkner's style, particularly its imagery drawn from art, is obtrusive in all five sections of the story. Muller apparently believes that the repeated references to art and to art forms create a desirable unity.

Because the essay does not contain a separate summary section, we can assume its author is addressing a group whose members have read the story but may not have noticed the wealth of references to art. Its publication in a scholarly journal for specialists in literature as well as its undocumented quotations obviously lend support to this assumption.

While Muller's own style is marked by the varied sentence structures associated with informative writing, we can also find characteristics that point to the researched aim. He presents plentiful examples from the story for each of his assertions, a habit associated with researched writing with its pervasive concern with proving or fortifying every major point. He has also deleted the first-person pronoun that usually surfaces in prewriting and that signals self-expressive composition. While we can still find the *I* in the researched model reproduced near the end of this chapter, the *I* is frequently absent in much published research, particularly in materials composed prior to the 1980's.

In spite of these traces of researched discourse, the Muller essay is best described as an example of informative writing. Its style is varied, and its word choices are conversational rather than academic. None of the three sentences of the first paragraph, for example, share a common structure, and the vocabulary choices that might require a dictionary—e.g., "penultimate," "tableau," "sublime," and "macabre"—are probably words with which most readers of news magazines would be familiar. Finally, the essay uses causal analysis, one of the most popular modes of informative writing, to structure its treatment of Emily; studies of motivation will usually trace causes and effects.

MODEL 2: INFORMATIVE AIM
"FAULKNER'S 'A ROSE FOR EMILY' "
BY J. F. KOBLER

William Faulkner's handling of Emily Grierson's name in both the story and the title of "A Rose for Emily" helps to reveal the attitude of Jefferson toward this "dear, inescapable" "idol in a niche." In both narrative passages and dialogue she is always called "Miss Emily," except for five references to her during her courting by Homer Barron, when she is called "Poor Emily."

Although such a title-name combination as "Miss Emily" is common in Mississippi for maiden ladies, all of them are not so designated by all other characters in Faulkner. Individual relationships can determine the name. For example, in *Intruder in the Dust* Chick refers to his maiden lady accomplice as "Miss Habersham" but the sheriff calls her "Miss Eunice." However, the whole town has a single feeling toward its "Miss Emily." The name assigned to her reveals those same paradoxical feelings evident in the old pattern of black servants calling young white children such names as "Mr. Bobby Joe" or "Miss Faye." The title of respect pulls one direction between the lower black and the higher white, but the use of the first name with it simultaneously indicates that the child, despite his whiteness, is still a child and therefore inferior in a way to the adult Negro. Thus the citizens of Jefferson by calling her "Miss Emily" give her the respect due a Grierson and at the same time indicate that they consider her inferior to them because she is peculiar, perhaps even crazy in their eyes.

Of the five references to "Poor Emily" (because she is being courted by a day-working Yankee), this one is the most telling: "And as soon as the old people said, 'Poor Emily,' the whispering began." The social arbiters announce her fallen state and their attitude toward it by calling her "Poor" (it should be capitalized as a title, as one use outside grammatical convention proves). Her actions have deprived her of the respect due a maiden Grierson; the change in form of address temporarily frees those beneath "Poor Emily" to whisper about her. The name-calling lasts only during the Barron episode.

However, the discovery of the skeleton at the end of the story causes the citizens to revert to the attitude expressed earlier about her consorting with the live Homer. Instead of having his citizens refer to her again as "Poor Emily," or worse, Faulkner makes his point about respect and condescension in his title, his gift at the funeral, and his message on her grave. The presence of "Rose" in the title indicates the respectful side of the coin, but the dropping of the "Miss" means two things: Emily Grierson has been proven to be something other than a true maiden lady and is no longer deserving of this particular appellation; she has also been completely humanized and brought down to earth out of her niche to the level of all other citizens of Jefferson. Therefore, she is now, and will remain to future generations, just plain Emily. Surely her tombstone reads "Emily Grierson."

Kobler's essay, like Muller's, is primarily informative. Its vocabulary is simple, its sentences are varied, and it uses comparison—a common mode of information—to discuss Faulkner's use of names in several of his books.

Kobler's essay also resembles the preceding one because it, too, carries traces of researched writing. It obviously draws upon several different texts (e.g., *Intruder in the Dust* and the unnamed resource for the information about black language), but it lacks the specific citations that mark researched writing. It does, however, assume that readers have either studied the story or have a copy of it before them as is evidenced by its unmarked direct quotations. Kobler joins Muller in addressing an audience of interested scholars who may not all be Faulkner specialists.

FOR PRACTICE

Review articles you have recently used for background or support in a research paper for this or for another class. Identify those that bear traces of the informative aim that are as strong or stronger than those of the researched aim. Be prepared to discuss the conception of the audience this tension between aims suggests.

MODEL 3: RESEARCHED AIM
"A NOTE ON ALLUSION IN 'DOVER BEACH' "
BY RONALD A. SHARP

"Dover Beach" has had its fair share of source studies, including U. C. Knoepflmacher's demonstrations of the influence of two Wordsworthian sonnets, "It Is a Beauteous Evening" and "Near Dover, September, 1802" (17–26). Knoepflmacher claims that "Dover Beach" 's melancholy inability to affirm belief is intensified by contrast with the Wordsworthian lines it recalls. I want to suggest that there are a number of other crucial echoes as well, none of which has been observed before and all of which play variations on the same theme of the withdrawal of the "Sea of Faith."

The first and most important allusion I wish to discuss is to *Paradise Lost*. As Adam and Eve leave the garden of Eden, Milton concludes his poem by telling us:

> *The World was all before them,* where to choose
> Thir place of rest, and Providence thir guide:
> They hand in hand with wandring steps and slow,
> Through *Eden* took thir solitarie way.
>> (12.646–649; *emphasis mine in first line*)

How strange that no one has remarked on Arnold's obvious reference to these famous lines towards the end of "Dover Beach":

> Ah, love, let us be true
> To one another! for *the world, which seems*
> *To lie before us* like a land of dreams,
> So various, so beautiful, so new,
> Hath really neither joy, nor love, nor light,
> Nor certitude, nor peace, nor help for pain.
>> (29–34; *emphasis mine*)

The turn from "was" to "seems" underlines Arnold's disillusionment with the Christian vision of joy, certainty, peace, and consolation, and it does so in the largest possible context. Confronting a painful world, the lovers are in both cases fortified by their love, but in Arnold's poem that love is not subordinate to—and connected with—faith in God; it is a substitute for it.

Arnold might well have had the recently published *Prelude* in mind here as well, since in the opening lines of his epic Wordsworth claims that "the earth is all before me" (1850 edition, 1.14), and later, that "the road lies plain before me" (1.641). Like Arnold, Wordsworth rejected Milton's theodicy but Wordsworth substituted his own, based on the holy marriage of mind and nature. For Arnold, however, "the eternal note of sadness" (1.14) could not be explained away by *any* principle of ultimate harmony, since

> we are here as on a darkling plain
> Swept with confused alarms of struggle and flight,
> Where ignorant armies clash by night.
>> (35–37)

The allusion to Thucydides is well known but one wonders if certain lines from Keats's "Hyperion" were not also in Arnold's imagination. In that poem Keats is concerned with the decay of old religious beliefs and he compares the Titans loitering in their den to old religious relics:

> Scarce images of life, one here, one there,
> Lay vast and edgeways; like a dismal cirque
> Of Druid stones, upon a *forlorn moor.*
> (2.33–35; emphasis mine)

Later, Keats says he must leave the Titans:

> Leave them, O Muse! for thou anon wilt find
> Many a fallen old Divinity
> Wandering in vain about *bewildered shores.*
> (3.709; emphasis mine)

"Bewildered shores," which now resemble a "forlorn moor," are what remain for Arnold when the "Sea of Faith" (21) withdraws, leaving an exposed "darkling plain." For Keats, however, there is still a certain holiness in the world. His "Bright Star" sonnet, which appeared in Milnes' edition just a few years before Arnold supposedly wrote "Dover Beach," speaks of "the moving waters at their priestlike task/ Of pure ablution *round earth's human shores* (5–6; emphasis mine). For Arnold, even that holiness has disappeared:

> The Sea of Faith
> Was once, too, at the full, and *round earth's shore*
> Lay like the folds of a bright girdle furled.
> But now I only hear
> Its melancholy, long, withdrawing roar.
> (21–25; emphasis mine)

Browning's Andrea del Sarto hears something of that same roar, though in a different key. It is odd to think of that poem as a possible source for "Dover Beach," partly because its overt subject is so different but mainly because it was written (1853) and published (1855) after "Dover Beach" was supposedly composed. But there are striking enough similarities of wording to suggest that Arnold may have done some revising of "Dover Beach" (if he did indeed write it in 1851) before he published it in 1867.

"Come from the window, love," Andrea tells his wife in lines that clearly recall "Dover Beach" 's "Come to the window" (6):

> *Come from the window, love,* —come in, at last,
> Inside the melancholy little house
> We built to be so gay with. God is just.
> . . . .
> *Let us but love each other.* Must you go?
> (211–213; emphasis mine)

Together with the earlier invitation for the lover to come from—or to—the window, "Let us but love each other" is close enough to Arnold's "Ah, love, let us be true/ To one another" (29–30) to suggest an intriguing parallel if not a direct allusion. Arnold's fragile solution to the problems posed by the decline of faith and by "human misery" (18) can be seen, as Anthony Hecht sees it in his wonderful parody "The Dover Bitch," as a "mournful cosmic last resort" (18). After all, Arnold's dilemma is directly related to his sense that the claim, "God is just," has lost its force. Not only has love failed for Andrea del Sarto; it has also cost him dearly as an artist. But like Arnold, if more pitifully, he clings to it.

The echoes in "Dover Beach" of Sophocles, Thucydides, Milton, Wordsworth, Keats, Browning, and others serve the special purpose, as a group, of distancing Arnold from his predecessors on the issue of religious belief. To be sure, the ebb and flow of faith can be seen even in these poets, but now, Arnold suggests, the big wave has gone out for good. The Sea of Faith that in one form or another had encircled each of these writers has retreated beyond reach, isolating him on the bewildered shores of modernity.

NOTES

[1] Kristian Smidt considers further parallels with "It Is a Beauteous Evening" in "The Beaches of Calais and Dover: Arnold's Counterstatement to Wordsworth's Confession of Faith."

[2] Richard Monckton Milnes' *Life, Letters, and Literary Remains, of John Keats* appeared in two volumes in 1848. Though the date of composition is uncertain, most scholars believe Arnold wrote "Dover Beach" in late June, 1851.

[3] Gerhard Joseph discusses the window imagery of both poems, along with many others, in his "Victorian Frames: The Windows and Mirrors of Browning, Arnold, and Tennyson." But beyond the fact that both poems include images of a window, Joseph never finds any connections that would link the two poems.

BIBLIOGRAPHY

Hecht, Anthony. "The Dover Bitch: A Criticism of Life." *The Hard Hours: Poems.* New York. 1968. 17.

Joseph, Gerhard. "Victorian Frames: The Windows and Mirrors of Browning, Arnold, and Tennyson." *Victorian Poetry* 16 (1978): 70–87.

Knoepflmacher, U. C. "Dover Revisited: the Wordsworthian Matrix in the Poetry of Matthew Arnold." *Victorian Poetry* 1 (1963): 17–26.

Smidt, Kristian. "The Beaches of Calais and Dover: Arnold's Counterstatement to Wordsworth's Confession of Faith." *Victorian Poetry* 14 (1976): 256–57.

Sharp's scrupulous attention to correct citations and documentation as well as his assumptions about his audience's background in poetry clearly mark this essay as an example of researched writing.

Unlike the writers of preceding papers, Sharp is addressing a group who demand careful notations within the body of his paper. This expectation leads him to mark "emphasis mine" within parentheses so that readers understand that he has added underscoring for emphasis to the original Arnold poem. It also leads him to note precisely the years of writing and of publication of several of his other resources (e.g., the "1850 edition" of Wordsworth's poetry, the appearance of Browning's "Andrea del Sarto").

Unlike preceding authors, Sharp assumes an audience whose members are both demanding and well read. This assumption causes him to draw upon a relatively wide range of resources himself and to leave some of his allusions unexplained; his remark that the "allusion to Thucydides is well known" reflects his belief that his readers, having probably read Arnold's critics, will accept the statement without question. His failure to explain fully the identities of Wordsworth, Keats, and Browning also supports the idea that he is addressing readers who are thoroughly familiar with the poets of the period.

Although Sharp uses the variety and the relatively simple diction we associate with informative writing, he is obviously a demanding and conscientious critic. Any time an author is speaking to fellow specialists, the researched aim will be dominant.

FOR PRACTICE

Study the following model to identify traces of the aims described above and in preceding chapters. Look specifically for elements in this list and make notes accordingly:

1. Sentence length (mostly long? many short? a combination?)
2. Sentence structure (mostly compound? mostly simple? filled with interrupting modifiers?)
3. Diction (appropriate to academic work? to conversation? a blend?)
4. Use of pronouns (many in first person?)
5. Personal references to the writer (who is he or she? what is his or her experience with the subject?)
6. Modes of organization
7. Definitions (at what level of difficulty are terms defined? what does this level suggest about readers addressed?)
8. Other traces to indicate the nature of the audience addressed

---

MODEL 4: FOR ANALYSIS
"OF THE DEVIL'S PARTY: UNDETECTED
WORDS OF MILTON'S SATAN IN
ARNOLD'S 'DOVER BEACH'"
BY MARTIN BIDNEY

"Dover Beach," one of the best-known poems in the language, might seem to offer few surprises. Yet nowhere in the critical literature can one find any mention of the striking fact that in the final, climactic lines of the poem, Arnold speaks the words of Milton's Satan, taken without alteration from *Paradise Lost*.[1] These words are few—only four in number: "neither joy, nor love" (DB 33; PL 4.509).[2] But they hardly stand alone. On the contrary, these quoted words combine with a series of other verbal and imaginal echoes and parallels to create a network of significant allusions to Milton's epic within Arnold's lyric. Milton's presence pervades all four stanzas of

"Dover Beach," even in ways of which Arnold need not have been fully aware, and Miltonic undercurrents lend the lyric much of its peculiar power.

The concluding lines of "Dover Beach" were probably the first that Arnold wrote (Allott 329–40), and they remain the most important in the finished version of the poem. In these lines Arnold presents a fallen world. Transfigured through lovers' eyes, this world may appear as untainted as an Eden, as "new" and "beautiful" as "dreams." But it is really a loveless, joyless nightmare, a benighted wilderness of internecine hostility:

> Ah, love, let us be true
> To one another! for the world, which seems
> To lie before us like a land of dreams,
> So various, so beautiful, so new,
> Hath really neither joy, nor love, nor light.
> Nor certitude, nor peace, nor help for pain;
> And we are here as on a darkling plain
> Swept with confused alarms of struggle and flight.
> Where ignorant armies clash by night.
>
> (29–37)

The only hope for our lives is conjugal love, and even this is a project, a resource, rather than a guaranteed refuge; "let us" make love our response to the world's chaos, Arnold suggests—but he does not affirm that it will suffice. Certainly there is no love or joy outside the lovers' window. Inside the room, the poet urges his beloved to help him try to recapture an Eden for which the external world no longer provides any parallels for precedents.

There was a time, of course—the time before paradise was lost—when the world outside the bower of two well-known lovers was indeed an objective correlative of their love: it was the perfect image of a perfect love, consummated in perfect joy. Satan realized this only too well when he paid Adam and Eve a visit:

> Sight hateful, sight tormenting! thus these two
> Imparadis't in one another's arms
> The happier *Eden,* shall enjoy thir fill
> Of bliss on bliss, while I to Hell am thrust,
> Where neither joy nor love, but fierce desire,
> Among our other torments not the least,
> Still unfulfill'd with pain of longing pines.
>
> (4.505–11)

Both Arnold and Milton's Satan contrast the world enjoyed by two lovers with a quite different world containing "neither joy nor love." For Arnold this joyless, loveless world is the one outside the lovers' window, while for Satan the description applies to Hell. By quoting Satan's words, Arnold implies that the world outside the lovers' window has become Hell. Other parallels bear this out. The external world in Arnold's poem offers no "light," no "peace," and no "help for pain" (33–34). All three of these deprivations are equally characteristic of Hell, where

> No light, but rather darkness visible
> Serv'd only to discover sights of woe,
> Regions of sorrow, doleful shades, where peace
> And rest can never dwell, hope never comes
> That comes to all; but torture without end
> Still urges.
>
> (PL 1.63–68)

No joy, no love, "No light," no possibility of "peace/And rest," and no help for the pain of "torture without end"—this takes care of five of the six Arnoldian negations. But what of "certitude"? Predictably, this too is absent in Hell. Only mazes of perplexity await the demonic seekers of philosophic knowledge:

> Others apart sat on a Hill retir'd,
> In thoughts more elevate, and reason'd high
> Of Providence, Foreknowledge, Will, and Fate,
> Fixt Fate, Free will, Foreknowledge absolute,
> And found no end, in wand'ring mazes lost.
> Of good and evil much they argu'd then,
> Of happiness and final misery,
> Passion and Apathy, and glory and shame,
> Vain wisdom all, and false Philosophie
> *(PL 2.557–565)*

Even the metaphorical "darkling plain" where Arnold hears the clashing of ignorant armies "by night" has its close counterpart in that "dreary Plain, forlorn and wild,/ The seat of desolation, void of light" (PL I.180–181), where Satan proposes that he and his fellow devils might do well to rest and lay their plans for further battle with the Almighty.

The cause of this transformation of earth into Hell is the withdrawal of the "Sea of Faith," which Arnold hears "Retreating, to the breath/ Of the night-wind, down the vast edges drear/ And naked shingles of the world" (26–28). As in the original story of the Fall, so here too the consciousness of nakedness, of vulnerability, becomes a problem only after "Faith" is broken or lost, or withdrawn. Appropriately, right after the passage in which Satan describes Hell as a place of "neither joy nor love," he immediately offers his thoughts on the question of "faith." Reflecting on what he has just overheard from the conversation of Adam and Eve, Satan says:

> Yet let me not forget what I have gain'd
> From thir own mouths; all is not theirs it seems:
> One fatal Tree there stands of Knowledge call'd,
> Forbidden them to taste: Knowledge forbidd'n?
> Suspicious, reasonless. Why should thir Lord
> Envy them that? can it be sin to know,
> Can it be death? and do they only stand
> By ignorance, is that this happy state,
> The proof of thir obedience and thir faith?
> *(PL 4.512–520)*

Both Satan and Arnold consider the question of faith in close conjunction with the question of the loss of joy and love. Arnold shares Satan's pessimism about the lack of happiness outside of Eden. Arnold clearly empathizes with Adam and Eve in their experience of the woeful consequences of loss of faith. Satan sees faith as a foolishness easy to challenge; Arnold sees its loss as a tragedy worthy of being sung by Sophocles. Satan created a tragedy; Arnold contemplates one.

By tempting Adam and Eve, Satan helped turn their world into something more closely resembling his own Hell, in which "fierce desire . . . Still unfulfill'd with pain of longing pines" (PL 4.509, 511). Similarly, in the second stanza of "Dover Beach," the withdrawal of the tide suggests to Arnold's Sophocles "the turbid ebb and flow/ Of human misery" (17–18). "The eternal note of sadness" that Arnold hears in stanza one seems to echo the concluding lines of Satan's speech on the "long woes" that will result from the loss of faith:

Live while ye may.
Yet happy pair; enjoy, til I return,
Short pleasures, for long woes are to succeed.
                              (*Pl 4.533–535*)

The method we have been using so far—that of moving backward in Arnold's poem as we move forward in Milton's—may strike the reader as curious. But this method yields results. If we continue this simultaneous backward and forward motion a couple of steps further, still more Arnold-Milton parallels appear. As soon as Satan has ended his envious, plotting speech, we see him departing while the sun sets in the west, "where Heav'n/ with Earth and Ocean meets" (PL 4.539–540). And as we move back still closer to the beginning of "Dover Beach," we see "the long line of spray/ Where the sea meets the moon-blanch'd land" (7–8). In both passages the meeting of elements is symbolic. In *Paradise Lost* at this point, the fall has not yet occurred, so one can still see an allegorical union of Heaven or sky with earth and ocean, just as at the beginning of "Dover Beach" the poet's mood is still relatively tranquil and serene, so the sea still seems "calm" (2). Yet in the Miltonic passage on cosmic unity the sun is already setting, perhaps an allegorical hint at coming trouble; and in the same way in Arnold's poem, "on the French coast the light/ Gleams and is gone" (3–4), rather like the vanishing of the visionary gleam itself, a forecast of the poet's later dejection.

After Satan has departed from Eden, Milton shows us the declining sunbeams illuminating the whiteness of the eastern gate of Paradise, "a Rock/ Of Alabaster, pil'd up to the Clouds," while surrounding it all "The rest was craggy cliff, that overhung/ Still as it rose, impossible to climb" (4.543–544, 547–548). And at the beginning of Arnold's poem, the chalky "cliffs of England stand,/ Glimmering and vast, out in the tranquil bay" (4–5), suggesting the security of a land-based Eden oblivious of the inconstant sea. In Arnold's perception of Dover cliffs we have a phenomenon analogous to Wordsworth's perception of Mount Snowdon in Book XIV of *The Prelude*. One need not doubt that Wordsworth actually saw Snowdon, despite the close resemblance of the scene in *The Prelude* to the landscape described in *Paradise Lost* (7.285–287). So too the reader of "Dover Beach" need hardly doubt that Arnold's firsthand observation of the Dover cliffs had left a lively record in his mind. Yet these cliffs might not have appeared to glimmer quite so brightly, or have loomed quite so vast, without the Miltonic precedent of the gleaming eastern gate of Eden and its surrounding unscalable rocky height.

These final Arnold-Milton parallels suggest that with Arnold, as with Coleridge, even a seemingly straightforward descriptive passage may travel to us by quite a labyrinthine route (a "road to Xanadu") from its hidden sources in the poet's mind. Yet these lesser corroborative landscape parallels will not all necessarily remain in our own minds with every reading of "Dover Beach." What we *will* find it difficult to forget on rereading the poem is the quotation from Satan embedded within the poet's final message, a quotation supported with additional parallels from Hell for every item in that final relentless litany of uncompromising negations: "neither joy, nor love, nor light,/ Nor certitude, nor peace, nor help for pain" (33–34). The parallels between the deprivations experienced in Milton's Hell and those felt in the external world of Arnold's poem greatly increase the pathos of the latter poet's plight. The embrace of Adam and Eve, as Satan accurately saw, was but "The happier Eden" within a wide Edenic space. But now that the world has become Hell, the embrace of two lovers stranded amid a dark expanse of aimless fury is a very precarious Eden indeed—an Eden internal, vulnerable, isolated, intermittent at best. The poet tenderly holds out

135

to his beloved the prospect of hope, but in the same sentence, almost in the same breath, he depicts their earthly world in the very words used by a despairing Devil to describe an eternal Hell. It takes a Milton-trained ear to appreciate the barely suppressed tension in the poet's voice as his pledge of love yields place to counter-revelations from the abyss.

NOTES [*MY ADDITION—WERE FOOTNOTES*]

[1] Not only have Satan's quoted words gone unrecognized, none of the Arnold-Milton parallels adduced in the present essay finds mention in any critical source I have been able to discover. Kenneth Allott, however, in his edition of *The Poems of Matthew Arnold* (London, 1965), p. 241, notes the "positioning of the adjectives" in "tremulous cadence slow" and "vast edges drear" (he might have added "bright girdle furled") as "Miltonic Grecism." And Paull F. Baum, in *Ten Studies in the Poetry of Matthew Arnold* (Duke University Press, 1958), p. 95, interestingly notes that "twenty of the thirty-seven lines as printed are 5-stress lines; but besides these there are several examples of concealed blank verse": Baum prints pairs of shorter lines together as single lines in order to show eight more "concealed" pentameters. Such experiments show additional affinities of Arnold's verse art with the tradition of the unrhymed pentameter verse as employed by Milton, though Baum does not make the connection with Milton.

[2] All Arnold citations refer to *The Poetical Works of Matthew Arnold,* ed. C. B. Tinker and H. F. Lowry (Oxford Univ. Press, 1950). All Milton citations refer to John Milton, *Complete Poems and Major Prose,* ed. Merritt Y. Hughes (Indianapolis and New York, 1957).

Appendix

Sherwood Anderson

THE EGG

My father was, I am sure, intended by nature to be a cheerful, kindly man. Until he was thirty-four years old he worked as a farm-hand for a man named Thomas Butterworth whose place lay near the town of Bidwell, Ohio. He had then a horse of his own and on Saturday evenings drove into town to spend a few hours in social intercourse with other farm-hands. In town he drank several glasses of beer and stood about in Ben Head's saloon—crowded on Saturday evenings with visiting farm-hands. Songs were sung and glasses thumped on the bar. At ten o'clock father drove home along a lonely country road, made his horse comfortable for the night and himself went to bed, quite happy in his position in life. He had at that time no notion of trying to rise in the world.

It was in the spring of his thirty-fifth year that father married my mother, then a country school-teacher, and in the following spring I came wriggling and crying into the world. Something happened to the two people. They became ambitious. The American passion for getting up in the world took possession of them.

It may have been that mother was responsible. Being a school-teacher she had no doubt read books and magazines. She had, I presume, read of how Garfield, Lincoln, and other Americans rose from poverty to fame and greatness and as I lay beside her—in the days of her lying-in—she may have dreamed that I would some day rule men and cities. At any rate she induced father to give up his place as a farm-hand, sell his horse and embark on an independent enterprise of his own. She was a tall silent woman with a long nose and troubled grey eyes. For herself she wanted nothing. For father and myself she was incurably ambitious.

The first venture into which the two people went turned out badly. They rented ten acres of poor stony land on Grigg's Road, eight miles from Bidwell, and launched into chicken raising. I grew into boyhood on the place and got my first impressions of life there. From the beginning they were impressions of disaster and if, in my turn, I am a gloomy man inclined to see the darker side of life, I attribute it to the fact that what should have been for me the happy joyous days of childhood were spent on a chicken farm.

One unversed in such matters can have no notion of the many and tragic things that can happen to a chicken. It is born out of an egg, lives for a few weeks as a tiny fluffy thing such as you will see pictured on Easter cards, then becomes hideously naked, eats quantities of corn and meal bought by the sweat of your father's brow, gets diseases called pip, cholera, and other names, stands looking with stupid eyes at the sun, becomes sick and dies. A few hens and now and then a rooster, intended to serve God's mysterious ends, struggle through to maturity. The hens lay eggs out of which come other chickens and the dreadful cycle is thus made complete. It is all unbelievably complex. Most philosophers must have been raised on chicken farms.

One hopes for so much from a chicken and is so dreadfully disillusioned. Small chickens, just setting out on the journey of life, look so bright and alert and they are in fact so dreadfully stupid. They are so much like people they mix one up in one's judgments of life. If disease does not kill them they wait until your expectations are thoroughly aroused and then walk under the wheels of a wagon—to go squashed and dead back to their maker. Vermin infest their youth, and fortunes must be spent for curative powders. In later life I have seen how a literature has been built up on the subject of fortunes to be made out of the raising of chickens. It is intended to be read by the gods who have just eaten of the tree of the knowledge of good and evil. It is a hopeful literature and declares that much may be done by simple ambitious people who own a few hens. Do not be led astray by it. It was not written for you. Go hunt for gold on the frozen hills of Alaska, put your faith in the honesty of a politician, believe if you will that the world is daily growing better and that good will triumph over evil, but do not read and believe the literature that is written concerning the hen. It was not written for you.

I, however, digress. My tale does not primarily concern itself with the hen. If correctly told it will center on the egg. For ten years my father and mother struggled to make our chicken farm pay and then they gave up that struggle and began another. They moved into the town of Bidwell, Ohio, and embarked in the restaurant business. After ten years of worry with incubators that did not hatch, and with tiny—and in their own way lovely—balls of fluff that passed on into semi-naked pullethood and from that into dead henhood, we threw all aside and packing our belongings on a wagon drove down Grigg's Road toward Bidwell, a tiny caravan of hope looking for a new place from which to start on our upward journey through life.

We must have been a sad looking lot, not, I fancy, unlike refugees fleeing from a battlefield. Mother and I walked in the road. The wagon that contained our goods had been borrowed for the day from Mr. Albert Griggs, a neighbor. Out of its sides stuck the legs of cheap chairs and at the back of the pile of beds, tables, and boxes filled with kitchen utensils was a crate of live chickens, and on top of that the baby carriage in which I had been wheeled about in my infancy. Why we stuck to the baby carriage I don't know. It was unlikely other children would be born and the wheels were broken. People who have few possessions cling tightly to those they have. That is one of the facts that make life so discouraging.

Father rode on top of the wagon. He was then a bald-headed man of forty-five, a little fat and from long association with mother and the chickens he had become habitually silent and discouraged. All during our ten years on the chicken farm he had worked as a laborer on neighboring farms and most of the money he had earned had been spent for remedies to cure chicken diseases, on Wilmer's White Wonder Cholera Cure or Professor Bidlow's Egg Producer or some other preparations that mother found advertised in the poultry papers. There were two little patches of hair on father's head just above his ears. I remember that as a child I used to sit looking at him when he had gone to sleep in a chair before the stove on Sunday afternoons in the winter. I had at that time already begun to read books and have notions of my own and the bald path that led over the top of his head was, I fancied, something like a broad road, such a road as Caesar might have made on which to lead his legions out of Rome and into the wonders of an unknown world. The tufts of hair that grew above father's ears were, I thought, like forests. I fell into a half-sleeping, half-waking state and dreamed I was a tiny thing going along the road into a far beautiful place where there were no chicken farms and where life was a happy eggless affair.

One might write a book concerning our flight from the chicken farm into town.

Mother and I walked the entire eight miles—she to be sure that nothing fell from the wagon and I to see the wonders of the world. On the seat of the wagon beside father was his greatest treasure. I will tell you of that.

On a chicken farm where hundreds and even thousands of chickens come out of eggs surprising things sometimes happen. Grotesques are born out of eggs as out of people. The accident does not often occur—perhaps once in a thousand births. A chicken is, you see, born that has four legs, two pairs of wings, two heads or what not. The things do not live. They go quickly back to the hand of their maker that has for a moment trembled. The fact that the poor little things could not live was one of the tragedies of life to father. He had some sort of notion that if he could but bring into henhood or roosterhood a five-legged hen or a two-headed rooster his fortune would be made. He dreamed of taking the wonder about to county fairs and of growing rich by exhibiting it to other farm-hands.

At any rate he saved all the little monstrous things that had been born on our chicken farm. They were preserved in alcohol and put each in its own glass bottle. These he had carefully put into a box and on our journey into town it was carried on the wagon seat beside him. He drove the horses with one hand and with the other clung to the box. When we got to our destination the box was taken down at once and the bottles removed. All during our days as keepers of a restaurant in the town of Bidwell, Ohio, the grotesques in their little glass bottles sat on a shelf back of the counter. Mother sometimes protested but father was a rock on the subject of his treasure. The grotesques were, he declared, valuable. People, he said, liked to look at strange and wonderful things.

Did I say that we embarked in the restaurant business in the town of Bidwell, Ohio? I exaggerated a little. The town itself lay at the foot of a low hill and on the shore of a small river. The railroad did not run through the town and the station was a mile away to the north at a place called Pickleville. There had been a cider mill and pickle factory at the station, but before the time of our coming they had both gone out of business. In the morning and in the evening busses came down to the station along a road called Turner's Pike from the hotel on the main street of Bidwell. Our going to the out of the way place to embark in the restaurant business was mother's idea. She talked of it for a year and then one day went off and rented an empty store building opposite the railroad station. It was her idea that the restaurant would be profitable. Travelling men, she said, would be always waiting around to take trains out of town and town people would come to the station to await incoming trains. They would come to the restaurant to buy pieces of pie and drink coffee. Now that I am older I know that she had another motive in going. She was ambitious for me. She wanted me to rise in the world, to get into a town school and become a man of the towns.

At Pickleville father and mother worked hard as they always had done. At first there was the necessity of putting our place into shape to be a restaurant. That took a month. Father built a shelf on which he put tins of vegetables. He painted a sign on which he put his name in large red letters. Below his name was the sharp command—"EAT HERE"—that was so seldom obeyed. A show case was bought and filled with cigars and tobacco. Mother scrubbed the floor and the walls of the room. I went to school in the town and was glad to be away from the farm and from the presence of the discouraged, sad-looking chickens. Still I was not very joyous. In the evening I walked home from school along Turner's Pike and remembered the children I had seen playing in the town school yard. A troop of little girls had gone hopping about and singing. I tried that. Down along the frozen road I went hopping solemnly on one leg. "Hippity Hop To The Barber Shop," I sang shrilly. Then I stopped and looked doubtfully about. I was afraid of being seen in my gay mood. It must have seemed to me that I was doing a thing that should not be done by one who, like myself, had been raised on a chicken farm where death was a daily visitor.

Mother decided that our restaurant should remain open at night. At ten in the evening a passenger train went north past our door followed by a local freight. The freight crew had switching to do in Pickleville and when the work was done they came to our restaurant for hot coffee and food. Sometimes one of them ordered a fried egg. In the morning at four they returned north-bound and again visited us. A little trade began to grow up. Mother slept at night and during the day tended the restaurant and fed our boarders while father slept. He slept in the same bed mother had occupied during the night and I went off to the town of Bidwell and to school. During the long nights, while mother and I slept, father cooked meats that were to go into sandwiches for the lunch baskets of our boarders. Then an idea in regard to getting up in the world came into his head. The American spirit took hold of him. He also became ambitious.

In the long nights when there was little to do father had time to think. That was his undoing. He decided that he had in the past been an unsuccessful man because he had not been cheerful enough and that in the future he would adopt a cheerful outlook on life. In the early morning he came upstairs and got into bed with mother. She woke and the two talked. From my bed in the corner I listened.

It was father's idea that both he and mother should try to entertain the people who came to eat at our restaurant. I cannot now remember his words, but he gave the impression of one about to become in some obscure way a kind of public entertainer. When people, particularly young people from the town of Bidwell, came into our place, as on very rare occasions they did, bright entertaining conversation was to be made. From father's words I gathered that something of the jolly inn-keeper effect was to be sought. Mother must have been doubtful from the first, but she said nothing discouraging. It was father's notion that a passion for the company of himself and mother would spring up in the breasts of the younger people of the town of Bidwell. In the evening bright happy groups would come singing down Turner's Pike. They would troop shouting with joy and laughter into our place. There would be song and festivity. I do not mean to give the impression that father spoke so elaborately of the matter. He was as I have said an uncommunicative man. "They want some place to go. I tell you they want some place to go," he said over and over. That was as far as he got. My own imagination has filled in the blanks.

For two or three weeks this notion of father's invaded our house. We did not talk much, but in our daily lives tried earnestly to make smiles take the place of glum looks. Mother smiled at the boarders and I, catching the infection, smiled at our cat. Father became a little feverish in his anxiety to please. There was no doubt, lurking somewhere in him, a touch of the spirit of the showman. He did not waste much of his ammunition on the railroad men he served at night but seemed to be waiting for a young man or woman from Bidwell to come in to show what he could do. On the counter in the restaurant there was a wire basket kept always filled with eggs, and it must have been before his eyes when the idea of being entertaining was born in his brain. There was something pre-natal about the way eggs kept themselves connected with the development of his idea. At any rate an egg ruined his new impulse in life. Late one night I was awakened by a roar of anger coming from father's throat. Both mother and I sat upright in our beds. With trembling hands she lighted a lamp that stood on a table by her head. Downstairs the front door of our restaurant went shut with a bang and in a few minutes father tramped up the stairs. He held an egg in his hand and his hand trembled as though he were having a chill. There was a half insane light in his eyes. As he stood glaring at us I was sure he intended throwing the egg at either mother or me. Then he laid it gently on the table beside the lamp and dropped on his knees beside mother's bed. He began to cry like a boy and I, carried away by his grief, cried with him. The two of us filled the little upstairs room with our wailing voices. It is ridiculous, but of the picture we made I can remember only the fact that mother's hand continually stroked the bald path that ran across the top of his head. I have forgotten what mother said to him and how she induced him to tell her of what had happened downstairs. His explanation also has gone out of my mind. I remember only my own grief and fright and the shiny path over father's head glowing in the lamp light as he knelt by the bed.

As to what happened downstairs. For some unexplainable reason I know the story as well as though I had been a witness to my father's discomfiture. One in time gets to know many unexplainable things. On that evening young Joe Kane, son of a merchant of Bidwell, came to Pickleville to meet his father, who was expected on the ten o'clock evening train from the South. The train was three hours late and Joe came into our place to loaf about and to wait for its arrival. The local freight train came in and the freight crew were fed. Joe was left alone in the restaurant with father.

From the moment he came into our place the Bidwell young man must have been puzzled by my father's actions. It was his notion that father was angry at him for hanging around. He noticed that the restaurant keeper was apparently disturbed by his presence and he thought of going out. However, it began to rain and he did not fancy the long walk to town and back. He bought a five-cent cigar and ordered a cup of coffee. He had a newspaper in his pocket and took it out and began to read. "I'm waiting for the evening train. It's late," he said apologetically.

For a long time father, whom Joe Kane had never seen before, remained silently gazing at his visitor. He was no doubt suffering from an attack of stage fright. As so often happens in life he had thought so much and so often of the situation that now confronted him that he was somewhat nervous in its presence.

For one thing, he did not know what to do with his hands. He thrust one of them nervously over the counter and shook hands with Joe Kane. "How-de-do," he said. Joe Kane put his newspaper down and stared at him. Father's eye lighted on the basket of eggs that sat on the counter and he began to talk. "Well," he began hesitatingly, "well, you have heard of Christopher Columbus, eh?" He seemed to be angry. "That Christopher Columbus was a cheat," he declared emphatically. "He talked of making an egg stand on its end. He talked, he did, and then he went and broke the end of the egg."

My father seemed to his visitor to be beside himself at the duplicity of Christopher Columbus. He muttered and swore. He declared it was wrong to teach children that Christopher Columbus was a great man when, after all, he cheated at the critical moment. He had declared he would make an egg stand on end and then when his bluff had been called he had done a trick. Still grumbling at Columbus, father took an egg from the basket on the counter and began to walk up and down. He rolled the egg between the palms of his hands. He smiled genially. He began to mumble words regarding the effect to be produced on an egg by the electricity that comes out of the human body. He declared that without breaking its shell and by virtue of rolling it back and forth in his hands he could stand the egg on its end. He explained that the warmth of his hands and the gentle rolling movement he gave the egg created a new center of gravity, and Joe Kane was mildly interested. "I have handled thousands of eggs," father said. "No one knows more about eggs than I do."

He stood the egg on the counter and it fell on its side. He tried the trick again and again, each time rolling the egg between the palms of his hands and saying the words regarding the wonders of electricity and the laws of gravity. When after a half hour's effort he did succeed in making the egg stand for a moment he looked up to find that his visitor was no longer watching. By the time he had succeeded in calling Joe Kane's attention to the success of his effort the egg had again rolled over and lay on its side.

Afire with the showman's passion and at the same time a good deal disconcerted by the failure of his first effort, father now took the bottles containing the poultry monstrosities down from their place on the shelf and began to show them to his visitor. "How would you like to have seven legs and two heads like this fellow?" he asked, exhibiting the most remarkable of his treasures. A cheerful smiled played over his face. He reached over the counter and tried to slap Joe Kane on the shoulder as he had seen men do in Ben Head's saloon when he was a young farm-hand and drove to town on Saturday evenings. His visitor was made a little ill by the sight of the body of the terribly deformed bird floating in the alcohol in the bottle and got up to go. Coming from behind the counter father took hold of the young man's arm and led him back to his seat. He grew a little angry and for a moment had to turn his face away and force himself to smile. Then he put the bottles back on the shelf. In an outburst of generosity he fairly compelled Joe Kane to have a fresh cup of coffee and another cigar at his expense. Then he took a pan and filling it with vinegar, taken from a jug that sat beneath the counter, he declared himself about to do a new trick. "I will heat this egg in this pan of vinegar," he said. "Then I will put it through the neck of a bottle without breaking the shell. When the egg is inside the bottle it will resume its normal shape and the shell will become hard again. Then I will give the bottle with the egg in it to you. You can take it about with you wherever you go. People will want to know how you got the egg in the bottle. Don't tell them. Keep them guessing. That is the way to have fun with this trick."

Father grinned and winked at his visitor. Joe Kane decided that the man who confronted him was mildly insane but harmless. He drank the cup of coffee that had been given him and began to read his paper again. When the egg had been heated in vinegar father carried it on a spoon to the counter and going into a back room got an empty bottle. He was angry because his visitor did not watch him as he began to do his trick, but nevertheless went cheerfully to work. For a long time, he struggled, trying to get the egg to go through the neck of the bottle. He put the pan of vinegar back on the stove, intending to reheat the egg, then picked it up and burned his fingers. After a second bath in the hot vinegar the shell of the egg had been softened a little but not enough for his purpose. He worked and worked and a spirit of desperate determination took possession of him. When he thought that at last the trick was about to be consummated the delayed train came in at the station and Joe Kane started to go nonchalantly out at the door. Father made a last desperate effort to conquer the egg and make it do the thing that would establish his reputation as one who knew how to entertain guests who came into his restaurant. He worried the egg. He attempted to be somewhat rough with it. He swore and the sweat stood out on his forehead. The egg broke under his hand. When the contents spurted over his clothes, Joe Kane, who had stopped at the door, turned and laughed.

A roar of anger rose from my father's throat. He danced and shouted a string of inarticulate words. Grabbing another egg from the basket on the counter, he threw it, just missing the head of the young man as he dodged through the door and escaped.

Father came upstairs to mother and me with an egg in his hand. I do not know what he intended to do. I imagine he had some idea of destroying it, of destroying all eggs, and that he intended to let mother and me see him begin. When, however, he got into the presence of mother something happened to him. He laid the egg gently on the table and dropped on his knees by the bed as I have already explained. He later decided to close the restaurant for the night and to come upstairs and get into bed. When he did so he blew out the light and after much muttered conversation both he and mother went to sleep. I suppose I went to sleep also, but my sleep was troubled. I awoke at dawn and for a long time looked at the egg that lay on the table. I wondered why eggs had to be and why from the egg came the hen who again laid the egg. The question got into my blood. It has stayed there, I imagine, because I am the son of my father. At any rate, the problem remains unsolved in my mind. And that, I conclude, is but another evidence of the complete and final triumph of the egg—at least as far as my family is concerned.

William Faulkner

A ROSE FOR EMILY

I

When Miss Emily Grierson died, our whole town went to her funeral: the men through a sort of respectful affection for a fallen monument, the women mostly out of curiosity to see the inside of her house, which no one save an old manservant—a combined gardener and cook—had seen in at least ten years.

It was a big, squarish frame house that had once been white, decorated with cupolas and spires and scrolled balconies in the heavily lightsome style of the seventies, set on what had once been our most select street. But garages and cotton gins had encroached and obliterated even the august names of that neighborhood; only Miss Emily's house was left, lifting its stubborn and coquettish decay above the cotton wagons and the gasoline pumps—an eyesore among eyesores. And now Miss Emily had gone to join the representatives of those august names where they lay in the cedar-bemused cemetery among the ranked and anonymous graves of Union and Confederate soldiers who fell at the battle of Jefferson.

Alive, Miss Emily had been a tradition, a duty, and a care; a sort of hereditary obligation upon the town, dating from that day in 1894 when Colonel Sartoris, the mayor—he who fathered the edict that no Negro woman should appear on the streets without an apron—remitted her taxes, the dispensation dating from the death of her father on into perpetuity. Not that Miss Emily would have accepted charity. Colonel Sartoris invented an involved tale to the effect that Miss Emily's father had loaned money to the town, which the town, as a matter of business, preferred this way of repaying. Only a man of Colonel Sartoris' generation and thought could have invented it, and only a woman could have believed it.

When the next generation, with its more modern ideas, became mayors and aldermen, this arrangement created some little dissatisfaction. On the first of the year they mailed her a tax notice. February came, and there was no reply. They wrote her a formal letter, asking her to call at the sheriff's office at her convenience. A week later the mayor wrote her himself, offering to call or to send his car for her, and received in reply a note on paper of an archaic shape, in a thin, flowing calligraphy in faded ink, to the effect that she no longer went out at all. The tax notice was also enclosed, without comment.

They called a special meeting of the Board of Aldermen. A deputation waited upon her, knocked at the door through which no visitor had passed since she ceased giving china-painting lessons eight or ten years earlier. They were admitted by the old Negro into a dim hall from which a stairway mounted into still more shadow. It smelled of dust and disuse—a close, dank smell. The Negro led them into the parlor. It was furnished in heavy, leather-covered furniture. When the Negro opened the blinds of one window, they could see that the leather was cracked; and when they sat down, a faint dust rose sluggishly about their thighs, spinning with slow motions in the single sun-ray. On a tarnished gilt easel before the fireplace stood a crayon portrait of Miss Emily's father.

They rose when she entered—a small, fat woman in black, with a thin gold chain descending to her waist and vanishing into her belt, leaning on an ebony cane with a tarnished gold head. Her skeleton was small and spare; perhaps that was why what would have been merely plumpness in another was obesity in her. She looked bloated, like a body long submerged in motionless water, and of that pallid hue. Her eyes, lost in the fatty ridges of her face, looked like two small pieces of coal pressed into a lump of dough as they moved from one face to another while the visitors stated their errand.

She did not ask them to sit. She just stood in the door and listened quietly until the spokesman came to a stumbling halt. Then they could hear the invisible watch ticking at the end of the gold chain.

Her voice was dry and cold. "I have no taxes in Jefferson. Colonel Sartoris explained it to me. Perhaps one of you can gain access to the city records and satisfy yourselves."

"But we have. We are the city authorities, Miss Emily. Didn't you get a notice from the sheriff, signed by him?"

"I received a paper, yes," Miss Emily said. "Perhaps he considers himself the sheriff . . . I have no taxes in Jefferson."

"But there is nothing on the books to show that, you see. We must go by the—"

"See Colonel Sartoris." (Colonel Sartoris had been dead almost ten years.) "I have no taxes in Jefferson. Tobe!" The Negro appeared. "Show these gentlemen out."

II

So she vanquished them, horse and foot, just as she had vanquished their fathers thirty years before about the smell. That was two years after her father's death and a short time after her sweetheart—the one we believed would marry her—had deserted her. After her father's death she went out very little; after her sweetheart went away, people hardly saw her at all. A few of the ladies had the temerity to call, but were not received, and the only sign of life about the place was the Negro man—a young man then—going in and out with a market basket.

"Just as if a man—any man—could keep a kitchen properly," the ladies said; so they were not surprised when the smell developed. It was another link between the gross, teeming world and the high and mighty Griersons.

A neighbor, a woman, complained to the mayor, Judge Stevens, eighty years old.

"But what will you have me do about it, madam?" he said.

"Why, send her word to stop it," the woman said. "Isn't there a law?"

"I'm sure that won't be necessary," Judge Stevens said. "It's probably just a snake or a rat that nigger of hers killed in the yard. I'll speak to him about it."

The next day he received two more complaints, one from a man who came in diffident deprecation. "We really must do something about it, Judge. I'd be the last one in the world to bother Miss Emily, but we've got to do something." That night the Board of Aldermen met—three graybeards and one younger man, a member of the rising generation.

"It's simple enough," he said. "Send her word to have her place cleaned up. Give her a certain time to do it in, and if she don't . . ."

"Dammit, sir," Judge Stevens said, "will you accuse a lady to her face of smelling bad?"

So the next night, after midnight, four men crossed Miss Emily's lawn and slunk about the house like burglars, sniffing along the base of the brickwork and at the cellar openings while one of them performed a regular sowing motion with his hand out of a sack slung from his shoulder. They broke open the cellar door and sprinkled lime there, and in all the outbuildings. As they recrossed the lawn, a window that had been dark was lighted and Miss Emily sat in it, the light behind her, and her upright torso motionless as that of an idol. They crept quietly across the lawn and into the shadow of the locusts that lined the street. After a week or two the smell went away.

That was when people had begun to feel really sorry for her. People in our town, remembering how old lady Wyatt, her great-aunt, had gone completely crazy at last, believed that the Griersons held themselves a little too high for what they really were. None of the young men were quite good enough for Miss Emily and such. We had long thought of them as a tableau, Miss Emily a slender figure in white in the background, her father a spraddled silhouette in the foreground, his back to her and clutching a horsewhip, the two of them framed by the back-flung front door. So when she got to be thirty and was still single, we were not pleased exactly, but vindicated; even with insanity in the family she wouldn't have turned down all of her chances if they had really materialized.

When her father died, it got about that the house was all that was left to her; and in a way, people were glad. At last they could pity Miss Emily. Being left alone, and a pauper, she had become humanized. Now she too would know the old thrill and the old despair of a penny more or less.

The day after his death all the ladies prepared to call at the house and offer condolence and aid, as is our custom. Miss Emily met them at the door, dressed as usual and with no trace of grief on her face. She told them that her father was not dead. She did that for three days, with the ministers calling on her, and the doctors, trying to persuade her to let them dispose of the body. Just as they were about to resort to law and force, she broke down, and they buried her father quickly.

We did not say she was crazy then. We believed she had to do that. We remembered all the young men her father had driven away, and we knew that with nothing left, she would have to cling to that which had robbed her, as people will.

III

She was sick for a long time. When we saw her again, her hair was cut short, making her look like a girl, with a vague resemblance to those angels in colored church windows—sort of tragic and serene.

The town had just let the contracts for paving the sidewalks, and in the summer after her father's death they began the work. The construction company came with niggers and mules and machinery, and a foreman named Homer Barron, a Yankee—a big, dark, ready man, with a big voice and eyes lighter than his face. The little boys would follow in groups to hear him cuss the niggers, and the niggers singing in time to the rise and fall of picks. Pretty soon he knew everybody in town. Whenever you heard a lot of laughing anywhere about the square, Homer Barron would be in the center of the group. Presently we began to see him and Miss Emily on Sunday afternoons driving in the yellow-wheeled buggy and the matched team of bays from the livery stable.

At first we were glad that Miss Emily would have an interest, because the ladies all said, "Of course a Grierson would not think seriously of a Northerner, a day laborer." But there were still others, older people, who said that even grief could not cause a real lady to forget *noblesse oblige*—without calling it *noblesse oblige*. They just said, "Poor Emily. Her kinsfolk should come to her." She had some kin in Alabama; but years ago her father had fallen out with them over the estate of old lady Wyatt, the crazy woman, and there was no communication between the two families. They had not even been represented at the funeral.

And as soon as the old people said, "Poor Emily," the whispering began. "Do you suppose it's really so?" they said to one another. "Of course it is. What else could . . ." This behind their hands; rustling of craned silk and satin behind jalousies closed upon the sun of Sunday afternoon as the thin, swift clop-clop-clop of the matched team passed: "Poor Emily."

She carried her head high enough—even when we believed that she was fallen. It was as if she demanded more than ever the recognition of her dignity as the last Grierson; as if it had wanted that touch of earthiness to reaffirm her imperviousness. Like when she bought the rat poison, the arsenic. That was over a year after they had begun to say "Poor Emily," and while the two female cousins were visiting her.

"I want some poison," she said to the druggist. She was over thirty then, still a slight woman, though thinner than usual, with cold, haughty black eyes in a face the flesh of which was strained across the temples and about the eye-sockets as you imagine a lighthouse-keeper's face ought to look. "I want some poison," she said.

"Yes, Miss Emily. What kind? For rats and such? I'd recom—"

"I want the best you have. I don't care what kind."

The druggist named several. "They'll kill anything up to an elephant. But what you want is—"

"Arsenic," Miss Emily said. "Is that a good one?"

"Is . . . arsenic? Yes, ma'am. But what you want—"

"I want arsenic."

The druggist looked down at her. She looked back at him, erect, her face like a strained flag. "Why, of course," the druggist said. "If that's what you want. But the law requires you to tell what you are going to use it for."

Miss Emily just stared at him, her head tilted back in order to look him eye for eye, until he looked away and went and got the arsenic and wrapped it up. The Negro delivery boy brought her the package; the druggist didn't come back. When she opened the package at home there was written on the box, under the skull and bones: "For rats."

IV

So the next day we all said, "She will kill herself"; and we said it would be the best thing. When she had first begun to be seen with Homer Barron, we had said, "She will marry him." Then we said, "She will persuade him yet," because Homer himself had remarked—he liked men, and it was known that he drank with the younger men in the Elks' Club—that he was not a marrying man. Later we said, "Poor Emily" behind the jalousies as they passed on Sunday afternoon in the glittering buggy, Miss Emily with her head high and Homer Barron with his hat cocked and a cigar in his teeth, reins and whip in a yellow glove.

Then some of the ladies began to say that it was a disgrace to the town and a bad example to the young people. The men did not want to interfere, but at last the ladies forced the Baptist minister—Miss Emily's people were Episcopal—to call upon her. He would never divulge what happened during that interview, but he refused to go back again. The next Sunday they again drove about the streets, and the following day the minister's wife wrote to Miss Emily's relations in Alabama.

So she had blood-kin under her roof again and we sat back to watch developments. At first nothing happened. Then we were sure that they were to be married. We learned that Miss Emily had been to the jeweler's and ordered a man's toilet set in silver, with the letters H. B. on each piece. Two days later we learned that she had bought a complete outfit of men's clothing, including a nightshirt, and we said, "They are married." We were really glad. We were glad because the two female cousins were even more Grierson than Miss Emily had ever been.

So we were not surprised when Homer Barron—the streets had been finished some time since—was gone. We were a little disappointed that there was not a public blowing-off, but we believed that he had gone on to prepare for Miss Emily's coming, or to give her a chance to get rid of the cousins. (By that time it was a cabal, and we were all Miss Emily's allies to help circumvent the cousins.) Sure enough, after another week they departed. And, as we had expected all along, within three days Homer Barron was back in town. A neighbor saw the Negro man admit him at the kitchen door at dusk one evening.

And that was the last we saw of Homer Barron. And of Miss Emily for some time. The Negro man went in and out with the market basket, but the front door remained closed. Now and then we would see her at a window for a moment, as the men did that night when they sprinkled the lime, but for almost six months she did not appear on the streets. Then we knew that this was to be expected too; as if that quality of her father which had thwarted her woman's life so many times had been too virulent and too furious to die.

When we next saw Miss Emily, she had grown fat and her hair was turning gray. During the next few years it grew grayer and grayer until it attained an even pepper-and-salt iron-gray, when it ceased turning. Up to the day of her death at seventy-four it was still that vigorous iron-gray, like the hair of an active man.

From that time on her front door remained closed, save for a period of six or seven years, when she was about forty, during which she gave lessons in china-painting. She fitted up a studio in one of the downstairs rooms, where the daughters and grand-daughters of Colonel Sartoris' contemporaries were sent to her with the same regularity and in the same spirit that they were sent to church on Sundays with a twenty-five-cent piece for the collection plate. Meanwhile her taxes had been remitted.

Then the newer generation became the backbone and the spirit of the town, and the painting pupils grew up and fell away and did not send their children to her with boxes of color and tedious brushes and pictures cut from the ladies' magazines. The front door closed upon the last one and remained closed for good. When the town got free postal delivery, Miss Emily alone refused to let them fasten the metal numbers above her door and attach a mailbox to it. She would not listen to them.

Daily, monthly, yearly we watched the Negro grow grayer and more stooped, going in and out with the market basket. Each December we sent her a tax notice, which would be returned by the post office a week later, unclaimed. Now and then we would see her in one of the downstairs windows—she had evidently shut up the top floor of the house—like the carven torso of an idol in a niche, looking or not looking at us, we could never tell which. Thus she passed from generation to generation— dear, inescapable, impervious, tranquil, and perverse.

And so she died. Fell ill in the house filled with dust and shadows, with only a doddering Negro man to wait on her. We did not even know she was sick; we had long since given up trying to get any information from the Negro. He talked to no one, probably not even to her, for his voice had grown harsh and rusty, as if from disuse.

She died in one of the downstairs rooms, in a heavy walnut bed with a curtain, her gray head propped on a pillow yellow and moldy with age and lack of sunlight.

V

The Negro met the first of the ladies at the front door and let them in, with their hushed, sibilant voices and their quick, curious glances, and then he disappeared. He walked right through the house and out the back and was not seen again.

The two female cousins came at once. They held the funeral on the second day, with the town coming to look at Miss Emily beneath a mass of bought flowers, with the crayon face of her father musing profoundly above the bier and the ladies sibilant and macabre; and the very old men—some in their brushed Confederate uniforms— on the porch and the lawn, talking of Miss Emily as if she had been a contemporary of theirs, believing that they had danced with her and courted her perhaps, confusing time with its mathematical progression, as the old do, to whom all the past is not a diminishing road but, instead, a huge meadow which no winter ever quite touches, divided from them now by the narrow bottle-neck of the most recent decade of years.

Already we knew that there was one room in that region above stairs which no one had seen in forty years, and which would have to be forced. They waited until Miss Emily was decently in the ground before they opened it.

The violence of breaking down the door seemed to fill this room with pervading dust. A thin, acrid pall as of the tomb seemed to lie everywhere upon this room decked and furnished as for a bridal: upon the valance curtains of faded rose color, upon the rose-shaded lights, upon the dressing table, upon the delicate array of crystal and the man's toilet things backed with tarnished silver, silver so tarnished that the monogram was obscured. Among them lay a collar and tie, as if they had just been removed, which, lifted, left upon the surface a pale crescent in the dust. Upon a chair hung the suit, carefully folded; beneath it the two mute shoes and the discarded socks.

The man himself lay in the bed.

For a long while we just stood there, looking down at the profound and fleshless grin. The body had apparently once lain in the attitude of an embrace, but now the long sleep that outlasts love, that conquers even the grimace of love, had cuckolded him. What was left of him, rotted beneath what was left of the nightshirt, had become inextricable from the bed in which he lay; and upon him and upon the pillow beside him lay that even coating of the patient and biding dust.

Then we noticed that in the second pillow was the indentation of a head. One of us lifted something from it, and leaning forward, that faint and invisible dust dry and acrid in the nostrils, we saw a long strand of iron-gray hair.

Nathaniel Hawthorne

YOUNG GOODMAN BROWN

Young Goodman Brown came forth at sunset into the street at Salem village; but put his head back, after crossing the threshold, to exchange a parting kiss with his young wife. And Faith, as the wife was aptly named, thrust her own pretty head into the street, letting the wind play with the pink ribbons of her cap while she called to Goodman Brown.

"Dearest heart," whispered she, softly and rather sadly, when her lips were close to his ear, "prithee put off your journey until sunrise and sleep in your own bed to-night. A lone woman is troubled with such dreams and such thoughts that she's afeard of herself sometimes. Pray tarry with me this night, dear husband, of all nights in the year."

"My love and my Faith," replied young Goodman Brown, "of all nights in the year, this one night must I tarry away from thee. My journey, as thou callest it, forth and back again, must needs be done 'twixt now and sunrise. What, my sweet, pretty wife, dost thou doubt me already, and we but three months married?"

"Then God bless you!" said Faith, with the pink ribbons; "and may you find all well when you come back."

"Amen!" cried Goodman Brown. "Say thy prayers, dear Faith, and go to bed at dusk, and no harm will come to thee."

So they parted; and the young man pursued his way until, being about to turn the corner by the meeting-house, he looked back and saw the head of Faith still peeping after him with a melancholy air, in spite of her pink ribbons.

"Poor little Faith!" thought he, for his heart smote him. "What a wretch am I to leave her on such an errand! She talks of dreams, too. Methought as she spoke there was trouble in her face, as if a dream had warned her what work is to be done tonight. But no, no; 't would kill her to think it. Well, she's a blessed angel on earth; and after this one night I'll cling to her skirts and follow her to heaven."

With this excellent resolve for the future, Goodman Brown felt himself justified in making more haste on his present evil purpose. He had taken a dreary road, darkened by all the gloomiest trees of the forest, which barely stood aside to let the narrow path creep through, and closed immediately behind. It was all as lonely as could be; and there is this peculiarity in such a solitude, that the traveller knows not who may be concealed by the innumerable trunks and the thick boughs overhead; so that with lonely footsteps he may yet be passing through an unseen multitude.

"There may be a devilish Indian behind every tree," said Goodman Brown to himself; and he glanced fearfully behind him as he added, ''What if the devil himself should be at my very elbow!''

His head being turned back, he passed a crook of the road, and, looking forward again, beheld the figure of a man, in grave and decent attire, seated at the foot of an old tree. He arose at Goodman Brown's approach and walked onward side by side with him.

''You are late, Goodman Brown,'' said he. ''The clock of the Old South was striking as I came through Boston, and that is full fifteen minutes agone.''

''Faith kept me back a while,'' replied the young man, with a tremor in his voice, caused by the sudden appearance of his companion, though not wholly unexpected.

It was now deep dusk in the forest, and deepest in that part of it where these two were journeying. As nearly as could be discerned, the second traveller was about fifty years old, apparently in the same rank of life as Goodman Brown, and bearing a considerable resemblance to him, though perhaps more in expression than features. Still they might have been taken for father and son. And yet, though the elder person was as simply clad as the younger, and as simple in manner too, he had an indescribable air of one who knew the world, and who would not have felt abashed at the governor's dinner table or in King William's court, were it possible that his affairs should call him thither. But the only thing about him that could be fixed upon as remarkable was his staff, which bore the likeness of a great black snake, so curiously wrought that it might almost be seen to twist and wriggle itself like a living serpent. This, of course, must have been an ocular deception, assisted by the uncertain light.

''Come, Goodman Brown,'' cried his fellow-traveller, ''this is a dull place for the beginning of a journey. Take my staff, if you are so soon weary.''

''Friend,'' said the other, exchanging his slow pace for a full stop, ''having kept covenant by meeting thee here, it is my purpose now to return whence I came. I have scruples touching the matter thou wot'st of.''

''Sayest thou so?'' replied he of the serpent, smiling apart. ''Let us walk on, nevertheless, reasoning as we go; and if I convince thee not thou shalt turn back. We are but a little way in the forest yet.''

''Too far! too far!'' exclaimed the goodman, unconsciously resuming his walk. ''My father never went into the woods on such an errand, nor his father before him. We have been a race of honest men and good Christians since the days of the martyrs; and shall I be the first of the name of Brown that ever took this path and kept''—

''Such company, thou wouldst say,'' observed the elder person, interpreting his pause. ''Well said, Goodman Brown! I have been as well acquainted with your family as with ever a one among the Puritans; and that's no trifle to say. I helped your grandfather, the constable, when he lashed the Quaker woman so smartly through the streets of Salem; and it was I that brought your father a pitch-pine knot, kindled at my own hearth, to set fire to an Indian village, in King Philip's war. They were my good friends, both; and many a pleasant walk have we had along this path, and returned merrily after midnight. I would fain be friends with you for their sake.''

''If it be as thou sayest,'' replied Goodman Brown, ''I marvel they never spoke of these matters; or, verily, I marvel not, seeing that the least rumor of the sort would have driven them from New England. We are a people of prayer, and good works to boot, and abide no such wickedness.''

''Wickedness or not,'' said the traveller with the twisted staff, ''I have a very general acquaintance here in New England. The deacons of many a church have drunk the communion wine with me; the selectmen of divers towns make me their chairman;

and a majority of the Great and General Court are firm supporters of my interest. The governor and I, too—But these are state secrets."

"Can this be so?" cried Goodman Brown, with a stare of amazement at his undisturbed companion. "Howbeit, I have nothing to do with the governor and council; they have their own ways, and are no rule for a simple husbandman like me. But, were I to go on with thee, how should I meet the eye of that good old man, our minister, at Salem village? Oh, his voice would make me tremble both Sabbath day and lecture day."

Thus far the elder traveller had listened with due gravity; but now burst into a fit of irrepressible mirth, shaking himself so violently that his snake-like staff actually seemed to wriggle in sympathy.

"Ha! ha! ha!" shouted he again and again; then composing himself, "Well, go on, Goodman Brown, go on; but, prithee, don't kill me with laughing."

"Well, then, to end the matter at once," said Goodman Brown, considerably nettled, "there is my wife, Faith. It would break her dear little heart; and I'd rather break my own."

"Nay, if that be the case," answered the other, "e'en go thy ways, Goodman Brown. I would not for twenty old women like the one hobbling before us that Faith should come to any harm."

As he spoke he pointed his staff at a female figure on the path, in whom Goodman Brown recognized a very pious and exemplary dame, who had taught him his catechism in youth, and was still his moral and spiritual adviser, jointly with the minister and Deacon Gookin.

"A marvel, truly, that Goody Cloyse should be so far in the wilderness at nightfall," said he. "But with your leave, friend, I shall take a cut through the woods until we have left this Christian woman behind. Being a stranger to you, she might ask whom I was consorting with and whither I was going."

"Be it so," said his fellow-traveller. "Betake you the woods, and let me keep the path."

Accordingly the young man turned aside, but took care to watch his companion, who advanced softly along the road until he had come within a staff's length of the old dame. She, meanwhile, was making the best of her way, with singular speed for so aged a woman, and mumbling some indistinct words—a prayer, doubtless—as she went. The traveller put forth his staff and touched her withered neck with what seemed the serpent's tail.

"The devil!" screamed the pious old lady.

"Then Goody Cloyse knows her old friend?" observed the traveller, confronting her and leaning on his writhing stick.

"Ah, forsooth, and is it your worship indeed?" cried the good dame. "Yea, truly is it, and in the very image of my old gossip, Goodman Brown, the grandfather of the silly fellow that now is. But—would your worship believe it?—my broomstick hath strangely disappeared, stolen, as I suspect, by that unhanged witch, Goody Cory, and that, too, when I was all anointed with the juice of smallage, and cinquefoil, and wolf's bane"—

"Mingled with fine wheat and the fat of a new-born babe," said the shape of old Goodman Brown.

"Ah, your worship knows the recipe," cried the old lady, cackling aloud. "So, as I was saying, being all ready for the meeting, and no horse to ride on, I made up my mind to foot it; for they tell me there is a nice young man to be taken into communion tonight. But now your good worship will lend me your arm, and we shall be there in a twinkling."

"That can hardly be," answered her friend. "I may not spare you my arm, Goody Cloyse; but here is my staff, if you will."

So saying, he threw it down at her feet, where, perhaps, it assumed life, being one of the rods which its owner had formerly lent to the Egyptian magi. Of this fact, however, Goodman Brown could not take cognizance. He had cast up his eyes in astonishment, and, looking down again, beheld neither Goody Cloyse nor the serpentine staff, but this fellow-traveller alone, who waited for him as calmly as if nothing had happened.

"That old woman taught me my catechism," said the young man; and there was a world of meaning in this simple comment.

They continued to walk onward, while the elder traveller exhorted his companion to make good speed and persevere in the path, discoursing so aptly that his arguments seemed rather to spring up in the bosom of his auditor than to be suggested by himself. As they went, he plucked a branch of maple to serve for a walking stick, and began to strip it of the twigs and little boughs, which were wet with evening dew. The moment his fingers touched them they became strangely withered and dried up as with a week's sunshine. Thus the pair proceeded, at a good free pace, until suddenly, in a gloomy hollow of the road, Goodman Brown sat himself down on the stump of a tree and refused to go any farther.

"Friend," said he, stubbornly, "my mind is made up. Not another step will I budge on this errand. What if a wretched old woman do choose to go to the devil when I thought she was going to heaven: is that any reason why I should quit my dear Faith and go after her?"

"You will think better of this by and by," said his acquaintance, composedly. "Sit here and rest yourself a while; and when you feel like moving again, there is my staff to help you along."

Without more words, he threw his companion the maple stick, and was as speedily out of sight as if he had vanished into the deepening gloom. The young man sat a few moments by the roadside, applauding himself greatly, and thinking with how clear a conscience he should meet the minister in his morning walk, nor shrink from the eye of good old Deacon Gookin. And what calm sleep would be his that very night, which was to have been spent so wickedly, but so purely and sweetly now, in the arms of Faith! Amidst these pleasant and praiseworthy meditations, Goodman Brown heard the tramp of horses along the road, and deemed it advisable to conceal himself within the verge of the forest, conscious of the guilty purpose that had brought him thither, though now so happily turned from it.

On came the hoof tramps and the voices of the riders, two grave old voices, conversing soberly as they drew near. These mingled sounds appeared to pass along the road, within a few yards of the young man's hiding-place; but, owing doubtless to the depth of the gloom at that particular spot, neither the travellers nor their steeds were visible. Though their figures brushed the small boughs by the wayside, it could not be seen that they intercepted, even for a moment, the faint gleam from the strip of bright sky athwart which they must have passed. Goodman Brown alternately crouched and stood on tiptoe, pulling aside the branches and thrusting forth his head as far as he durst without discerning so much as a shadow. It vexed him the more, because he could have sworn, were such a thing possible, that he recognized the voices of the minister and Deacon Gookin, jogging along quietly, as they were wont to do, when bound to some ordination or ecclesiastical council. While yet within hearing, one of the riders stopped to pluck a switch.

"Of the two, reverend sir," said the voice like the deacon's, "I had rather miss an ordination dinner than to-night's meeting. They tell me that some of our community are to be here from Falmouth and beyond, and others from Connecticut and Rhode Island, besides several of the Indian powwows, who, after their fashion, know almost as much deviltry as the best of us. Moreover, there is a goodly young woman to be taken into communion."

"Mighty well, Deacon Gookin!" replied the solemn old tones of the minister. "Spur up, or we shall be late. Nothing can be done, you know, until I get on the ground."

The hoofs clattered again; and the voices, talking so strangely in the empty air, passed on through the forest, where no church had ever been gathered or solitary Christian prayed. Whither, then, could these holy men be journeying so deep into the heathen wilderness? Young Goodman Brown caught hold of a tree for support, being ready to sink down on the ground, faint and overburdened with the heavy sickness of his heart. He looked up to the sky, doubting whether there really was a heaven above him. Yet there was the blue arch, and the stars brightening in it.

"With heaven above and Faith below, I will yet stand firm against the devil!" cried Goodman Brown.

While he still gazed upward into the deep arch of the firmament and had lifted his hands to pray, a cloud, though no wind was stirring, hurried across the zenith and hid the brightening stars. The blue sky was still visible, except directly overhead, where this black mass of cloud was sweeping swiftly northward. Aloft in the air, as if from the depths of the cloud, came a confused and doubtful sound of voices. Once the listener fancied that he could distinguish the accents of towns-people of his own, men and women, both pious and ungodly, many of whom he had met at the communion table, and had seen others rioting at the tavern. The next moment, so indistinct were the sounds, he doubted whether he had heard aught but the murmur of the old forest, whispering without a wind. Then came a stronger swell of those familiar tones, heard daily in the sunshine at Salem village, but never until now from a cloud of night. There was one voice, of a young woman, uttering lamentations, yet with an uncertain sorrow, and entreating for some favor, which, perhaps, it would grieve her to obtain; and all the unseen multitude, both saints and sinners, seemed to encourage her onward.

"Faith!" shouted Goodman Brown, in a voice of agony and desperation; and the echoes of the forest mocked him, crying, "Faith! Faith!" as if bewildered wretches were seeking her all through the wilderness.

The cry of grief, rage, and terror was yet piercing the night, when the unhappy husband held his breath for a response. There was a scream, drowned immediately in a louder murmur of voices, fading into far-off laughter, as the dark cloud swept away, leaving the clear and silent sky above Goodman Brown. But something fluttered lightly down through the air and caught on the branch of a tree. The young man seized it, and beheld a pink ribbon.

"My Faith is gone!" cried he, after one stupefied moment. "There is no good on earth; and sin is but a name. Come, devil; for to thee is this world given."

And, maddened with despair, so that he laughed loud and long, did Goodman Brown grasp his staff and set forth again, at such a rate that he seemed to fly along the forest path rather than to walk or run. The road grew wilder and drearier and more faintly traced, and vanished at length, leaving him in the heart of the dark wilderness, still rushing onward with the instinct that guides mortal man to evil. The whole forest was peopled with frightful sounds—the creaking of the trees, the howling of wild beasts, and the yell of Indians; while sometimes the wind tolled like a distant church bell, and sometimes gave a broad roar around the traveller, as if all Nature were laughing him to scorn. But he was himself the chief horror of the scene and shrank not from its other horrors.

"Ha! ha! ha!" roared Goodman Brown when the wind laughed at him. "Let us hear which will laugh loudest. Think not to frighten me with your deviltry. Come witch, come wizard, come Indian powwow, come devil himself, and here comes Goodman Brown. You may as well fear him as he fear you."

In truth, all through the haunted forest there could be nothing more frightful than the figure of Goodman Brown. On he flew among the black pines, brandishing his staff with frenzied gestures, now giving vent to an inspiration of horrid blasphemy, and now shouting forth such laughter as set all the echoes of the forest laughing like demons around him. The fiend in his own shape is less hideous than when he rages in the breast of man. Thus sped the demoniac on his course, until, quivering among the trees, he saw a red light before him, as when the felled trunks and branches of a clearing have been set on fire, and throw up their lurid blaze against the sky, at the hour of midnight. He paused, in a lull of the tempest that had driven him onward, and heard the swell of what seemed a hymn, rolling solemnly from a distance with the weight of many voices. He knew the tune; it was a familiar one in the choir of the village meeting-house. The verse died heavily away, and was lengthened by a chorus, not of human voices, but of all the sounds of the benighted wilderness pealing in awful harmony together. Goodman Brown cried out, and his cry was lost to his own ear by its unison with the cry of the desert.

In the interval of silence he stole forward until the light glared full upon his eyes. At one extremity of an open space, hemmed in by the dark wall of the forest, arose a rock, bearing some rude, natural resemblance either to an altar or a pulpit, and surrounded by four blazing pines, their tops aflame, their stems untouched, like candles at an evening meeting. The mass of foliage that had overgrown the summit of the rock was all on fire, blazing high into the night and fitfully illuminating the whole field. Each pendent twig and leafy festoon was in a blaze. As the red light arose and fell, a numerous congregation alternately shone forth, then disappeared in shadow, and again grew, as it were, out of the darkness, peopling the heart of the solitary woods at once.

"A grave and dark-clad company," quoth Goodman Brown.

In truth they were such. Among them, quivering to and fro between gloom and splendor, appeared faces that would be seen next day at the council board of the province, and others which, Sabbath after Sabbath, looked devoutly heavenward, and benignantly over the crowded pews, from the holiest pulpits in the land. Some affirm that the lady of the governor was there. At least there were high dames well known to her, and wives of honored husbands, and widows, a great multitude, and ancient maidens, all of excellent repute, and fair young girls, who trembled lest their mothers should espy them. Either the sudden gleams of light flashing over the obscure field bedazzled Goodman Brown, or he recognized a score of the church members of Salem village famous for their especial sanctity. Good old Deacon Gookin had arrived, and waited at the skirts of that venerable saint, his revered pastor. But, irreverently consorting with these grave, reputable, and pious people, these elders of the church, these chaste dames and dewy virgins, there were men of dissolute lives and women of spotted fame, wretches given over to all mean and filthy vice, and suspected even of horrid crimes. It was strange to see that the good shrank not from the wicked, nor were the sinners abashed by the saints. Scattered also among their pale-faced enemies were the Indian priests, or powwows, who had often scared their native forest with more hideous incantations than any known to English witchcraft.

"But where is Faith?" thought Goodman Brown; and, as hope came into his heart, he trembled.

Another verse of the hymn arose, a slow and mournful strain, such as the pious love, but joined to words which expressed all that our nature can conceive of sin, and darkly hinted at far more. Unfathomable to mere mortals is the lore of fiends. Verse after verse was sung; and still the chorus of the desert swelled between like the deepest tone of a mighty organ; and with the final peal of that dreadful anthem there came a sound, as if the roaring wind, the rushing streams, the howling beasts, and every other voice of the unconcerted wilderness were mingling and according with the voice of guilty man in homage to the prince of all. The four blazing pines threw up a loftier flame, and obscurely discovered shapes and visages of horror on the smoke wreaths above the impious assembly. At the same moment the fire on the rock shot redly forth and formed a glowing arch above its base, where now appeared a figure. With reverence be it spoken, the figure bore no slight similitude, both in garb and manner, to some grave divine of the New England churches.

"Bring forth the converts!" cried a voice that echoed through the field and rolled into the forest.

At the word, Goodman Brown stepped forth from the shadow of the trees and approached the congregation, with whom he felt a loathful brotherhood by the sympathy of all that was wicked in his heart. He could have well-nigh sworn that the shape of his own dead father beckoned him to advance, looking downward from a smoke wreath, while a woman, with dim features of despair, threw out her hand to warn him back. Was it his mother? But he had no power to retreat one step, nor to resist, even in thought, when the minister and good old Deacon Gookin seized his arms and led him to the blazing rock. Thither came also the slender form of a veiled female, led between Goody Cloyse, that pious teacher of the catechism, and Martha Carrier, who had received the devil's promise to be queen of hell. A rampant hag was she. And there stood the proselytes beneath the canopy of fire.

"Welcome, my children," said the dark figure, "to the communion of your race. Ye have found thus young your nature and your destiny. My children, look behind you!"

They turned; and flashing forth, as it were, in a sheet of flame, the fiend worshippers were seen; the smile of welcome gleamed darkly on every visage.

"There," resumed the sable form, "are all whom ye have reverenced from youth. Ye deemed them holier than yourselves, and shrank from your own sin, contrasting it with their lives of righteousness and prayerful aspirations heavenward. Yet here are they all in my worshipping assembly. This night it shall be granted you to know their secret deeds: how hoary-bearded elders of the church have whispered wanton words to the young maids of their households; how many a woman, eager for widows' weeds, has given her husband a drink at bedtime and let him sleep his last sleep in her bosom; how beardless youths have made haste to inherit their fathers' wealth; and how fair damsels—blush not, sweet ones—have dug little graves in the garden, and bidden me, the sole guest, to an infant's funeral. By the sympathy of your human hearts for sin ye shall scent out all the places—whether in church, bed-chamber, street, field, or forest—where crime has been committed, and shall exult to behold the whole earth one stain of guilt, one mighty blood spot. Far more than this. It shall be yours to penetrate, in every bosom, the deep mystery of sin, the fountain of all wicked arts, and which inexhaustibly supplies more evil impulses than human power—than my power at its utmost—can make manifest in deeds. And now, my children, look upon each other.''

They did so; and, by the blaze of the hell-kindled torches, the wretched man beheld his Faith, and the wife her husband, trembling before that unhallowed altar.

''Lo, there ye stand, my children,'' said the figure, in a deep and solemn tone, almost sad with its despairing awfulness, as if his once angelic nature could yet mourn for our miserable race. ''Depending upon one another's hearts, ye had still hoped that virtue were not all a dream. Now are ye undeceived. Evil is the nature of mankind. Evil must be your only happiness. Welcome again, my children, to the communion of your race.''

''Welcome,'' repeated the fiend worshippers, in one cry of despair and triumph.

And there they stood, the only pair, as it seemed, who were yet hesitating on the verge of wickedness in this dark world. A basin was hollowed, naturally, in the rock. Did it contain water, reddened by the lurid light? or was it blood? or, perchance, a liquid flame? Herein did the shape of evil dip his hand and prepare to lay the mark of baptism upon their foreheads, that they might be partakers of the mystery of sin, more conscious of the secret guilt of others, both in deed and thought, than they could now be of their own. The husband cast one look at his pale wife, and Faith at him. What polluted wretches would the next glance show them to each other, shuddering alike at what they disclosed and what they saw!

''Faith! Faith!'' cried the husband, ''look up to heaven, and resist the wicked one.''

Whether Faith obeyed he knew not. Hardly had he spoken when he found himself amid calm night and solitude, listening to a roar of the wind which died heavily away through the forest. He staggered against the rock, and felt it chill and damp; while a hanging twig, that had been all on fire, besprinkled his cheek with the coldest dew.

The next morning young Goodman Brown came slowly into the street of Salem village, staring around him like a bewildered man. The good old minister was taking a walk along the graveyard to get an appetite for breakfast and meditate his sermon, and bestowed a blessing, as he passed, on Goodman Brown. He shrank from the venerable saint as if to avoid an anathema. Old Deacon Gookin was at domestic worship, and the holy words of his prayer were heard through the open window. ''What God doth the wizard pray to?'' quoth Goodman Brown. Goody Cloyse, that excellent old Christian, stood in the early sunshine at her own lattice, catechizing a little girl who had brought her a pint of morning's milk. Goodman Brown snatched away the child as from the grasp of the fiend himself. Turning the corner by the meeting-house, he spied the head of Faith, with the pink ribbons, gazing anxiously forth, and bursting into such joy at sight of him that she skipped along the street and almost kissed her husband before the whole village. But Goodman Brown looked sternly and sadly into her face, and passed on without a greeting.

Had Goodman Brown fallen asleep in the forest and only dreamed a wild dream of a witch-meeting?

Be it so if you will; but, alas! it was a dream of evil omen for young Goodman Brown. A stern, a sad, a darkly meditative, a distrustful, it not a desperate man did he become from the night of that fearful dream. On the Sabbath day, when the congregation were singing a holy psalm, he could not listen because an anthem of sin rushed loudly upon his ear and drowned all the blessed strain. When the minister spoke from the pulpit with power and fervid eloquence, and, with his hand on the open Bible, of the sacred truths of our religion, and of saint-like lives and triumphant deaths, and of future bliss or misery unutterable, then did Goodman Brown turn pale, dreading lest the roof should thunder down upon the gray blasphemer and his hearers. Often, awaking suddenly at midnight, he shrank from the bosom of Faith; and at morning or eventide, when the family knelt down at prayer, he scowled and muttered to himself, and gazed sternly at his wife, and turned away. And when he had lived long, and was borne to his grave, a hoary corpse, followed by Faith, an aged woman, and children and grandchildren, a goodly procession, besides neighbors not a few, they carved no hopeful verse upon his tombstone, for his dying hour was gloom.

D. H. Lawrence

THE ROCKING-HORSE WINNER

There was a woman who was beautiful, who started with all the advantages, yet she had no luck. She married for love, and the love turned to dust. She had bonny children, yet she felt they had been thrust upon her, and she could not love them. They looked at her coldly, as if they were finding fault with her. And hurriedly she felt she must cover up some fault in herself. Yet what it was that she must cover up she never knew. Nevertheless, when her children were present, she always felt the centre of her heart go hard. This troubled her, and in her manner she was all the more gentle and anxious for her children, as if she loved them very much. Only she herself knew that at the centre of her heart was a hard little place that could not feel love, no, not for anybody. Everybody else said of her, "She is such a good mother. She adores her children." Only she herself, and her children themselves, knew it was not so. They read it in each other's eyes.

There were a boy and two little girls. They lived in a pleasant house, with a garden, and they had discreet servants, and felt themselves superior to anyone in the neighbourhood.

Although they lived in style, they felt always an anxiety in the house. There was never enough money. The mother had a small income, and the father had a small income, but not nearly enough for the social position which they had to keep up. The father went into town to some office. But though he had good prospects, these prospects never materialised. There was always the grinding sense of the shortage of money, though the style was always kept up.

At last the mother said: "I will see if *I* can't make something." But she did not know where to begin. She racked her brains, and tried this thing and the other, but could not find anything successful. The failure made deep lines come into her face. Her children were growing up, they would have to go to school. There must be more money, there must be more money. The father, who was always very handsome and expensive in his tastes, seemed as if he never *would* be able to do anything worth doing. And the mother, who had a great belief in herself, did not succeed any better, and her tastes were just as expensive.

And so the house came to be haunted by the unspoken phrase: *There must be more money! There must be more money!* The children could hear it all the time, though nobody said it aloud. They heard it at Christmas, when the expensive and splendid toys filled the nursery. Behind the shining modern rocking-horse, behind the smart doll's house, a voice would start whispering: "There *must* be more money!

There *must* be more money!'' And the children would stop playing, to listen for a moment. They would look into each other's eyes, to see if they had all heard. And each one saw in the eyes of the other two that they too had heard. ''There *must* be more money! There *must* be more money!''

It came whispering from the springs of the still-swaying rocking-horse, and even the horse, bending his wooden, champing head, heard it. The big doll, sitting so pink and smirking in her new pram, could hear it quite plainly, and seemed to be smirking all the more self-consciously because of it. The foolish puppy, too, that took the place of the teddy-bear, he was looking so extraordinarily foolish for no other reason but that he heard the secret whisper all over the house: ''There *must* be more money!''

Yet nobody ever said it aloud. The whisper was everywhere, and therefore no one spoke it. Just as no one ever says: ''We are breathing!'' in spite of the fact that breath is coming and going all the time.

''Mother,'' said the boy Paul one day, ''why don't we keep a car of our own? Why do we always use uncle's, or else a taxi?''

''Because we're the poor members of the family,'' said the mother.

''But why *are* we, mother?''

''Well—I suppose,'' she said slowly and bitterly, ''it's because your father has no luck.''

The boy was silent for some time.

''Is luck money, mother?'' he asked, rather timidly.

''No, Paul. Not quite. It's what causes you to have money.''

''Oh!'' said Paul vaguely. ''I thought when Uncle Oscar said *filthy lucker,* it meant money.''

''*Filthy lucre* does mean money,'' said the mother. ''But it's lucre, not luck.''

''Oh!'' said the boy. ''Then what *is* luck, mother?''

''It's what causes you to have money. If you're lucky you have money. That's why it's better to be born lucky than rich. If you're rich, you may lose your money. But if you're lucky, you will always get more money.''

''Oh! Will you? And is father not lucky?''

''Very unlucky, I should say,'' she said bitterly.

The boy watched her with unsure eyes.

''Why?'' he asked.

''I don't know. Nobody ever knows why one person is lucky and another unlucky.''

''Don't they? Nobody at all? Does *nobody* know?''

''Perhaps God. But He never tells.''

''He ought to, then. And aren't you lucky either, mother?''

''I can't be, if I married an unlucky husband.''

''But by yourself, aren't you?''

''I used to think I was, before I married. Now I think I am very unlucky indeed.''

''Why?''

''Well—never mind! Perhaps I'm not really,'' she said.

The child looked at her to see if she meant it. But he saw, by the lines of her mouth, that she was only trying to hide something from him.

''Well, anyhow,'' he said stoutly, ''I'm a lucky person.''

''Why?'' said, his mother, with a sudden laugh.

He stared at her. He didn't even know why he had said it.

''God told me,'' he asserted, brazening it out.

''I hope he did, dear!'' she said, again with a laugh, but rather bitter.

''He did, mother!''

"Excellent!" said the mother, using one of her husband's exclamations.

The boy saw she did not believe him; or rather, that she paid no attention to his assertion. This angered him somewhere, and made him want to compel her attention.

He went off by himself, vaguely, in a childish way, seeking for the clue to "luck." Absorbed, taking no heed of other people, he went about with a sort of stealth, seeking inwardly for luck. He wanted luck, he wanted it, he wanted it. When the two girls were playing dolls in the nursery, he would sit on his big rocking-horse, charging madly into space, with a frenzy that made the little girls peer at him uneasily. Wildly the horse careered, the waving dark hair of the boy tossed, his eyes had a strange glare in them. The little girls dared not speak to him.

When he had ridden to the end of his mad little journey, he climbed down and stood in front of his rocking-horse, staring fixedly into its lowered face. Its red mouth was slightly open, its big eye was wide and glassy-bright.

"Now!" he would silently command the snorting steed. "Now, take me to where there is luck! Now take me!"

And he would slash the horse on the neck with the little whip he had asked Uncle Oscar for. He *knew* the horse could take him to where there was luck, if only he forced it. So he would mount again and start on his furious ride, hoping at last to get there. He knew he could get there.

"You'll break your horse, Paul!" said the nurse.

"He's always riding like that! I wish he'd leave off!" said his elder sister Joan.

But he only glared down on them in silence. Nurse gave him up. She could make nothing of him. Anyhow, he was growing beyond her.

One day his mother and his Uncle Oscar came in when he was on one of his furious rides. He did not speak to them.

"Hallo, you young jockey! Riding a winner?" said his uncle.

"Aren't you growing too big for a rocking-horse? You're not a very little boy any longer, you know," said his mother.

But Paul only gave a blue glare from his big, rather close-set eyes. He would speak to nobody when he was in full tilt. His mother watched him with an anxious expression on her face.

At last he suddenly stopped racing his horse into the mechanical gallop and slid down.

"Well, I got there!" he announced fiercely, his blue-eyes still flaring, and his sturdy long legs straddling apart.

"Where did you get to?" asked his mother.

"Where I wanted to go," he flared back at her.

"That's right, son!" said Uncle Oscar. "Don't you stop till you get there. What's the horse's name?"

"He doesn't have a name," said the boy.

"Gets on without all right?" asked the uncle.

"Well, he has different names. He was called Sansovino last week."

"Sansovino, eh? Won the Ascot. How did you know this name?"

"He always talks about horse-races with Bassett," said Joan.

The uncle was delighted to find that his small nephew was posted with all the racing news. Bassett, the young gardener, who had been wounded in the left foot in the war and had got his present job through Oscar Cresswell, whose batman he had been, was a perfect blade of the "turf." He lived in the racing events, and the small boy lived with him.

Oscar Cresswell got it all from Bassett.

"Master Paul comes and asks me, so I can't do more than tell him, sir," said Bassett, his face terribly serious, as if he were speaking of religious matters.

"And does he ever put anything on a horse he fancies?"

"Well—I don't want to give him away—he's a young sport, a fine sport, sir. Would you mind asking him himself? He sort of takes a pleasure in it, and perhaps he'd feel I was giving him away, sir, if you don't mind."

Bassett was serious as a church.

The uncle went back to his nephew and took him off for a ride in the car.

"Say, Paul, old man, do you ever put anything on a horse?" the uncle asked.

The boy watched the handsome man closely.

"Why, do you think I oughtn't to?" he parried.

"Not a bit of it! I thought perhaps you might give me a tip for the Lincoln."

"The car sped on into the country, going down to Uncle Oscar's place in Hampshire.

"Honour bright?" said the nephew.

"Honour bright, son!" said the uncle.

"Well, then, Daffodil."

"Daffodil! I doubt it, sonny. What about Mirza?"

"I only know the winner," said the boy. "That's Daffodil."

"Daffodil, eh?"

There was a pause. Daffodil was an obscure horse comparatively.

"Uncle!"

"Yes, son?"

"You won't let it go any further, will you? I promised Bassett."

"Bassett be damned, old man! What's he got to do with it?"

"We're partners. We've been partners from the first. Uncle, he lent me my first five shillings, which I lost. I promised him, honour bright, it was only between me and him; only you gave me that ten-shilling note I started winning with, so I thought you were lucky. You won't let it go any further, will you?"

The boy gazed at his uncle from those big, hot, blue eyes, set rather close together. The uncle stirred and laughed uneasily.

"Right you are, son! I'll keep your tip private. Daffodil, eh? How much are you putting on him?"

"All except twenty pounds," said the boy. "I keep that in reserve."

The uncle thought it a good joke.

"You keep twenty pounds in reserve, do you, you young romancer? What are you betting, then?"

"I'm betting three hundred," said the boy gravely. "But it's between you and me, Uncle Oscar! Honour bright?"

The uncle burst into a roar of laughter.

"It's between you and me all right, you young Nat Gould," he said laughing. "But where's your three hundred?"

"Bassett keeps it for me. We're partners."

"You are, are you! And what is Bassett putting on Daffodil?"

"He won't go quite as high as I do, I expect. Perhaps he'll go a hundred and fifty."

"What, pennies?" laughed the uncle.

"Pounds," said the child, with a surprised look at his uncle. "Bassett keeps a bigger reserve than I do."

160

Between wonder and amusement Uncle Oscar was silent. He pursued the matter no further, but he determined to take his nephew with him to the Lincoln races.

"Now, son," he said, "I'm putting twenty on Mirza, and I'll put five on for you on any horse you fancy. What's your pick?"

"Daffodil, uncle."

"No, not the fiver on Daffodil!"

"I should if it was my own fiver," said the child.

"Good! Good! Right you are! A fiver for me and a fiver for you on Daffodil."

The child had never been to a race-meeting before, and his eyes were blue fire. He pursed his mouth tight and watched. A Frenchman just in front had put his money on Lancelot. Wild with excitement, he flayed his arms up and down, yelling, *"Lancelot! Lancelot!"* in his French accent.

Daffodil came in first, Lancelot second, Mirza third. The child, flushed and with eyes blazing, was curiously serene. His uncle brought him four five-pound notes, four to one.

"What am I do with these?" he cried, waving them before the boy's eyes.

"I suppose we'll talk to Bassett," said the boy. "I expect I have fifteen hundred by now; and twenty in reserve; and this twenty."

His uncle studied him for some moments.

"Look here, son!" he said. "You're not serious about Bassett and that fifteen hundred, are you?"

"Yes, I am. But it's between you and me, uncle. Honour bright?"

"Honour bright all right, son! But I must talk to Bassett."

"If you'd like to be a partner, uncle, with Bassett and me, we could all be partners. Only, you'd have to promise, honour bright, uncle, not to let it go beyond us three. Bassett and I are lucky, and you must be lucky, because it was your ten shillings I started winning with. . . ."

Uncle Oscar took both Bassett and Paul into Richmond Park for an afternoon, and there they talked.

"It's like this, you see, sir," Bassett said. "Master Paul would get me talking about racing events, spinning yarns, you know, sir. And he was always keen on knowing if I'd made or if I'd lost. It's about a year since, now, that I put five shillings on Blush of Dawn for him: and we lost. Then the luck turned, with that ten shillings he had from you: that we put on Singhalese. And since that time, it's been pretty steady, all things considering. What do you say, Master Paul?"

"We're all right when we're sure," said Paul. "It's when we're not quite sure that we go down."

"Oh, but we're careful then," said Bassett.

"But when are you *sure?*" smiled Uncle Oscar.

"It's Master Paul, sir," said Bassett in a secret, religious voice. "It's as if he had it from heaven. Like Daffodil, now, for the Lincoln. That was as sure as eggs."

"Did you put anything on Daffodil?" asked Oscar Cresswell.

"Yes, sir. I made my bit."

"And my nephew?"

Bassett was obstinately silent, looking at Paul.

"I made twelve hundred, didn't I, Bassett? I told uncle I was putting three hundred on Daffodil."

"That's right," said Bassett, nodding.

"But where's the money?" asked the uncle.

"I keep it safe locked up, sir. Master Paul he can have it any minute he likes to ask for it."

"What, fifteen hundred pounds?"

"And twenty! And *forty,* that is, with the twenty he made on the course."

"It's amazing!" said the uncle.

"If Master Paul offers you to be partners, sir, I would, if I were you: if you'll excuse me," said Bassett.

Oscar Cresswell thought about it.

"I'll see the money," he said.

They drove home again, and, sure enough, Bassett came round to the garden-house with fifteen hundred pounds in notes. The twenty pounds reserve was left with Joe Glee, in the Turf Commission deposit.

"You see, it's all right, uncle, when I'm *sure!* Then we go strong, for all we're worth. Don't we, Bassett?"

"We do that, Master Paul."

"And when are you sure?" said the uncle, laughing.

"Oh, well, sometimes I'm *absolutely* sure, like about Daffodil," said the boy; "and sometimes I have an idea; and sometimes I haven't even an idea, have I, Bassett? Then we're careful, because we mostly go down."

"You do, do you! And when you're sure, like about Daffodil, what makes you sure, sonny?"

"Oh, well, I don't know," said the boy uneasily. "I'm sure, you know, uncle; that's all."

"It's as if he had it from heaven, sir," Bassett reiterated.

"I should say so!" said the uncle.

But he became a partner. And when the Leger was coming on Paul was "sure" about Lively Spark, which was a quite inconsiderable horse. The boy insisted on putting a thousand on the horse, Bassett was for five hundred, and Oscar Cresswell two hundred. Lively Spark came in first, and the betting had been ten to one against him. Paul had made ten thousand.

"You see," he said, "I was absolutely sure of him."

Even Oscar Cresswell had cleared two thousand.

"Look here, son," he said, "this sort of thing makes me nervous."

"It needn't, uncle! Perhaps I shan't be sure again for a long time."

"But what are you going to do with your money?" asked the uncle.

"Of course," said the boy, "I started it for mother. She said she had no luck, because father is unlucky, so I thought if *I* was lucky, it might stop whispering."

"What might stop whispering?"

"Our house. I *hate* our house for whispering."

"'What does it whisper?"

"Why—why"—the boy fidgeted—"why, I don't know. But it's always short of money, you know, uncle."

"I know it, son, I know it."

"You know people send mother writs, don't you, uncle?"

"I'm afraid I do," said the uncle.

"And then the house whispers, like people laughing at you behind your back. It's awful, that is! I thought if I was lucky——"

"You might stop it," added the uncle.

The boy watched him with big blue eyes, that had an uncanny cold fire in them, and he said never a word.

"Well, then!" said the uncle. "What are we doing?"

"I shouldn't like mother to know I was lucky," said the boy.

"Why not, son?"

"She'd stop me."

"I don't think she would."

"Oh!"—and the boy writhed in an odd way—"I *don't* want her to know, uncle."

"All right, son! We'll manage it without her knowing."

They managed it very easily. Paul, at the other's suggestion, handed over five thousand pounds to his uncle, who deposited it with the family lawyer, who was then to inform Paul's mother that a relative had put five thousand pounds into his hands, which sum was to be paid out a thousand pounds at a time, on the mother's birthday, for the next five years.

"So she'll have a birthday present of a thousand pounds for five successive years," said Uncle Oscar. "I hope it won't make it all the harder for her later."

Paul's mother had her birthday in November. The house had been "whispering" worse than ever lately, and, even in spite of his luck, Paul could not bear up against it. He was very anxious to see the effect of the birthday letter, telling his mother about the thousand pounds.

When there were no visitors, Paul now took his meals with his parents, as he was beyond the nursery control. His mother went into town nearly every day. She had discovered that she had an odd knack of sketching furs and dress materials, so she worked secretly in the studio of a friend who was the chief "artist" for the leading drapers. She drew the figures of ladies in furs and ladies in silk and sequins for the newspaper advertisements. This young woman artist earned several thousand pounds a year, but Paul's mother only made several hundreds, and she was again dissatisfied. She so wanted to be first in something, and she did not succeed, even in making sketches for drapery advertisements.

She was down to breakfast on the morning of her birthday. Paul watched her face as she read her letters. He knew the lawyer's letter. As his mother read it, her face hardened and became more expressionless. Then a cold, determined look came on her mouth. She hid the letter under the pile of others, and said not a word about it.

"Didn't you have anything nice in the post for your birthday, mother?" said Paul.

"Quite moderately nice," she said, her voice cold and absent.

She went away to town without saying more.

But in the afternoon Uncle Oscar appeared. He said Paul's mother had had a long interview with the lawyer, asking if the whole five thousand could not be advanced at once, as she was in debt.

"What do you think, uncle?" said the boy.

"I leave it to you, son."

"Oh, let her have it, then! We can get some more with the other," said the boy.

"A bird in the hand is worth two in the bush, laddie!" said Uncle Oscar.

"But I'm sure to *know* for the Grand National; or the Lincolnshire; or else the Derby. I'm sure to know for *one* of them," said Paul.

So Uncle Oscar signed the agreement, and Paul's mother touched the whole five thousand. Then something very curious happened. The voices in the house suddenly went mad, like a chorus of frogs on a spring evening. There were certain new furnishings, and Paul had a tutor. He was *really* going to Eton, his father's school, in the following autumn. There were flowers in the winter, and a blossoming of the luxury Paul's mother had been used to. And yet the voices in the house, behind the sprays of mimosa and almondblossom, and from under the piles of iridescent cushions, simply trilled and screamed in a sort of ecstasy: "There *must* be more money! Oh-h-h; there *must* be more money. Oh, now, now-w! Now-w-w—there *must* be more money!—more than ever! More than ever!"

It frightened Paul terribly. He studied away at his Latin and Greek with his tutor. But his intense hours were spent with Bassett. The Grand National had gone by: he had not "known," and had lost a hundred pounds. Summer was at hand. He was in agony for the Lincoln. But even for the Lincoln he didn't "know," and he lost fifty pounds. He became wild-eyed and strange, as if something were going to explode in him.

"Let it alone, son! Don't you bother about it!" urged Uncle Oscar. But it was as if the boy couldn't really hear what his uncle was saying.

"I've got to know for the Derby! I've got to know for the Derby!" the child reiterated, his big blue eyes blazing with a sort of madness.

His mother noticed how overwrought he was.

"You'd better go to the seaside. Wouldn't you like to go now to the seaside, instead of waiting? I think you'd better," she said, looking down at him anxiously, her heart curiously heavy because of him.

But the child lifted his uncanny blue eyes.

"I couldn't possibly go before the Derby, mother!" he said. 'I couldn't possibly."

"Why not?" she said, her voice becoming heavy when she was opposed. "Why not? You can still go from the seaside to see the Derby with your Uncle Oscar, if that's what you wish. No need for you to wait here. Besides, I think you care too much about these races. It's a bad sign. My family has been a gambling family, and you won't know till you grow up how much damage it has done. But it has done damage. I shall have to send Bassett away, and ask Uncle Oscar not to talk racing to you, unless you promise to be reasonable about it: go away to the seaside and forget it. You're all nerves!"

"I'll do what you like, mother, so long as you don't send me away till after the Derby," the boy said.

"Send you away from where? Just from this house?"

"Yes," he said, gazing at her.

"Why, you curious child, what makes you care about this house so much, suddenly? I never knew you loved it."

He gazed at her without speaking. He had a secret within a secret, something he had not divulged, even to Bassett or to his Uncle Oscar.

But his mother, after standing undecided and a little bit sullen for some moments, said:

"Very well, then! Don't go to the seaside till after the Derby, if you don't wish it. But promise me you won't let your nerves go to pieces. Promise you won't think so much about horse-racing and *events,* as you call them!"

"Oh no," said the boy casually. "I won't think much about them, mother. You needn't worry. I wouldn't worry, mother, if I were you."

"If you were me and I were you," said his mother,"I wonder what we *should* do!"

"But you know you needn't worry, mother, don't you?" the boy repeated.

"I should be awfully glad to know it," she said wearily.

"Oh, well, you *can,* you know. I mean, you *ought* to know you needn't worry," he insisted.

"Ought I? Then I'll see about it," she said.

Paul's secret of secrets was his wooden horse, that which had no name. Since he was emancipated from a nurse and a nursery-governess, he had had his rocking-horse removed to his own bedroom at the top of the house.

"Surely you're too big for a rocking-horse!" his mother had remonstrated.

"Well, you see, mother, till I can have a *real* horse, I like to have *some* sort of animal about," had been his quaint answer.

"Do you feel he keeps you company?" she laughed.

"Oh yes! He's very good, he always keeps me company, when I'm there," said Paul.

So the horse, rather shabby, stood in an arrested prance in the boy's bedroom.

The Derby was drawing near, and the boy grew more and more tense. He hardly heard what was spoken to him, he was very frail, and his eyes were really uncanny. His mother had sudden strange seizures of uneasiness about him. Sometimes, for half an hour, she would feel a sudden anxiety about him that was almost anguish. She wanted to rush to him at once, and know he was safe.

Two nights before the Derby, she was at a big party in town, when one of her rushes of anxiety about her boy, her first-born, gripped her heart till she could hardly speak. She fought with the feeling, might and main, for she believed in common sense. But it was too strong. She had to leave the dance and go downstairs to telephone to the country. The children's nursery-governess was terribly surprised and startled at being rung up in the night.

"Are the children all right, Miss Wilmot?"

"Oh yes, they are quite all right."

"Master Paul? Is he all right?"

"He went to bed as right as a trivet. Shall I run up and look at him?"

"No," said Paul's mother reluctantly. "No! Don't trouble. It's all right. Don't sit up. We shall be home fairly soon." She did not want her son's privacy intruded upon.

"Very good," said the governess.

It was about one o'clock when Paul's mother and father drove up to their house. All was still. Paul's mother went to her room and slipped off her white fur cloak. She had told her maid not to wait up for her. She heard her husband downstairs, mixing a whisky and soda.

And then, because of the strange anxiety at her heart, she stole upstairs to her son's room. Noiselessly she went along the upper corridor. Was there a faint noise? What was it?

She stood, with arrested muscles, outside his door, listening. There was a strange, heavy, and yet not loud noise. Her heart stood still. It was a soundless noise, yet rushing and powerful. Something huge, in violent, hushed motion. What was it? What in God's name was it? She ought to know. She felt that she knew the noise. She knew what it was.

Yet she could not place it. She couldn't say what it was. And on and on it went, like a madness.

Softly, frozen with anxiety and fear, she turned the doorhandle.

The room was dark. Yet in the space near the window, she heard and saw something plunging to and fro. She gazed in fear and amazement.

Then suddenly she switched on the light, and saw her son, in his green pyjamas, madly surging on the rocking-horse. The blaze of light suddenly lit him up, as he urged the wooden horse, and lit her up, as she stood, blonde, in her dress of pale green and crystal, in the doorway.

"Paul!" she cried "Whatever are you doing?"

"It's Malabar!" he screamed in a powerful, strange voice. "It's Malabar!"

His eyes blazed at her for one strange and senseless second, as he ceased urging his wooden horse. Then he fell with a crash to the ground, and she, all her tormented motherhood flooding upon her, rushed to gather him up.

But he was unconscious, and unconscious he remained, with some brain-fever. He talked and tossed, and his mother sat stonily by his side.

"Malabar! It's Malabar! Bassett, Bassett, I *know*! It's Malabar!"

So the child cried, trying to get up and urge the rocking-horse that gave him his inspiration.

"What does he mean by Malabar?" asked the heart-frozen mother.

"I don't know," said the father stonily.

"What does he mean by Malabar?" she asked her brother Oscar.

"It's one of the horses running for the Derby," was the answer.

And, in spite of himself, Oscar Cresswell spoke to Bassett, and himself put a thousand on Malabar: at fourteen to one.

The third day of the illness was critical: they were waiting for a change. The boy, with his rather long, curly hair, was tossing ceaselessly on the pillow. He neither slept nor regained consciousness, and his eyes were like blue stones. His mother sat, feeling her heart had gone, turned actually into a stone.

In the evening, Oscar Cresswell did not come, but Bassett sent a message, saying could he come up for one moment, just one moment? Paul's mother was very angry at the intrusion, but on second thoughts she agreed. The boy was the same. Perhaps Bassett might bring him to consciousness.

The gardener, a shortish fellow with a little brown moustache and sharp little brown eyes, tiptoed into the room, touched his imaginary cap to Paul's mother, and stole to the bedside, staring with glittering, smallish eyes at the tossing, dying child.

"Master Paul!" he whispered. "Master Paul! Malabar came in first all right, a clean win. I did as you told me. You've made over seventy thousand pounds, you have; you've got over eighty thousand. Malabar came in all right, Master Paul."

"Malabar! Malabar! Did I say Malabar, mother? Did I say Malabar? Do you think I'm lucky, mother? I knew Malabar, didn't I? Over eighty thousand pounds! I call that lucky, don't you, mother? Over eighty thousands pounds! I knew, didn't I know I knew? Malabar came in all right. If I ride my horse till I'm sure, then I tell you, Bassett, you can go as high as you like. Did you go for all you were worth, Bassett?"

"I went a thousand on it, Master Paul."

"I never told you, mother, that if I can ride my horse, and *get there,* then I'm absolutely sure—oh, absolutely! Mother, did I ever tell you? I *am* lucky!"

"No, you never did," said his mother.

But the boy died in the night.

And even as he lay dead, his mother heard her brother's voice saying to her: "My God, Hester, you're eighty-odd thousand to the good, and a poor devil of a son to the bad. But, poor devil, poor devil, he's best gone out of a life where he rides his rocking-horse to find a winner."

Herman Melville

BARTLEBY THE SCRIVENER: A STORY OF WALL STREET

I am a rather elderly man. The nature of my avocations, for the last thirty years, has brought me into more than ordinary contact with what would seem an interesting and somewhat singular set of men, of whom, as yet, nothing, that I know of, has ever been written—I mean, the law-copyists, or scriveners. I have known very many of them, professionally and privately, and, if I pleased, could relate divers histories, at which good-natured gentlemen might smile, and sentimental souls might weep. But I waive the biographies of all other scriveners, for a few passages in the life of Bartleby, who was a scrivener, the strangest I ever saw, or heard of. While, of other law-copyists, I might write the complete life, of Bartleby nothing of that sort can be done. I believe that no materials exist for a full and satisfactory biography of this man. It is an irreparable loss to literature. Bartleby was one of those beings of whom nothing is ascertainable, except from the original sources, and, in his case, those are very small. What my own astonished eyes saw of Bartleby, *that* is all I know of him, except, indeed, one vague report, which will appear in the sequel.

Ere introducing the scrivener, as he first appeared to me, it is fit I make some mention of myself, my employees, my business, my chambers, and general surroundings; because some such description is indispensable to an adequate understanding of the chief character about to be presented. Imprimis: I am a man who, from his youth upwards, has been filled with a profound conviction that the easiest way of life is the best. Hence, though I belong to a profession proverbially energetic and nervous, even to turbulence, at times, yet nothing of that sort have I ever suffered to invade my peace. I am one of those unambitious lawyers who never addresses a jury, or in any way draws down public applause; but, in the cool tranquillity of a snug retreat, do a snug business among rich men's bonds, and mortgages, and title-deeds. All who know me, consider me an eminently *safe* man. The late John Jacob Astor, a personage little given to poetic enthusiasm, had no hesitation in pronouncing my first grand point to be prudence; my next, method. I do not speak it in vanity, but simply record the fact, that I was not unemployed in my profession by the late John Jacob Astor; a name which, I admit, I love to repeat; for it hath a rounded and orbicular sound to it, and rings like unto bullion. I will freely add, that I was not insensible to the late John Jacob Astor's good opinion.

Some time prior to the period at which this little history begins, my avocations had been largely increased. The good old office, now extinct in the State of New York, of a Master in Chancery, had been conferred upon me. It was not a very arduous office, but very pleasantly remunerative. I seldom lose my temper; much more seldom indulge in dangerous indignation at wrongs and outrages; but, I must be permitted to be rash here, and declare that I consider the sudden and violent abrogation of the office of Master in Chancery, by the new Constitution, as a —premature act; inasmuch as I had counted upon a life-lease of the profits, whereas I only received those of a few short years. But this is by the way.

My chambers were up stairs, at No.——Wall Street. At one end, they looked upon the white wall of the interior of a spacious sky-light shaft, penetrating the building from top to bottom.

This view might have been considered rather tame than otherwise, deficient in what landscape painters call "life." But, if so, the view from the other end of my chambers offered, at least, a contrast, if nothing more. In that direction, my windows commanded an unobstructed view of a lofty brick wall, black by age and everlasting shade; which wall required no spyglass to bring out its lurking beauties, but, for the benefit of all near-sighted spectators, was pushed up to within ten feet of my window panes. Owing to the great height of the surrounding buildings, and my chambers being on the second floor, the interval between this wall and mine not a little resembled a huge square cistern.

At the period just preceding the advent of Bartleby, I had two persons as copyists in my employment, and a promising lad as an office-boy. First, Turkey; second, Nippers; third, Ginger Nut. These may seem names, the like of which are not usually found in the Directory. In truth, they were nicknames, mutually conferred upon each other by my three clerks, and were deemed expressive of their respective persons or characters. Turkey was a short, pursy Englishman, of about my own age—that is, somewhere not far from sixty. In the morning, one might say, his face was of a fine florid hue, but after twelve o'clock, meridian—his dinner hour—it blazed like a grate full of Christmas coals; and continued blazing—but, as it were, with a gradual wane—till six o'clock P.M., or thereabouts; after which, I saw no more of the proprietor of the face, which, gaining its meridian with the sun, seemed to set with it, to rise, culminate, and decline the following day, with the like regularity and undiminished glory. There are many singular coincidences I have known in the course of my life, not the least among which was the fact, that, exactly when Turkey displayed his fullest beams from his red and radiant countenance, just then, too, at that critical moment, began the daily period when I considered his business capacities as seriously disturbed for the remainder of the twenty-four hours. Not that he was absolutely idle, or averse to business, then; far from it. The difficulty was, he was apt to be altogether too energetic. There was a strange, inflamed, flurried, flighty recklessness of activity about him. He would be incautious in dipping his pen into his inkstand. All his blots upon my documents were dropped there after twelve o'clock meridian. Indeed, not only would he be reckless, and sadly given to making blots in the afternoon, but, some days, he went further, and was rather noisy. At such times, too, his face flamed with augmented blazonry, as if cannel coal had been heaped on anthracite. He made an unpleasant racket with his chair; spilled his sand-box; in mending his pens, impatiently split them all to pieces, and threw them on the floor in a sudden passion; stood up, and leaned over his table, boxing his papers about in a most indecorous manner, very sad to behold in an elderly man like him. Nevertheless, as he was in many ways a most valuable person to me, and all the time before twelve o'clock meridian, was the quickest, steadiest creature, too, accomplishing a great deal of work in a style not easily to be matched—for these reasons, I was willing to overlook his eccentricities, though, indeed, occasionally, I remonstrated with him. I did this very gently, however, because, though the civilest, nay, the blandest and most reverential of men in the morning, yet, in the afternoon, he was disposed, upon provocation, to be slightly rash with his tongue—in fact, insolent. Now, valuing his morning services as I did, and resolved not to lose them—yet, at the same time, made uncomfortable by his inflamed ways after twelve o'clock—and being a man of peace, unwilling by my admonitions to call forth unseemly retorts from him, I took upon me, one Saturday noon (he was always worse on Saturdays) to hint to him, very kindly, that, perhaps, now that he was growing old, it might be well to abridge in his labors; in short, he need not come to my chambers after twelve o'clock, but, dinner over, had best go home to his lodgings, and rest himself till tea-time. But no; he insisted upon his afternoon devotions. His countenance became intolerably fervid, as he oratorically assured me—gesticulating with a long ruler at the other end of the room—that if his services in the morning were useful, how indispensable, then, in the afternoon?

"With submission, sir," said Turkey, on this occasion, "I consider myself your right-hand man. In the morning I but marshal and deploy my columns; but in the afternoon I put myself at their head, and gallantly charge the foe, thus"—and he made a violent thrust with the ruler.

"But the blots, Turkey," intimated I.

"True; but, with submission, sir, behold these hairs! I am getting old. Surely, sir, a blot or two of a warm afternoon is not to be severely urged against gray hairs. Old age—even if it blot the page—is honorable. With submission, sir, we *both* are getting old."

This appeal to my fellow-feeling was hardly to be resisted. At all events, I saw that go he would not. So, I made up my mind to let him stay, resolving, nevertheless, to see to it that, during the afternoon, he had to do with my less important papers.

Nippers, the second on my list, was a whiskered, sallow, and upon the whole, rather piratical-looking young man, of about five and twenty. I always deemed him the victim of two evil powers—ambition and indigestion. The ambition was evinced by a certain impatience of the duties of a mere copyist, an unwarrantable usurpation of strictly professional affairs, such as the original drawing up of legal documents. The indigestion seemed betokened in an occasional nervous testiness and grinning irritability, causing the teeth to audibly grind together over mistakes committed in copying; unnecessary maledictions, hissed, rather than spoken, in the heat of business; and especially by a continual discontent with the height of the table where he worked. Though of a very ingenious, mechanical turn, Nippers could never get his table to suit him. He put chips under it, blocks of various sorts, bits of pasteboard, and at last went so far as to attempt an exquisite adjustment, by final pieces of folded blotting-paper. But no invention would answer. If, for the sake of easing his back, he brought the table lid at a sharp angle well up towards his chin, and wrote there like a man using the steep roof of a Dutch house for his desk, then he declared that it stopped the circulation in his arms. If now he lowered the table to his waistbands, and stooped over it in writing, then there was a sore aching in his back. In short, the truth of the matter was, Nippers knew not what he wanted. Or, if he wanted anything, it was to be rid of a scrivener's table altogether. Among the manifestations of his diseased ambition was a fondness he had for receiving visits from certain ambiguous-looking fellows in seedy coats, whom he called his clients. Indeed, I was aware that not only was he, at times, considerable of a ward-politician, but he occasionally did a little business at the Justices' courts, and was not unknown on the steps of the Tombs. I have good reason to believe, however, that one individual who called upon him at my chambers, and who, with a grand air, he insisted was his client, was no other than a dun, and the alleged title-deed, a bill. But, with all his failings, and the annoyances he caused me, Nippers, like his compatriot Turkey, was a very useful man to me; wrote a neat, swift hand; and, when he chose, was not deficient in a gentlemanly sort of deportment. Added to this, he always dressed in a gentlemanly sort of way; and so, incidentally, reflected credit upon my chambers. Whereas, with respect to Turkey, I had much ado to keep him from being a reproach to me. His clothes were apt to look oily, and smell of eating-houses. He wore his pantaloons very loose and baggy in summer. His coats were execrable; his hat not be handled. But while the hat was a thing of indifference to me, inasmuch as his natural civility and deference, as a dependent Englishman, always led him to doff it the moment he entered the room, yet his coat was another matter. Concerning his coats, I reasoned with him; but with no effect.

The truth was, I suppose, that a man with so small an income could not afford to sport such a lustrous face and a lustrous coat at one and the same time. As Nippers once observed, Turkey's money went chiefly for red ink. One winter day, I presented Turkey with a highly respectable-looking coat of my own—a padded gray coat, of a most comfortable warmth, and which buttoned straight up from the knee to the neck. I thought Turkey would appreciate the favor, and abate his rashness and obstreperousness of afternoons. But no; I verily believe that buttoning himself up in so downy and blanket-like a coat had a pernicious effect upon him—upon the same principle that too much oats are bad for horses. In fact, precisely as a rash, restive horse is said to feel his oats, so Turkey felt his coat. It made him insolent. He was a man whom prosperity harmed.

Though, concerning the self-indulgent habits of Turkey, I had my own private surmises, yet, touching Nippers, I was well persuaded that, whatever might be his faults in other respects, he was, at least, a temperate young man. But, indeed, nature herself seemed to have been his vintner, and, at his birth, charged him so thoroughly with an irritable, brandy-like disposition, that all subsequent potations were needless. When I consider how, amid the stillness of my chambers, Nippers would sometimes impatiently rise from his seat, and stopping over his table, spread his arms wide apart, seize the whole desk, and move it, and jerk it, with a grim, grinding motion on the floor, as if the table were a perverse voluntary agent and vexing him, I plainly perceive that, for Nippers, brandy-and-water were altogether superfluous.

It was fortunate for me that, owing to its peculiar cause—indigestion—the irritability and consequent nervousness of Nippers were mainly observable in the morning, while in the afternoon he was comparatively mild. So that, Turkey's paroxysms only coming on about twelve o'clock, I never had to do with their eccentricities at one time. Their fits relieved each other, like guards. When Nippers's was on, Turkey's was off; and *vice versa*. This was a good natural arrangement, under the circumstances.

Ginger Nut, the third on my list, was a lad, some twelve years old. His father was a car-man, ambitious of seeing his son on the bench instead of a cart, before he died. So he sent him to my office, as a student at law, errand-boy, cleaner and sweeper, at the rate of one dollar a week. He had a little desk to himself; but he did not use it much. Upon inspection, the drawer exhibited a great array of shells of various sorts of nuts. Indeed, to this quick-witted youth, the whole noble science of the law was contained in a nutshell. Not the least among the employments of Ginger Nut, as well as one which he discharged with the most alacrity, was his duty as cake and apple purveyor for Turkey and Nippers. Copying law-papers being proverbially a dry, husky sort of business, my two scriveners were fain to moisten their mouths very often with Spitzenbergs, to be had at the numerous stalls nigh the Custom House and Post Office. Also, they sent Ginger Nut very frequently for that peculiar cake—small, flat, round, and very spicy—after which he had been named by them. Of a cold morning, when business was but dull, Turkey would gobble up scores of these cakes, as if they were mere wafers—indeed, they did sell them at the rate of six or eight for a penny—the scrape of his pen blending with the crunching of the crisp particles in his mouth. Rashest of all the fiery afternoon blunders and flurried rashnesses of Turkey, was his once moistening a ginger-cake between his lips, and clapping it on to a mortgage, for a seal. I came within an ace of dismissing him then. But he mollified me by making an oriental bow, and saying—

"With submission, sir, it was generous of me to find you in stationery on my own account."

Now my original business—that of a conveyancer and title hunter, and drawer-up of recondite documents of all sorts—was considerably increased by receiving the master's office. There was now great work for scriveners. Not only must I push the clerks already with me, but I must have additional help.

In answer to my advertisement, a motionless young man one morning stood upon my office threshold, the door being open, for it was summer. I can see that figure now—pallidly neat, pitiably respectable, incurably forlorn! It was Bartleby.

After a few words touching his qualifications, I engaged him, glad to have among my corps of copyists a man of so singularly sedate an aspect, which I thought might operate beneficially upon the flighty temper of Turkey, and the fiery one of Nippers.

I should have stated before that ground glass folding-doors divided my premises into two parts, one of which was occupied by my scriveners, the other by myself. According to my humor, I threw open these doors, or closed them. I resolved to assign Bartleby a corner by the folding-doors, but on my side of them, so as to have this quiet man within easy call, in case any trifling thing was to be done. I placed his desk close up to a small side-window in that part of the room, a window which originally had afforded a lateral view of certain grimy backyards and bricks, but which, owing to subsequent erections, commanded at present no view at all, though it gave some light. Within three feet of the panes was a wall, and the light came down from far above, between two lofty buildings, as from a very small opening in a dome. Still further to a satisfactory arrangement, I procured a high green folding screen, which might entirely isolate Bartleby from my sight, though not remove him from my voice. And thus, in a manner, privacy and society were conjoined.

At first, Bartleby did an extraordinary quantity of writing. As if long famishing for something to copy, he seemed to gorge himself on my documents. There was no pause for digestion. He ran a day and night line, copying by sun-light and by candle-light. I should have been quite delighted with his application, had he been cheerfully industrious. But he wrote on silently, palely, mechanically.

It is, of course, an indispensable part of a scrivener's business to verify the accuracy of his copy, word by word. Where there are two or more scriveners in an office, they assist each other in this examination, one reading from the copy, the other holding the original. It is a very dull, wearisome, and lethargic affair. I can readily imagine that, to some sanguine temperaments, it would be altogether intolerable. For example, I cannot credit that the mettlesome poet, Byron, would have contentedly sat down with Bartleby to examine a law document of, say five hundred pages, closely written in a crimpy hand.

Now and then, in the haste of business, it had been my habit to assist in comparing some brief document myself, calling Turkey or Nippers for this purpose. One object I had, in placing Bartleby so handy to me behind the screen, was to avail myself of his services on such trivial occasions. It was on the third day, I think, of his being with me, and before any necessity had arisen for having his own writing examined, that, being much hurried to complete a small affair I had in hand, I abruptly called to Bartleby. In my haste and natural expectancy of instant compliance, I sat with my head bent over the original on my desk, and my right hand sideways, and somewhat nervously extended with the copy, so that, immediately upon emerging from his retreat, Bartleby might snatch it and proceed to business without the least delay.

In this very attitude did I sit when I called to him, rapidly stating what it was I wanted him to do—namely, to examine a small paper with me. Imagine my surprise, nay, my consternation, when, without moving from his privacy, Bartleby, in a singularly mild, firm voice, replied, "I would prefer not to."

I sat awhile in perfect silence, rallying my stunned faculties. Immediately it occurred to me that my ears had deceived me, or Bartleby had entirely misunderstood my meaning. I repeated my request in the clearest tone I could assume; but in quite as clear a one came the previous reply, "I would prefer not to."

"Prefer not to," echoed I, rising in high excitement, and crossing the room with a stride. "What do you mean? Are you moon-struck? I want you to help me compare this sheet here—take it," and I thrust it towards him.

"I would prefer not to," said he.

I looked at him steadfastly. His face was leanly composed; his gray eyes dimly calm. Not a wrinkle of agitation rippled him. Had there been the least uneasiness, anger, impatience, or impertinence in his manner; in other words, had there been any thing ordinarily human about him, doubtless I should have violently dismissed him from the premises. But as it was, I should have as soon thought of turning my pale plaster-of-paris bust of Cicero out of doors. I stood gazing at him awhile, as he went on with his own writing, and then reseated myself at my desk. This is very strange, thought I. What had one best do? But my business hurried me. I concluded to forget the matter for the present, reserving it for my future leisure. So calling Nippers from the other room, the paper was speedily examined.

A few days after this, Bartleby concluded four lengthy documents, being quadruplicates of a week's testimony taken before me in my High Court of Chancery. It became necessary to examine them. It was an important suit, and great accuracy was imperative. Having all things arranged, I called Turkey, Nippers, and Ginger Nut from the next room, meaning to place the four copies in the hands of my four clerks, while I should read from the original. Accordingly, Turkey, Nippers, and Ginger Nut had taken their seats in a row, each with his document in his hand, when I called to Bartleby to join this interesting group.

"Bartleby! quick, I am waiting."

I heard a slow scrape of his chair legs on the uncarpeted floor, and soon he appeared standing at the entrance of his hermitage.

"What is wanted?" said he, mildly.

"The copies, the copies," said I, hurriedly. "We are going to examine them. There—" and I held towards him the fourth quadruplicate.

"I would prefer not to," he said, and gently disappeared behind the screen.

For a few moments I was turned into a pillar of salt, standing at the head of my seated column of clerks. Recovering myself, I advanced towards the screen, and demanded the reason for such extraordinary conduct.

"*Why* do you refuse?"

"I would prefer not to."

With any other man I should have flown outright into a dreadful passion, scorned all further words, and thrust him ignominiously from my presence. But there was something about Bartleby that not only strangely disarmed me, but in a wonderful manner, touched and disconcerted me. I began to reason with him.

"These are your own copies we are about to examine. It is labor saving to you, because one examination will answer for your four papers. It is common usage. Every copyist is bound to help examine his copy. Is it not so? Will you not speak? Answer!"

"I prefer not to," he replied in a flutelike tone. It seemed to me that, while I had been addressing him, he carefully revolved every statement that I made; fully comprehended the meaning; could not gainsay the irresistible conclusion; but, at the same time, some paramount consideration prevailed with him to reply as he did.

"You are decided, then, not to comply with my request—a request made according to common usage and common sense?"

He briefly gave me to understand, that on that point my judgment was sound. Yes: his decision was irreversible.

It is not seldom the case that, when a man is browbeaten in some unprecedented and violently unreasonable way, he begins to stagger in his own plainest faith. He begins, as it were, vaguely to surmise that, wonderful as it may be, all the justice and all the reason is on the other side. Accordingly, if any disinterested persons are present, he turns to them for some reinforcement of his own faltering mind.

"Turkey," said I, "what do you think of this? Am I not right?"

"With submission, sir," said Turkey, in his blandest tone, "I think that you are."

"Nippers," said I, "what do *you* think of it?"

"I think I should kick him out of the office."

(The reader, of nice perceptions, will here perceive that, it being morning, Turkey's answer is couched in polite and tranquil terms, but Nippers replies in ill-tempered ones. Or, to repeat a previous sentence, Nippers's ugly mood was on duty, and Turkey's off.)

"Ginger Nut," said I, willing to enlist the smallest suffrage in my behalf, "what do *you* think of it?"

"I think, sir, he's a little *luny*," replied Ginger Nut, with a grin.

"You hear what they say," said I, turning towards the screen, "come forth and do your duty."

But he vouchsafed no reply. I pondered a moment in sore perplexity. But once more business hurried me. I determined again to postpone the consideration of this dilemma to my future leisure. With a little trouble we made out to examine the papers without Bartleby, though at every page or two Turkey deferentially dropped his opinion, that this proceeding was quite out of the common; while Nippers, twitching in his chair with a dyspeptic nervousness, ground out, between his set teeth, occasional hissing maledictions against the stubborn oaf behind the screen. And for his (Nippers's) part, this was the first and the last time he would do another man's business without pay.

Meanwhile Bartleby sat in his hermitage, oblivious to everything but his own peculiar business there.

Some days passed, the scrivener being employed upon another lengthy work. His late remarkable conduct led me to regard his ways narrowly. I observed that he never went to dinner; indeed, that he never went anywhere. As yet I had never, of my personal knowledge, known him to be outside of my office. He was a perpetual sentry in the corner. At about eleven o'clock though, in the morning, I noticed that Ginger Nut would advance toward the opening in Bartleby's screen, as if silently beckoned thither by a gesture invisible to me where I sat. The boy would then leave the office, jingling a few pence, and reappear with a handful of ginger-nuts, which he delivered in the hermitage, receiving two of the cakes for his trouble.

He lives, then, on ginger-nuts, thought I; never eats a dinner, properly speaking; he must be a vegetarian, then; but no; he never eats even vegetables, he eats nothing but giner-nuts. My mind then ran on in reveries concerning the probable effects upon the human constitution of living entirely on ginger-nuts. Ginger-nuts are so called, because they contain ginger as one of their peculiar constituents, and the final flavoring one. Now, what was ginger? A hot, spicy thing. Was Bartleby hot and spicy? Not at all. Ginger, then, had no effect upon Bartleby. Probably he preferred it should have none.

Nothing so aggravates an earnest person as a passive resistance. If the individual so resisted be of a not inhumane temper, and the resisting one perfectly harmless in his passivity, then, in the better moods of the former, he will endeavor charitably to construe to his imagination what proves impossible to be solved by his judgement. Even so, for the most part, I regarded Bartleby and his ways. Poor fellow! thought I, he means no mischief; it is plain he intends no insolence; his aspect sufficiently evinces that his eccentricities are involuntary. He is useful to me. I can get along with him. If I turn him away, the chances are he will fall in with some less-indulgent employer, and then he will be rudely treated, and perhaps driven forth miserably to starve. Yes. Here I can cheaply purchase a delicious self-approval. To befriend Bartleby; to humor him in his strange willfulness, will cost me little or nothing, while I lay up in my soul what will eventually prove a sweet morsel for my conscience. But this mood was not invariable with me. The passiveness of Bartleby sometimes irritated me. I felt strangely goaded on to encounter him in new opposition—to elicit some angry spark from him answerable to my own. But, indeed, I might as well have essayed to strike fire with my knuckles against a bit of Windsor soap. But one afternoon the evil impulse in me mastered me, and the following little scene ensued:

"Bartleby," said I, "when those papers are all copied, I will compare them with you."

"I would prefer not to."

"How? Surely you do not mean to persist in that mulish vagary?"

No answer.

I threw open the folding-doors near by, and, turning upon Turkey and Nippers exclaimed:

"Bartleby a second time says, he won't examine his papers. What do you think of it, Turkey?"

It was afternoon, be it remembered. Turkey sat glowing like a brass boiler; his bald head steaming; his hands reeling among his blotted papers.

"Think of it?" roared Turkey; "I think I'll just step behind his screen, and black his eyes for him!"

So saying, Turkey rose to his feet and threw his arms into a pugilistic position. He was hurrying away to make good his promise, when I detained him, alarmed at the effect of incautiously rousing Turkey's combativeness after dinner.

"Sit down, Turkey," said I, "and hear what Nippers has to say. What do you think of it, Nippers? Would I not be justified in immediately dismissing Bartleby?"

"Excuse me, that is for you to decide, sir. I think his conduct quite unusual, and, indeed, unjust, as regards Turkey and myself. But it may only be a passing whim."

"Ah," exclaimed I, "you have strangely changed your mind, then—you speak very gently of him now."

"All beer," cried Turkey: "gentleness is effects of beer—Nippers and I dined to-gether to-day. You see how gentle *I* am, sir. Shall I go and black his eyes?"

"You refer to Bartleby, I suppose. No, not to-day, Turkey," I replied: "pray, put up your fists."

I closed the doors, and again advanced towards Bartleby. I felt additional incentives tempting me to my fate. I burned to be rebelled against again. I remembered that Bartleby never left the office.

"Bartleby," said I, "Ginger Nut is away; just step around to the Post Office, won't you? (it was but a three minutes' walk), and see if there is anything for me."

"I would prefer not to."

"You *will* not?"

"I *prefer* not."

I staggered to my desk, and sat there in a deep study. My blind inveteracy returned. Was there any other thing in which I could procure myself to be ignominiously repulsed by this lean, penniless wight?—my hired clerk? What added thing is there, perfectly reasonable, that he will be sure to refuse to do? "Bartleby!"

No answer.

"Bartleby," in a louder tone.

No answer.

"Bartleby," I roared.

Like a very ghost, agreeably to the laws of magical invocation, at the third summons, he appeared at the entrance of his hermitage.

"Go to the next room, and tell Nippers to come to me."

"I prefer not to," he respectfully and slowly said and mildly disappeared.

"Very good, Bartleby," said I, in a quiet sort of serenely-severe, self-possessed tone, intimating the unalterable purpose of some terrible retribution very close at hand. At the moment I half intended something of the kind. But upon the whole, as it was drawing towards my dinner-hour, I thought it best to put on my hat and walk home for the day, suffering much from perplexity and distress of mind.

Shall I acknowledge it? The conclusion of this whole business was, that it soon became a fixed fact of my chambers, that a pale young scrivener, by the name of Bartleby, had a desk there; that he copied for me at the usual rate of four cents a folio (one hundred words); but he was permanently exempt from examining the work done by him, that duty being transferred to Turkey and Nippers, out of compliment, doubtless, to their superior acuteness; moreover, said Bartleby was never, on any account, to be dispatched on the most trivial errand of any sort; and that even if entreated to take upon him such a matter, it was generally understood that he would "prefer not to"—in other words, he would refuse point blank.

As days passed on, I became considerably reconciled to Bartleby. His steadiness, his freedom from all dissipation, his incessant industry (except when he chose to throw himself into a standing revery behind his screen), his great stillness, his unalterableness of demeanor under all circumstances, made him a valuable acquisition. One prime thing was this—*he was always there*—first in the morning, continually through the day, and the last at night. I had a singular confidence in his honesty. I felt my most precious papers perfectly safe in his hands. Sometimes, to be sure, I could not, for the very soul of me, avoid falling into sudden spasmodic passions with him. For it was exceeding difficult to bear in mind all the time those strange peculiarities, privileges, and unheard of exemptions, forming the tacit stipulations on Bartleby's part under which he remained in my office. Now and then, in the eagerness of dispatching pressing business, I would inadvertently summon Bartleby, in a short, rapid tone, to put his finger, say, on the incipient tie of a bit of red tape with which I was about compressing some papers. Of course, from behind the screen the usual answer, "I prefer not to," was sure to come; and then, how could a human creature, with the common infirmities of our nature, refrain from bitterly exclaiming upon such perverseness–such unreasonableness. However, every added repulse of this sort which I received only tended to lessen the probability of my repeating the inadvertence.

Here it must be said, that according to the custom of most legal gentlemen occupying chambers in densely-populated law buildings, there were several keys to my door. One was kept by a woman residing in the attic, which person weekly scrubbed and daily swept and dusted my apartments. Another was kept by Turkey for convenience sake. The third I sometimes carried in my own pocket. The fourth I knew not who had.

Now, one Sunday morning I happened to go to Trinity Church, to hear a celebrated preacher, and finding myself rather early on the ground I thought I would walk around to my chambers for a while. Luckily I had my key with me; but upon applying it to the lock, I found it resisted by something inserted from the inside. Quite surprised, I called out; when to my consternation a key was turned from within; and thrusting his lean visage at me, and holding the door ajar, the apparition of Bartleby appeared, in his shirt sleeves, and otherwise in a strangely tattered *déshabillé,* saying quietly that he was sorry, but he was deeply engaged just then, and—preferred not admitting me at present. In a brief word or two, he moreover added, that perhaps I had better walk around the block two or three times, and by that time he would probably have concluded his affairs.

Now, the utterly unsurmised appearance of Bartleby, tenanting my law-chambers of a Sunday morning, with his cadaverously gentlemanly *nonchalance,* yet withal firm and self-possessed, had such a strange effect upon me, that incontinently I slunk away from my own door, and did as desired. But not without sundry twinges of impotent rebellion against the mild effrontery of this unaccountable scrivener. Indeed, it was his wonderful mildness chiefly, which not only disarmed me, but unmanned me as it were. For I consider that one, for the time, is somehow unmanned when he tranquilly permits his hired clerk to dictate to him, and order him away from his own premises. Furthermore, I was full of uneasiness as to what Bartleby could possibly be doing in my office in his shirt sleeves, and in an otherwise dismantled condition of a Sunday morning. Was anything amiss going on? Nay, that was out of the question. It was not to be thought of for a moment that Bartleby was an immoral person. But what could he be doing there?—copying? Nay again, whatever might be his eccentricities, Bartleby was an eminently decorous person. He would be the last man to sit down to his desk in any state approaching to nudity. Besides, it was Sunday; and there was something about Bartleby that forbade the supposition that he would by any secular occupation violate the proprieties of the day.

Nevertheless, my mind was not pacified; and full of a restless curiosity, at last I returned to the door. Without hindrance I inserted my key, opened it, and entered. Bartleby was not to be seen. I looked round anxiously, peeped behind his screen; but it was very plain that he was gone. Upon more closely examining the place, I surmised that for an indefinite period Bartleby must have eaten, dressed, and slept in my office, and that, too, without plate, mirror, or bed. The cushioned seat of a rickety old sofa in one corner bore the faint impress of a lean, reclining form. Rolled away under his desk, I found a blanket; under the empty grate, a blacking box and brush; on a chair, a tin basin, with soap and a ragged towel; in a newspaper a few crumbs of ginger-nuts and a morsel of cheese. Yes, thought I, it is evident enough that Bartleby has been making his home here, keeping bachelor's hall all by himself. Immediately then the thought came sweeping across me, what miserable friendlessness and loneliness are here revealed! His poverty is great; but his solitude, how horrible! Think of it. Of a Sunday, Wall Street is deserted as Petra; and every night of every day it is an emptiness. This building, too, which of week-days hums with industry and life, at nightfall echoes with sheer vacancy, and all through Sunday is forlorn. And here Bartleby makes his home; sole spectator of a solitude which he has seen all populous—a sort of innocent and transformed Marius brooding among the ruins of Carthage!

For the first time in my life a feeling of over-powering stinging melancholy seized me. Before, I had never experienced aught but a not unpleasing sadness. The bond of a common humanity now drew me irresistibly to gloom. A fraternal melancholy! for both I and Bartleby were sons of Adam. I remembered the bright silks and sparkling faces I had seen that day, in gala trim, swan-like sailing down the Mississippi of Broadway; and I contrasted them with the pallid copyist, and thought to myself, Ah, happiness courts the light, so we deem the world is gay; but misery hides aloof, so we deem that misery there is none. These sad fancyings—chimeras, doubtless, of a sick and silly brain—led on to other and more special thoughts, concerning the eccentricities of Bartleby. Presentiments of strange discoveries hovered round me. The scrivener's pale form appeared to me laid out, among uncaring strangers, in its shivering winding sheet.

Suddenly I was attracted by Bartleby's closed desk, the key in open sight left in the lock.

I mean no mischief, seek the gratification of no heartless curiosity, thought I; besides, the desk is mine, and its contents, too, so I will make bold to look within. Everything was methodically arranged, the papers smoothly placed. The pigeon holes were deep, and removing the files of documents, I groped into their recesses. Presently I felt something there, and dragged it out. It was an old bandanna handkerchief, heavy and knotted. I opened it, and saw it was a savings bank.

I now recalled all the quiet mysteries which I had noted in the man. I remembered that he never spoke but to answer; that, though at intervals he had considerable time to himself, yet I had never seen him reading—no, not even a newspaper; that for long periods he would stand looking out, at his pale window behind the screen, upon the dead brick wall; I was quite sure he never visited any refectory or eating house; while his pale face clearly indicated that he never drank beer like Turkey, or tea and coffee even, like other men; that he never went anywhere in particular that I could learn; never went out for a walk, unless, indeed, that was the case at present; that he had declined telling who he was, or whence he came, or whether he had any relatives in the world; that though so thin and pale, he never complained of ill health. And more than all, I remembered a certain unconscious air of pallid—how shall I call it?—of pallid haughtiness, say, or rather an austere reserve about him, which had positively awed me into my tame compliance with his eccentricities, when I had feared to ask him to do the slightest incidental thing for me, even though I might know, from his long-continued motionlessness, that behind his screen he must be standing in one of those dead-wall reveries of his.

Revolving all these things, and coupling them with the recently discovered fact, that he made my office his constant abiding place and home, and not forgetful of his morbid moodiness; revolving all these things, a prudential feeling began to steal over me. My first emotions had been those of pure melancholy and sincerest pity; but just in proportion as the forlornness of Bartleby grew and grew to my imagination, did that same melancholy merge into fear, that pity into repulsion. So true it is, and so terrible, too, that up to a certain point the thought or sight of misery enlists our best affections; but, in certain special cases, beyond that point it does not. They err who would assert that invariably this is owing to the inherent selfishness of the human heart. It rather proceeds from a certain hopelessness of remedying excessive and organic ill. To a sensitive being, pity is not seldom pain. And when at last it is perceived that such pity cannot lead to effectual succor, common sense bids the soul be rid of it. What I saw that morning persuaded me that the scrivener was the victim of innate and incurable disorder. I might give alms to his body; but his body did not pain him; it was his soul that suffered, and his soul I could not reach.

I did not accomplish the purpose of going to Trinity Church that morning. Somehow, the things I had seen disqualified me for the time from churchgoing. I walked homeward, thinking what I would do with Bartleby. Finally, I resolved upon this—I would put certain calm questions to him the next morning, touching his history, etc., and if he declined to answer them openly and unreservedly (and I supposed he would prefer not), then to give him a twenty dollar bill over and above whatever I might owe him, and tell him his services were no longer required; but that if in any other way I could assist him, I would be happy to do so, especially if he desired to return to his native place, wherever that might be, I would willingly help to defray the expenses. Moreover, if, after reaching home, he found himself at any time in want of aid, a letter from him would be sure of a reply.

The next morning came.

"Bartleby," said I, gently calling to him behind his screen.

No reply.

"Bartleby," said I, in a still gentler tone, "come here; I am not going to ask you to do anything you would prefer not to do—I simply wish to speak to you."

Upon this he noiselessly slid into view.

"Will you tell me, Bartleby, where you were born?"

"I would prefer not to."

"Will you tell me *anything* about yourself?"

"I would prefer not to."

"But what reasonable objection can you have to speak to me? I feel friendly towards you."

He did not look at me while I spoke, but kept his glance fixed upon my bust of Cicero, which, as I then sat, was directly behind me, some six inches above my head.

"What is your answer, Bartleby," said I, after waiting a considerable time for a reply, during which his countenance remained immovable, only there was the faintest conceivable tremor of the white attenuated mouth.

"At present I prefer to give no answer," he said, and retired into his hermitage.

It was rather weak in me I confess, but his manner, on this occasion, nettled me. Not only did there seem to lurk in it a certain calm disdain, but his perverseness seemed ungrateful, considering the undeniable good usage and indulgence he had received from me.

Again I sat ruminating what I should do. Mortified as I was at his behavior, and resolved as I had been to dismiss him when I entered my office, nevertheless I strangely felt something superstitious knocking at my heart, and forbidding me to carry out my purpose, and denouncing me for a villain if I dared to breathe one bitter word against this forlornest of mankind. At last, familiarly drawing my chair behind his screen, I sat down and said: "Bartleby, never mind, then, about revealing your history; but let me entreat you, as a friend, to comply as far as may be with the usages of this office. Say now, you will help to examine papers to-morrow or next day: in short, say now, that in a day or two you will begin to be a little reasonable:—say so, Bartleby."

"At present I would prefer not to be a little reasonable," was his mildly cadaverous reply.

Just then the folding-doors opened, and Nippers approached. He seemed suffering from an unusually bad night's rest, induced by severer indigestion than common. He overheard those final words of Bartleby.

"*Prefer not*, eh?" gritted Nippers—"I'd *prefer* him, if I were you, sir," addressing me—"I'd *prefer* him; I'd give him preferences, the stubborn mule! What is it, sir, pray, that he *prefers* not to do now?"

Bartleby moved not a limb.

"Mr. Nippers," said I, "I'd prefer that you would withdraw for the present."

Somehow, of late, I had got into the way of involuntarily using this word "prefer" upon all sorts of not exactly suitable occasions. And I trembled to think that my contact with the scrivener had already and seriously affected me in a mental way. And what

178

further and deeper aberration might it not yet produce? This apprehension had not been without efficacy in determining me to summary measures.

As Nippers, looking very sour and sulky, was departing, Turkey blandly and deferentially approached.

"With submission, sir," said he, "yesterday I was thinking about Bartleby here, and I think that if he would but prefer to take a quart of good ale every day, it would do much towards mending him, and enabling him to assist in examining his papers."

"So you have got the word, too," said I, slightly excited.

"With submission, what word, sir," asked Turkey, respectfully crowding himself into the contracted space behind the screen, and by so doing, making me jostle the scrivener. "What word, sir?"

"I would prefer to be left alone here," said Bartleby, as if offended at being mobbed in his privacy.

"*That*'s the word, Turkey," said I—"*that*'s it."

"Oh, *prefer?* oh yes—queer word. I never use it myself. But, sir, as I was saying, if he would but prefer—"

"Turkey," interrupted I, "you will please withdraw."

"Oh certainly, sir, if you prefer that I should."

As he opened the folding-door to retire, Nippers at his desk caught a glimpse of me, and asked whether I would prefer to have a certain paper copied on blue paper or white. He did not in the least roguishly accent the word prefer. It was plain that it involuntarily rolled from his tongue. I thought to myself, surely I must get rid of a demented man, who already has in some degree turned the tongues, if not the heads of myself and clerks. But I thought it prudent not to break the dismission at once.

The next day I noticed that Bartleby did nothing but stand at his window in his dead-wall revery. Upon asking him why he did not write, he said that he had decided upon doing no more writing."

"Why, how now? What next?" exclaimed I, "do no more writing?"

"No more."

"And what is the reason?"

"Do you not see the reason for yourself?" he indifferently replied.

I looked steadfastly at him, and perceived that his eyes looked dull and glazed. Instantly it occurred to me, that his unexampled diligence in copying by his dim window for the first few weeks of his stay with me might have temporarily impaired his vision.

I was touched. I said something in condolence with him. I hinted that of course he did wisely in abstaining from writing for a while; and urged him to embrace the opportunity of taking wholesome exercise in the open air. This, however, he did not do. A few days after this, my other clerks being absent, and being in a great hurry to dispatch certain letters by the mail, I thought that, having nothing else earthly to do, Bartleby would surely be less inflexible than usual, and carry these letters to the post-office. But he blankly declined. So, much to my inconvenience, I went myself.

Still added days went by. Whether Bartleby's eyes improved or not, I could not say. To all appearance I thought they did. But when I asked him if they did, he vouchsafed no answer. At all events, he would do no copying. At last, in reply to my urgings, he informed me that he had permanently given up copying.

"What!" exclaimed I; "suppose your eyes should get entirely well—better than ever before—would you not copy then?"

"I have given up copying," he answered, and slid aside.

He remained as ever, a fixture in my chamber. Nay—if that were possible—he became still more of a fixture than before. What was to be done? He would do nothing in the office; why should he stay there? In plain fact, he had now become a millstone to me, not only useless as a necklace, but afflictive to bear. Yet I was sorry for him. I speak less than truth when I say that, on his own account, he occasioned me uneasiness. If he would but have named a single relative or friend, I would instantly have written, and urged their taking the poor fellow away to some convenient retreat. But he seemed alone, absolutely alone in the universe. A bit of wreck in the mid Atlantic. At length, necessities connected with my business tyrannized over all other considerations. Decently, as I could, I told Bartleby that in six days time he must unconditionally leave the office. I warned him to take measures, in the interval, for procuring some other abode. I offered to assist him in his endeavor, if he himself would but take the first step towards a removal. "And when you finally quit me, Bartleby," added I, "I shall see that you go not away entirely unprovided. Six days from this hour, remember."

At the expiration of that period, I peeped behind the screen, and lo! Bartleby was there.

I buttoned up my coat, balanced myself; advanced slowly towards him, touched his shoulder, and said, "The time has come; you must quit this place; I am sorry for you; here is money; but you must go."

"I would prefer not" he replied, with his back still towards me.

"You *must*."

He remained silent.

Now I had an unbounded confidence in this man's common honesty. He had frequently restored to me sixpences and shillings carelessly dropped upon the floor, for I am apt to be very reckless in such shirt-button affairs. The proceeding, then, which followed will not be deemed extraordinary.

"Bartleby," said I, "I owe you twelve dollars on account; here are thirty-two; the odd twenty are yours—Will you take it?" and I handed the bills towards him.

But he made no motion.

"I will leave them here, then," putting them under a weight on the table. Then taking my hat and cane and going to the door, I tranquilly turned and added—"After you have removed your things from these offices, Bartleby, you will of course lock the door—since every one is now gone for the day but you—and if you please, slip your key underneath the mat, so that I may have it in the morning. I shall not see you again; so good-by to you. If, hereafter, in your new place of abode, I can be of any service to you, do not fail to advise me by letter. Good-by, Bartleby, and fare you well."

But he answered not a word; like the last column of some ruined temple, he remained standing mute and solitary in the middle of the otherwise deserted room.

As I walked home in a pensive mood, my vanity got the better of my pity. I could not but highly plume myself on my masterly management in getting rid of Bartleby. Masterly I call it, and such it must appear to any dispassionate thinker. The beauty of my procedure seemed to consist in its perfect quietness. There was no vulgar bullying, no bravado of any sort, no choleric hectoring, and striding to and fro across the apartment, jerking out vehement commands for Bartleby to bundle himself off with his beggarly traps. Nothing of the kind. Without loudly bidding Bartleby depart—as an inferior genius might have done—I *assumed* the ground that depart he must; and upon that assumption built all I had to say. The more I thought over my procedure, the more I was charmed with it. Nevertheless, next morning, upon awakening, I had my doubts—I had somehow slept off the fumes of vanity. One of the coolest and wisest hours a man has, is just after he awakes in the morning. My procedure seemed as sagacious as ever—but only in theory. How it would prove in practice—there was the rub. It was truly a beautiful thought to have assumed Bartleby's departure; but, after all, that assumption was simply my own, and none of Bartleby's. The great point was, not whether I had assumed that he would quit me, but whether he would prefer so to do. He was more a man of preferences than assumptions.

After breakfast, I walked down town, arguing the probabilities *pro* and *con*. One moment I thought it would prove a miserable failure, and Bartleby would be found all alive at my office as usual; the next moment it seemed certain that I should find his chair empty. And so I kept veering about. At the corner of Broadway and Canal Street, I saw quite an excited group of people standing in earnest conversation.

"I'll take odds he doesn't," said a voice as I passed.

"Doesn't go?—done!" said I; "put up your money."

I was instinctively putting my hand in my pocket to produce my own, when I remembered that this was an election day. The words I had overheard bore no reference to Bartleby, but to the success or non-success of some candidate for the mayoralty. In my intent frame of mind, I had, as it were, imagined that all Broadway shared in my excitement, and were debating the same question with me. I passed on, very thankful that the uproar of the street screened my momentary absent-mindedness.

As I had intended, I was earlier than usual at my office door. I stood listening for a moment. All was still. He must be gone. I tried the knob. The door was locked! Yes, my procedure had worked to a charm; he indeed must be vanished. Yet a certain melancholy mixed with this: I was almost sorry for my brilliant success. I was fumbling under the door mat for key, which Bartleby was to have left there for me, when accidentally my knee knocked againt a panel, producing a summoning sound, and in response a voice came to me from within—"Not yet; I am occupied."

It was Bartleby.

I was thunderstruck. For an instant I stood like the man who, pipe in mouth, was killed one cloudless afternoon long ago in Virginia, by summer lightning; at his own warm open window he was killed, and remained leaning out there upon the dreamy afternoon, till some one touched him, when he fell.

"Not gone!" I murmured at last. But again obeying that wondrous ascendancy which the inscrutable scrivener had over me, and from which ascendancy, for all my chafing, I could not completely escape, I slowly went down stairs and out into the street, and while walking round the block, considered what I should next do in this unheard-of perplexity. Turn the man out by an actual thrusting I could not; to drive him away by calling him hard names would not do; calling in the police was an unpleasant idea; and yet, permit him to enjoy his cadaverous triumph over me—this, too, I could not think of. What was to be done? or, if nothing could be done, was there anything further that I could *assume* in the matter? Yes, as before I had prospectively assumed that Bartleby would depart, so now I might retrospectively assume that departed he was. In the legitimate carrying out of this assumption, I might enter my office in a great hurry, and pretending not to see Bartleby at all, walk straight against him as if he were air. Such a proceeding would in a singular degree have the appearance of a home-thrust. It was hardly possible that Bartleby could withstand such an application of the doctrine of assumptions. But upon second thoughts the success of the plan seemed rather dubious. I resolved to argue the matter over with him again.

"Bartleby," said I, entering the office, with a quietly severe expression, "I am seriously displeased. I am pained, Bartleby. I had thought better of you. I had imagined you of such a gentlemanly organization, that in any delicate dilemma a slight hint would suffice—in short, an assumption. But it appears I am deceived. Why," I added, unaffectedly starting, "you have not even touched that money yet," pointing to it, just where I had left it the evening previous.

He answered nothing.

"Will you, or will you not, quit me?" I now demanded in a sudden passion, advancing close to him.

"I would prefer *not* to quit you," he replied, gently emphasizing the *not.*

"What earthly right have you to stay here? Do you pay any rent? Do you pay my taxes? Or is this property yours?"

He answered nothing.

"Are you ready to go on and write now? Are your eyes recovered? Could you copy a small paper for me this morning? or help examine a few lines? or step round to the post-office? In a word, will you do anything at all, to give a coloring to your refusal to depart the premises?"

He silently retired into his hermitage.

I was now in such a state of nervous resentment that I thought it but prudent to check myself at present from further demonstrations. Bartleby and I were alone. I remembered the tragedy of the unfortunate Adams and the still more unfortunate Colt in the solitary office of the latter; and how poor Colt, being dreadfully incensed by Adams, and imprudently permitting himself to get wildly excited, was at unawares hurried into his fatal act—an act which certainly no man could possibly deplore more than the actor himself. Often it had occurred to me in my ponderings upon the subject, that had that altercation taken place in the public street, or at a private residence, it would not have terminated as it did. It was the circumstance of being alone in a solitary office, up stairs, of a building entirely unhallowed by humanizing domestic associations—an uncarpeted office, doubtless, of a dusty, haggard sort of appearance—this it must have been, which greatly helped to enhance the irritable desperation of the hapless Colt.

But when this old Adam of resentment rose in me and tempted me concerning Bartleby, I grappled him and threw him. How? Why, simply by recalling the divine injunction: "A new commandment give I unto you, that ye love one another." Yes, this it was that saved me. Aside from higher considerations, charity often operates as a vastly wise and prudent principle—a great safeguard to its possessor. Men have committed murder for jealousy's sake, and anger's sake, and hatred's sake, and selfishness' sake, and spiritual pride's sake; but no man that ever I heard of, ever committed a diabolical murder for sweet charity's sake. Mere self-interest, then, if no better motive can be enlisted, should, especially with high-tempered men, prompt all beings to charity and philanthropy. At any rate, upon the occasion in question, I strove to drown my exasperated feelings towards the scrivener by benevolently construing his conduct. Poor fellow, poor fellow! thought I, he don't mean anything; and besides, he has seen hard times, and ought to be indulged.

I endeavored, also, immediately to occupy myself, and at the same time to comfort my despondency. I tried to fancy, that in the course of the morning, at such time as might prove agreeable to him, Bartleby, of his own free accord, would emerge from his hermitage and take up some decided line of march in the direction of the door. But no. Half-past twelve o'clock came; Turkey began to glow in the face, overturn his inkstand, and become generally obstreperous; Nippers abated down into quietude and courtesy; Ginger Nut munched his noon apple; and Bartleby remained standing at his window in one of his profoundest dead-wall reveries. Will it be credited? Ought I to acknowledge it? That afternoon I left the office without saying one further word to him.

Some days now passed, during which, at leisure intervals I looked a little into "Edwards on the Will," and "Priestley on Necessity." Under the circumstances, those books induced a salutary feeling. Gradually I slid into the persuasion that these troubles of mine, touching the scrivener, had been all predestinated from eternity, and Bartleby was billeted upon me for some mysterious purpose of an all-wise Providence, which it was not for a mere mortal like me to fathom. Yes, Bartleby, stay there behind your screen, thought I; I shall persecute you no more; you are harmless and noiseless as any of these old chairs; in short, I never feel so private as when I know you are here. At last I see it, I feel it; I penetrate to the predestinated purpose of my life. I am content. Others may have loftier parts to enact; but my mission in this world, Bartleby, is to furnish you with office-room for such period as you may see fit to remain.

I believe that this wise and blessed frame of mind would have continued with me, had it not been for the unsolicited and uncharitable remarks obtruded upon me by my professional friends who visited the rooms. But thus it often is, that the constant friction of illiberal minds wears out at last the best resolves of the more generous. Though to be sure, when I reflected upon it, it was not strange that people entering my office should be struck by the peculiar aspect of the unaccountable Bartleby, and so be tempted to throw out some sinister observations concerning him. Sometimes an attorney, having business with me, and calling at my office, and finding no one but the scrivener there, would undertake to obtain some sort of precise information from him touching my whereabouts; but without heeding his idle talk, Bartleby would remain standing immovable in the middle of the room. So after contemplating him in that position for a time, the attorney would depart, no wiser than he came.

Also, when a reference was going on, and the room full of lawyers and witnesses, and business driving fast, some deeply-occupied legal gentlemen present, seeing Bartleby wholly unemployed, would request him to run round to his (the legal gentleman's) office and fetch some papers for him. Thereupon, Bartleby would tranquilly decline, and yet remain idle as before. Then the lawyer would give a great stare, and turn to me. And what could I say? At last I was made aware that all through the circle of my professional acquaintance, a whisper of wonder was running round, having reference to the strange creature I kept at my office. This worried me very much. And as the idea came upon me of his possibly turning out a long-lived man, and keep occupying my chambers, and denying my authority; and perplexing my visitors; and scandalizing my professional reputation; and casting a general gloom over the premises; keeping soul and body together to the last upon his savings (for doubtless he spent but half a dime a day), and in the end perhaps outlive me, and claim possession of my office by right of his perpetual occupancy: as all these dark anticipations crowded upon me more and more, and my friends continually intruded their relentless remarks upon the apparition in my room; a great change was wrought in me. I resolved to gather all my faculties together, and forever rid me of this intolerable incubus.

Ere revolving any complicated project, however, adapted to this end, I first simply suggested to Bartleby the propriety of his permanent departure. In a calm and serious tone, I commended the idea to his careful and mature consideration. But, having taken three days to meditate upon it, he apprised me, that his original determination remained the same; in short, that he still preferred to abide with me.

What shall I do? I now said to myself, buttoning up my coat to the last button. What shall I do? what ought I to do? what does conscience say I *should* do with this man, or, rather, ghost. Rid myself of him, I must; go, he shall. But how? You will not thrust him, the poor, pale, passive mortal—you will not thrust such a helpless creature out of your door? you will not dishonor yourself by such cruelty? No, I will not, I cannot do that. Rather would I let him live and die here, and then mason up his remains in the wall. What, then, will you do? For all your coaxing, he will not budge. Bribes he leaves under your own paper-weight on your table; in short, it is quite plain that he prefers to cling to you.

Then something severe, something unusual must be done. What! surely you will not have him collared by a constable, and commit his innocent pallor to the common jail? And upon what ground could you procure such a thing to be done?—a vagrant, is he? What! he a vagrant, a wanderer, who refuses to budge? It is because he will *not* be a vagrant, then, that you seek to count him *as* a vagrant. This is too absurd. No visible means of support: there I have him. Wrong again: for indubitably he *does* support himself, and that is the only unanswerable proof that any man can show of his possessing the means so to do. No more, then. Since he will not quit me, I must quit him. I will change my offices; I will move elsewhere, and give him fair notice, that if I find him on my new premises I will then proceed against him as a common trespasser.

Acting accordingly, next day I thus addressed him: "I find these chambers too far from the City Hall; the air is unwholesome. In a word, I propose to remove my offices next week, and shall no longer require your services. I tell you this now, in order that you may seek another place."

He made no reply; and nothing more was said.

On the appointed day I engaged carts and men, proceeded to my chambers, and, having but little furniture, everything was removed in a few hours. Throughout, the scrivener remained standing behind the screen, which I directed to be removed the last thing. It was withdrawn; and, being folded up like a huge folio, left him the motionless occupant of a naked room. I stood in the entry watching him a moment, while something from within me upbraided me.

I re-entered, with my hand in my pocket—and—and my heart in my mouth.

"Good-by, Bartleby; I am going—good-by, and God some way bless you; and take that," slipping something in his hand. But it dropped upon the floor, and then—strange to say—I tore myself from him whom I had so longed to be rid of.

Established in my new quarters, for a day or two I kept the door locked, and started at every footfall in the passages. When I returned to my rooms, after any little absence, I would pause at the threshold for an instant, and attentively listen, ere applying my key. But these fears were needless. Bartleby never came nigh me.

I thought all was going well, when a perturbed-looking stranger visited me, inquiring whether I was the person who had recently occupied rooms at No.——Wall Street.

Full of forebodings, I replied that I was.

"Then, sir," said the stranger, who proved a lawyer, "you are responsible for the man you left there. He refuses to do any copying; he refuses to do anything; he says he prefers not to; and he refuses to quit the premises."

"I am very sorry, sir," said I, with assumed tranquillity, but an inward tremor, "but, really, the man you allude to is nothing to me—he is no relation or apprentice of mine, that you should hold me responsible for him."

"In mercy's name, who is he?"

"I certainly cannot inform you. I know nothing about him. Formerly I employed him as a copyist; but he has done nothing for me now for some time past."

"I shall settle him then—good morning, sir."

Several days passed, and I heard nothing more; and, though I often felt a charitable prompting to call at the place and see poor Bartleby, yet a certain squeamishness, of I know not what, withheld me.

All is over with him, by this time, thought I, at last, when, through another week, no further intelligence reached me. But, coming to my room the day after, I found several persons waiting at my door in a high state of nervous excitement.

"That's the man—here he comes," cried the foremost one, whom I recognized as the lawyer who had previously called upon me alone.

"You must take him away, sir, at once," cried a portly person among them, advancing upon me, and whom I knew to be the landlord of No.——Wall Street. "These gentlemen, my tenants, cannot stand it any longer; Mr. B—," pointing to the lawyer, "has turned him out of his room, and he now persists in haunting the building generally, sitting upon the banisters of the stairs by day, and sleeping in the entry by night. Everybody is concerned; clients are leaving the offices; some fears are entertained of a mob; something you must do, and that without delay."

Aghast at this torrent, I fell back before it, and would fain have locked myself in my new quarters. In vain I persisted that Bartleby was nothing to me—no more than to any one else. In vain—I was the last person known to have anything to do with him, and they held me to the terrible account. Fearful, then, of being exposed in the papers (as one person present obscurely threatened), I considered the matter, and, at length, said, that if the lawyer would give me a confidential interview with the scrivener, in his (the lawyer's) own room, I would, that afternoon, strive my best to rid them of the nuisance they complained of.

Going up stairs to my old haunt, there was Bartleby silently sitting upon the banister at the landing.

"What are you doing here, Bartleby?" said I.

"Sitting upon the banister," he mildly replied.

I motioned him into the lawyer's room, who then left us.

"Bartleby," said I, "are you aware that you are the cause of great tribulation to me, by persisting in occupying the entry after being dismissed from the office?"

No answer.

"Now one of two things must take place. Either you must do something, or something must be done to you. Now what sort of business would you like to engage in? Would you like to re-engage in copying for some one?"

"No; I would prefer not to make any change."

"Would you like a clerkship in a dry-goods store?"

"There is too much confinement about that. No, I would not like a clerkship; but I am not particular."

"Too much confinement," I cried, "why you keep yourself confined all the time!"

"I would prefer not to take a clerkship," he rejoined, as if to settle that little item at once.

"How would a bar-tender's business suit you? There is no trying of the eyesight in that."

"I would not like it at all; though, as I said before, I am not particular."

His unwonted wordiness inspirited me. I returned to the charge.

"Well, then, would you like to travel through the country collecting bills for the merchants? That would improve your health."

"No, I would prefer to be doing something else."

"How, then, would going as a companion to Europe, to entertain some young gentlemen with your conversation—how would that suit you?"

"Not at all. It does not strike me that there is anything definite about that. I like to be stationary. But I am not particular."

"Stationary you shall be, then," I cried, now losing all patience, and, for the first time in all my exasperating connection with him, fairly flying into a passion. "If you do not go away from these premises before night, I shall feel bound—indeed, I *am* bound—to—to—to quit the premises myself!" I rather absurdly concluded, knowing not with what possible threat to try to frighten his immobility into compliance. Despairing of all further efforts, I was precipitately leaving him, when a final thought occurred to me—one which had not been wholly unindulged before.

"Bartleby," said I, in the kindest tone I could assume under such exciting circumstances, "will you go home with me now—not to my office, but my dwelling—and remain there till we can conclude upon some convenient arrangement for you at our leisure? Come, let us start now, right away."

"No: at present I would prefer not to make any change at all."

I answered nothing; but, effectually dodging every one by the suddenness and rapidity of my flight, rushed from the building, ran up Wall Street towards Broadway, and, jumping into the first omnibus, was soon removed from pursuit. As soon as tranquillity returned, I distinctly perceived that I had now done all that I possibly could, both in respect to the demands of the landlord and his tenants, and with regard to my own desire and sense of duty, to benefit Bartleby, and shield him from rude persecution. I now strove to be entirely care-free and quiescent; and my conscience justified me in the attempt; though, indeed, it was not so successful as I could have wished. So fearful was I of being again hunted out by the incensed landlord and his exasperated tenants, that, surrendering my business to Nippers, for a few days, I drove about the upper part of the town and through the suburbs, in my rockaway; crossed over to Jersey City and Hoboken, and paid fugitive visits to Manhattanville and Astoria. In fact, I almost lived in my rockaway for the time.

When again I entered my office, lo, a note from the landlord lay upon the desk. I opened it with trembling hands. It informed me that the writer had sent to the police, and had Bartleby removed to the Tombs as a vagrant. Moreover, since I knew more about him than any one else, he wished me to appear at that place, and make a suitable statement of the facts. These tidings had a conflicting effect upon me. At first I was indignant; but, at last, almost approved. The landlord's energetic, summary disposition, had led him to adopt a procedure which I do not think I would have decided upon myself; and yet, as a last resort, under such peculiar circumstances, it seemed the only plan.

As I afterwards learned, the poor scrivener, when told that he must be conducted to the Tombs, offered not the slightest obstacle, but, in his pale, unmoving way, silently acquiesced.

Some of the compassionate and curious bystanders joined the party; and headed by one of the constables arm in arm with Bartleby, the silent procession filed its way through all the noise, and heat, and joy of the roaring thoroughfares at noon.

The same day I received the note, I went to the Tombs, or, to speak more properly the Halls of Justice. Seeking the right officer, I stated the purpose of my call, and was informed that the individual I described was, indeed, within. I then assured the functionary that Bartleby was a perfectly honest man, and greatly to be compassionated, however unaccountably eccentric. I narrated all I knew, and closed by suggesting the idea of letting him remain in as indulgent confinement as possible, till something less harsh might be done—though, indeed, I hardly knew what. At all events, if nothing else could be decided upon, the alms-house must receive him. I then begged to have an interview.

Being under no disgraceful charge, and quite serene and harmless in all his ways, they had permitted him freely to wander about the prison, and, especially, in the inclosed grass-platted yards thereof. And so I found him there, standing all alone in the quietest of the yards, his face towards a high wall, while all around, from the narrow slits of the jail windows, I thought I saw peering out upon him the eyes of murderers and thieves.

"Bartleby!"

"I know you," he said, without looking round—"and I want nothing to say to you."

"It was not I that brought you here, Bartleby," said I, keenly pained at his implied suspicion. "And to you, this should not be so vile a place. Nothing reproachful attaches to you by being here. And see, it is not so sad a place as one might think. Look, there is the sky, and here is the grass."

"I know where I am," he replied, but would say nothing more, and so I left him.

As I entered the corridor again, a broad meat-like man, in an apron, accosted me, and, jerking his thumb over his shoulder, said—"Is that your friend?"

"Yes."

"Does he want to starve? If he does, let him live on the prison fare, that's all."

"Who are you?" asked I, not knowing what to make of such an unofficially speaking person in such a place.

"I am the grub-man. Such gentlemen as have friends here, hire me to provide them with something good to eat."

"Is this so?" said I, turning to the turnkey.

He said it was.

"Well, then," said I, slipping some silver into the grub-man's hands (for so they called him), "I want you to give particular attention to my friend there; let him have the best dinner you can get. And you must be as polite to him as possible."

"Introduce me, will you?" said the grub-man, looking at me with an expression which seemed to say he was all impatience for an opportunity to give a specimen of his breeding.

Thinking it would prove of benefit to the scrivener, I acquiesced; and, asking the grub-man his name, went up with him to Bartleby.

"Bartleby, this is a friend; you will find him very useful to you."

"Your sarvant, sir, your sarvant," said the grub-man, making a low salutation behind his apron. "Hope you find it pleasant here, sir; nice grounds—cool apartments—hope you'll stay with us sometime—try to make it agreeable. What will you have for dinner to-day?"

"I prefer not to dine to-day," said Bartleby, turning away. "It would disagree with me; I am unused to dinners." So saying, he slowly moved to the other side of the inclosure, and took up a position fronting the dead-wall.

"How's this?" said the grub-man, addressing me with a stare of astonishment. "He's odd, ain't he?"

"I think he is a little deranged," said I, sadly.

"Deranged? deranged is it? Well, now, upon my word, I thought that friend of yourn was a gentleman forger; they are always pale and genteel-like, them forgers. I can't help pity 'em—can't help it, sir. Did you know Monroe Edwards?" he added, touchingly, and paused. Then, laying his hand piteously on my shoulder, sighed, "he died of consumption at Sing-Sing. So you weren't acquainted with Monroe?"

"No, I was never socially acquainted with any forgers. But I cannot stop longer. Look to my friend yonder. You will not lose by it. I will see you again."

Some few days after this, I again obtained admission to the Tombs, and went through the corridors in quest of Bartleby; but without finding him.

"I saw him coming from his cell not long ago," said a turnkey, "may be he's gone to loiter in the yards."

So I went in that direction.

"Are you looking for the silent man?" said another turnkey, passing me. "Yonder he lies—sleeping in the yard there. 'Tis not twenty minutes since I saw him lie down."

The yard was entirely quiet. It was not accessible to the common prisoners. The surrounding walls of amazing thickness, kept off all sounds behind them. The Egyptian character of the masonry weighed upon me with its gloom. But a soft imprisoned turf grew under foot. The heart of the eternal pyramids, it seemed, wherein, by some strange magic, through the clefts, grass-seed, dropped by birds, had sprung.

Strangely huddled at the base of the wall, his knees drawn up, and lying on his side, his head touching the cold stones, I saw the wasted Bartleby. But nothing stirred. I paused; then went close up to him; stooped over, and saw that his dim eyes were open; otherwise he seemed profoundly sleeping. Something prompted me to touch him. I felt his hand, when a tingling shiver ran up my arm and down my spine to my feet.

The round face of the grub-man peered upon me now. "His dinner is ready. Won't he dine to-day, either? Or does he live without dining?"

"Lives without dining," said I, and closed the eyes.

"Eh—He's asleep, ain't he?"

"With kings and counselors," murmured I.

There would seem little need for proceeding further in this history. Imagination will readily supply the meagre recital of poor Bartleby's interment. But, ere parting with the reader, let me say, that if this little narrative has sufficiently interested him, to awaken curiosity as to who Bartleby was, and what manner of life he led prior to the present narrator's making his acquaintance, I can only reply, that in such curiosity I fully share, but am wholly unable to gratify it. Yet here I hardly know whether I should divulge one little item of rumor, which came to my ear a few months after the scrivener's decease. Upon what basis it rested, I could never ascertain; and hence, how true it is I cannot now tell. But, inasmuch as this vague report has not been without a certain suggestive interest to me, however said, it may prove the same with some others; and so I will briefly mention it. The report was this: that Bartleby had been a subordinate clerk in the Dead Letter Office at Washington, from which he had been suddenly removed by a change in the administration. When I think over this rumor, hardly can I express the emotions which seize me. Dead letters! does it not sound like dead men? Conceive a man by nature and misfortune prone to a pallid hopelessness, can any business seem more fitted to heighten it than that of continually handling these dead letters, and assorting them for the flames? For by the cart-load they are annually burned. Some times from out the folded paper the pale clerk takes a ring—the finger it was meant for, perhaps, moulders in the grave; a bank-note sent in swiftest charity—he whom it would relieve, nor eats nor hungers any more; pardon for those who died despairing; hope for those who died unhoping; good tidings for those who died stifled by unrelieved calamities. On errands of life, these letters speed to death.

Ah, Bartleby! Ah, humanity!

Index